Contributions to Management Science

For further volumes:
http://www.springer.com/series/1505

Olof Arwinge

Internal Control

A Study of Concept and Themes

Physica-Verlag
A Springer Company

Olof Arwinge
Department of Finance and Accounting
Uppsala University
Uppsala
Sweden

ISSN 1431-1941
ISBN 978-3-7908-2881-8 ISBN 978-3-7908-2882-5 (eBook)
DOI 10.1007/978-3-7908-2882-5
Springer Heidelberg New York Dordrecht London

Library of Congress Control Number: 2012951400

Printed on acid-free paper

Physica-Verlag is a brand of Springer

Springer is part of Springer Science+Business Media (www.springer.com)

Foreword

Internal control remains an important topic in business and organisational life. This is also the reason for why this book on the concept and themes of internal control is highly relevant for business professionals as well as students and scholars. Representing the partner team in the accounting and auditing firm Grant Thornton in Sweden, which is Olof's professional home base, we take pride in the fact that we are able to attract and support professionals that want to do exciting and relevant research while remaining in practice. Olof's book is intriguing as well as current and relevant as it summarises and discusses various perspectives on internal control, a subject that has proven to be even more in focus today than ever.

While it seems at times that internal control is an accountant's term only, this is of course not true. Internal control is most of all important for firms themselves, and for the investors that invest in them. But also important for legislators that need to understand internal control-related regulation, as well as the supervisory authorities that enforce them.

Having served as a member of management teams, IT compliance manager and IT internal audit manager at major financial institutions, I do not have to be convinced about the importance of having adequate and effective internal controls in place. This is what directors of boards as well as managers depend on in the day-to-day activity in order to survive and remain on track. For me, this is what internal control is all about. Being able to trust data and business-related information and therefore the processes that are performed and decisions that are made based on that information. In the end, I think it is about being prepared and geared up in order to meet and tackle various market-related challenges head-on. A robust internal control system makes us prepared to go fast while not taking too many chances, much like how a car needs effective brakes in order to be able to go fast, and not slow. Hence, internal control is not primarily or solely an accounting term, as pointed out by Olof, but of vital interest for directors, managers, regulators, investors and customers. A book like this may thus increase awareness and knowledge about the different perspectives and facets of the concept of internal control. It can enable the different stakeholders to better understand what internal controls are, and how it may contribute to long-term business success. This book is accordingly an excellent example that deals with the way in which internal control is important for customers or the internal control designer, the director and manager, the legislators and supervisory authorities and for those that make investments in firms. As the recent credit and liquidity crisis has shown us, the business system is complex and interrelated. And while business opportunities are perhaps more than ever, ineffective risk management and internal control have proven to have severe negative consequences. I am convinced that a book such as this one may therefore add to our understanding about the way in which adequate and effective internal control keep firms safe, while allowing them also to aggressively pursue business return. I congratulate Olof on this achievement and recommend the book to the various professionals, students and scholars that are concerned with internal control.

August 2011

Tomas Munkby,
Partner and Head of Business Risk Services
Grant Thornton,
Stockholm Sweden.

Preface

In recent years, there have been increasing demands for improved governance and control of all types of organisations. Quite understandably, different stakeholders have differing views both about what should be achieved and how. To some, it seems a simple matter of truthful reporting, sometimes disregarding the problems of objective valuation in an uncertain world. To others, it is more a matter of avoiding fraud and questionable reward systems. Many link improved control to management of the risks facing the organisation. Others ask whether organisations, their boards and their management really have incentives to act in the best interests of their owners. Shareholders expect them to develop and exploit the organisation's assets in an optimal way, as probably do employees and other stakeholders. Today, such assets include market positions, brand names, available talent and other immaterial assets as well as more traditional ones such as plants, equipment and financial positions. Governance and control should encourage strategically appropriate actions and risk-taking that is reasonable and well considered. How can all these aims be achieved? And should they all be included in what we call *internal control*?

This book by Olof Arwinge is almost entirely based on his licentiate thesis for which we served as thesis advisors. An important aim for Olof's work was to clarify the origins and alternative interpretations given to the concept 'internal control'. It turned out to be older than we had expected, and its alternative contents – more or less those we described in the previous paragraph – were also suggested early in its history. At least from the mid-1950s, from time to time there has been a debate about what should be achieved for internal control to be considered good or even adequate.

Why then is this issue receiving more attention than ever now, a half century later?

We believe it has to do with increasing awareness that competitiveness or even survival is becoming more complex, as most organisations, at least in Europe and the USA, depend heavily on rapidly changing markets, both for demand and supply. Their developments are hard to predict, yet preparing for future scenarios through development efforts, new learning and investments may take longer than before.

The resulting risks are huge, exacerbated through uncertainties about protection of immaterial assets such as intellectual property and reputation.

As a consequence, we see even organisations with leading positions in their industries lose their grip, disappointing owners and employees. In such situations, it is natural to question the actions of boards and management. Did they know enough? Did they really act as stewards of the interests they should represent? Or was something wrong with internal information, processes and incentives?

Internal control thus becomes more difficult at the same time as it is more important. Its scope and what reasonably can be expected from it need to be discussed. For this purpose, we instigated a research programme with an advisory board consisting of representatives of The IIA's Swedish chapter and Far, the professional institute for public accountants and other accountancy professionals in Sweden. This programme is financed – including funding for the final stage of completing and publishing Olof's licentiate thesis – by the research foundation of Jan Wallander and Tom Hedelius as well as that of Tore Browaldh.

This book provides an up-to-date summary of the emergence and use of the term *internal control* in the literature, and an analysis of some themes concerning how it can be designed and used. Like with all academic dissertations in Sweden, this book is the work of its author and does not necessarily represent the views of his advisors or of the practitioners on the programme's advisory board. It has, however, already led to valuable discussions among researchers and practitioners in Sweden and will certainly continue to do so now that the programme has continued with additional projects.

Uppsala 8 September 2011

Fredrik Nilsson
Professor of Business Studies,
especially Accounting
Department of Business Studies
Uppsala University

Nils-Göran Olve
Guest professor
Department of Business Studies
Uppsala University

Summary

This thesis studies the accounting and auditing approach to control where the concept of internal control has developed along with the theory and practice of accounting and auditing and its stated objectives. In this context, internal control has traditionally been regarded as a means of ensuring financial reporting quality as well as a way of preventing and detecting fraudulent activity.

We have surveyed scientific research on the subject of internal control and reviewed regulatory texts as well as practical frameworks and standards. Based on this literature study, we have investigated some of the findings from previous research. Components and particular features of internal control were described and discussed. We have also identified and summarised themes and issues that frequently occur in writings on the subject.

During recent years, demands have been made for greater accountability and transparency in corporate governance. The independent audit activity has become the primary tool for securing accountability. Some regard this as the emergence of an audit society. An important joint development has been the rise of internal control systems. Internal control, once a private matter for technical assurance specialists, has risen to be an autonomous field of expertise and a mode of organising uncertainty. Traditionally, internal control has had a fairly direct relationship to the accounting records. The wider approaches to internal control have expanded its boundaries significantly, far beyond the financial reports and the duties of the accountant. Internal control has become an all-encompassing process.

Enterprise risk management practices are growing and evolving. An associated development has been that internal control has become more closely tied to these risk management practices, and therefore also to the formulation and execution of strategies. New risk-related regulations and practical frameworks have contributed to the transformation of internal control into an extension of risk management. Internal control is now considered to be a form of risk treatment through which risk may be managed in different ways.

Internal control is today a primary regulatory and formal policy object. Lawmakers and supervisory authorities are increasingly concerned with the design and operating effectiveness of internal controls. Disclosure requirements imposed on firms are forcing them to provide public disclosures about their internal control systems, which were previously private to firms.

Both scientific research and practical writings suggest that internal control designs are contingent upon certain variables. These variables include company objectives and strategies, regulatory characteristics, risk and risk appetite, firm size and managements' attitudes to risk and control. Building internal control capabilities is important if firms are to be able to design balanced, integrated, dynamic and cost-effective internal controls.

Internal control is considered to be a key corporate governance mechanism. Some researchers however, have pointed out that there is still much to learn about internal control quality and how internal control is associated with corporate governance quality. The fact that internal control is an inherently complex concept poses a significant research barrier, and while all research methods are valid, it is unlikely that archival studies or experiments are able to measure internal control quality. Instead, we recommend case studies of how firms design, apply, and oversee their systems of internal control.

This study was made possible through the research collaboration between my former employer, Skandia, and Linköping University through the Research Programme for Auditors and Consultants. During the final stage, generous funding was provided by the Jan Wallanders and Tom Hedelius foundation as well as the Tore Browaldhs foundation.

Acknowledgements

Writing this thesis could not have been done without the input, support and guidance from a number of people. First of all, I am grateful to my supervisors, professors Fredrik Nilsson and Nils-Göran Olve, for their patience and intellectual support and whose advice has helped me significantly in my work. I would also like to express my gratitude to the senior researchers and Ph.D. colleagues at EIS and the Research Program for Auditors and Consultants at Linköping University, especially Dr. Mikael Scheja (econ), econ.lic. Jesper Fagerberg and econ.lic. Elisabeth Styf have been supportive and helpful throughout the process. My stay at the Manchester Business School at an early stage of the research process allowed me to develop and refine my research idea. Advice from professors Stuart Turley and Sven Modell were of great value. Other Marie Curie Fellows were also of great help through their insightful comments and moral support.

The completion of the doctoral studies is taking place at the department of business studies at Uppsala University and I am thankful to my fellow doctoral colleagues and senior researchers. My research at Uppsala University has allowed me to refine and develop my insights regarding governance, risk management and internal control. Along with my lead supervisors, assisting supervisor Dr. Gunilla Eklöv Alander (econ.) deserves recognition.

I would also like to express my gratitude to my former employer Skandia, for their flexibility and professional approach which allowed me to do research while still working with auditing. I am also grateful to my current employer, Grant Thornton, for their people-oriented approach which has allowed me to move forward in my Ph.D. studies in a professional and exciting work environment. Their support is vital and I am grateful to Tomas Munkby, Roland Dansell and my other colleagues at Grant Thornton. My family and friends are obviously extremely important in anything I do and there are a number of people that have helped and supported me throughout this process: I would like to thank you. Finally, Pamela Vang's efforts to improve my English must also be acknowledged.

This study was made possible through the research collaboration between my former employer Skandia and Linköping University. During the final stage, generous funding was provided by the Jan Wallanders and Tom Hedelius foundation as well as the Tore Browaldhs foundation. This book is based on my thesis for the degree of licentiate of economics, Linköping University.

Stockholm Olof Arwinge

Contents

List of Figures

List of Tables

Chapter 1
Introduction

Abstract

Purpose: The aim of this chapter is to introduce the general research idea, purpose and the research method as well as to provide an overview of the general thesis structure and content.

Synopsis: This thesis will study the accounting and auditing approach to control where the concept of internal control has developed along with the theory and practice of auditing and its stated objectives. The concept of internal control goes back over 100 years and was first recognized in formal literature on auditing in 1892. Since the concept was first established, there has been a century of debate as to its definition and content and official definitions have often proven to be controversial. During the last 15 years, there have been loud calls for better and stronger corporate governance. Continuing corporate malfunctions, changes in shareholder patterns and the legal climate are some of the key drivers behind these calls. Demands have been made for greater accountability and transparency and the independent audit activity has hereby become the primary tool for securing accountability. An important joint development with the emerging audit society has been the rise of internal control systems. Internal control, once a private matter for technical assurance specialists, has risen to be an autonomous field or expertise and a mode of organizing uncertainty. Traditionally internal control had a fairly direct relationship to the accounting records. With the introduction of broader definitions, internal control has significantly expanded its domains into general management control and corporate governance. However the concept seems to be under-explored by social scientists and thus there is a need for more research into this area. The purpose of this research enterprise is to provide an account of existing research on internal controls. This will be done based on a literature review where academic papers published by other researchers on the subject have been surveyed. This thesis comprises of six chapters in total. Chapter 1 provides an introduction to the general research idea and method. In the following chapters, theories that explain the need for control systems will be discussed as well as a practical framework on internal control. Chapter 4 provides a regulatory perspective and

O. Arwinge, *Internal Control*, Contributions to Management Science,
DOI 10.1007/978-3-7908-2882-5_1,

Chap. 5 takes up those common themes and issues which frequently occur in existing research on internal control. The final chapter makes concluding observations and provides suggestions for future research.

1.1 Call for Improved Corporate Governance

The concepts of governance and internal control are by no means new (see Haun, 1955; Zannetos, 1964; Lee, 1971). Even the Bible makes explicit references to the rationale for installing internal controls and gives a number of examples of traditional controls, such as the restriction of access, the segregation of work duties and the importance of having honest and competent staff (Ramamoorti, 2003, p. 3). In fact, research on the historical development of internal controls shows that signs of internal control can be found as early as 3600–3200 B.C in the early Mesopotamian civilization. In a paper by Lee (1971) on the historical development of internal control, Kenneth S. Most is quoted. Most claims that:

> It was customary for summaries to be prepared by scribes other than those who had provided original lists of payments. Further, the documents of the period reveal tiny marks, dots, ticks and circles at the side of the figures, indicating that checking had been performed. (p. 151)

Accordingly, it seems that already then "business managers" had established a system of controls where certain accounting duties were segregated in order to prevent fraud and protect assets. Traditionally, the rationale behind effective governance and control is closely related to the custody and protection of assets.

The problems resulting from the separation of ownership and control (Jensen & Meckling, 1976; Fama & Jensen, 1983) have a long time now researched. Adam Smith (1776), the father of scientific economics, pointed to the dangers of people being in charge of other people's money rather than their own. Smith claimed that "it cannot be expected that they should watch over it with the same anxious vigilances which the partners in a private copartnery frequently watch over their own" (p. 700). Following the early work by Berle and Means (1932), the problems that arise as a result from large corporate size, including issues such as how shareholders should best control large corporations, have been widely researched.

During the last 15 years, there have been loud calls for strengthened corporate governance. Governance, organizational governance and corporate governance are terms which are increasingly emphasized today (Netter, Poulsen, & Stegemoller, 2009). Not surprisingly, different definitions of the concept exist although most exhibit significant similarities. Corporate governance focuses attention on the relationship between two key parties: the shareholders and the managers of the firm. Debt-holders, however, sometimes assume the status of owners or shareholders (Williamson, 1985, p. 304). Shareholders are represented by the board of directors and its committees. The traditional school of corporate governance with roots in *free market theory* focuses exclusively on maximizing profits for stockholders. Accordingly the corporate governance relationship only includes managers and shareholders.

This traditional free market view is supplemented by the *stakeholder-view* where additional parties are included in the governance relationships (Bhasa, 2004, pp. 8–9). Here, the responsibilities of the corporation clearly extend beyond the shareholders (DesJardins & McCall, 2005, pp. 6–7, 66–67).

The Cadbury Code (1992) in the United Kingdom refers to corporate governance as "the system by which companies are directed and controlled" (Handley-Schachler, Juleff, & Paton, 2007, p. 624). Handley-Schachler, Juleff and Paton (2007) argue that the definition of corporate governance provided by the OECD (Organization for Economic Co-operation and Development) from 1999, whereas emphasizing the relationship between shareholders, its representatives and the management of the firm, builds on the stakeholder view and accordingly suggests a somewhat wider relationship. The definition from 2004 (OECD, 2004, p. 11) reads:

> Corporate governance involves a set of relationships between a company's management, its board, its shareholders and other stakeholders. Corporate governance also provides the structure through which the objectives of the company are set, and the means of attaining those objectives and monitoring performance are determined. Good corporate governance should provide proper incentives for the board and management to pursue objectives that are in the interests of the company and its shareholders and should facilitate effective monitoring.

For the purpose of this thesis, we will apply a rather simple and straightforward definition of corporate governance obtained from Lazarides and Drimpetas (2008). The authors refer to "management as running the business and governance as overseeing that the firm is run properly"(p. 74). It follows that governance is about the duties and responsibilities of the board of directors and its committees and the way they oversee and monitor management and business activity.

As mentioned earlier, there have lately been loud calls for a better governance of firms. According to Hermanson and Rittenberg (2003) these loud calls for improved corporate governance may be divided into three key drivers. These drivers are illustrated in Fig. 1.1 below.

As seen from Fig. 1.1, continuing corporate mal-functions and disasters have been a key driver in corporate governance developments. In the United Kingdom, a number of incidents in the early 1990s stimulated discussion about the effectiveness of governance mechanisms established to avoid such incidents, including the financial reporting mechanism and the independent audit (see Power, 1997, pp. 22, 33, 54; also 2007, p. 34).

As a result, The Cadbury Code, released in 1992, formed a part of the following agenda for reforming corporate governance in the United Kingdom (Solomon, Solomon, Norton, & Joseph, 2000, p. 48). The Cadbury Report was named after its author, Sir Adrian Cadbury, and defined effective corporate governance through a number of basic principles. The Cadbury Code became a pioneer in corporate governance and has been widely influential and exported to countries all over the world (Chapman, 2003a, p. 38; Power, 2007, pp. 34–35).

Similarly, in the United States a number of well-known corporate malfunctions, such as the Enron-disaster occurred and shook investor's confidence as enormous assets were wiped out and one of the biggest audit firms, Arthur Andersen, went out

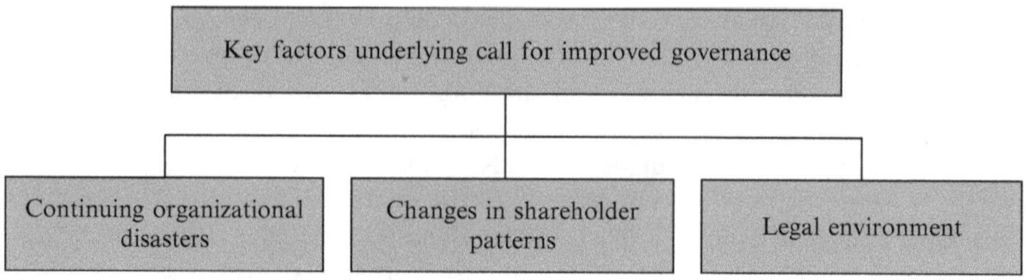

Fig. 1.1 Demands for better corporate governance (Hermanson & Rittenberg, 2003, p. 39)

of business (Vinten, 2002, 2003; Yakhou & Dorweiler, 2004; Tackett, Wolf, & Claypool, 2004) The response was quick in 2002 when President George W. Bush made the Sarbanes-Oxley Bill into a law which imposed a number of significant governance rules on public companies listed on the New York stock exchange in the United States.[1]

Sweden too has been unable to escape from corporate malfunctions and high-profile fraud cases. As a result a government commission, the commission for trust [Förtroendekomissionen], was established in order to restore trust in the Swedish business community and financial markets. A Code group [Kodgruppen] was formed by the commission which subsequently in 2004 developed a proposal for a corporate governance code of conduct, Sweden's first. This new corporate governance code was modeled after the pioneering code in the United Kingdom and thus followed the *comply-or-explain* nature of the Cadbury Code (see SOU, 2004b: 130, p. 5; SOU 2004a: 46, pp. 10–11; also see Jonnergård & Larsson, 2007, p. 467).[2]

The current global turmoil in financial institutions, with a number of collapses including the high-profile collapse of Lehman Brothers, is only the most recent example that shows how organizational disasters put focus on the effectiveness of the governance arrangements and risk oversight of firms (see Kirkpatrick, 1962; and OECD, 2009a, b; also Birkenshaw & Jenkins, 2009; Senior Supervisors Group, 2009).

[1] The complete name of this law is: *An act to protect investors by improving the accuracy and reliability of corporate disclosures made pursuant to the securities laws, for other purposes*. This is the public law 107–204 by the 107th Congress, United States, dated July 30 2002. The law may be cited in short as the "Sarbanes-Oxley Act of 2002" but we will repeatedly refer to this Act as SOX (2002) as this is common in papers on the subject.

[2] See proposal from the Code group in SOU 2004, p. 46 [Svensk Kod för Bolagsstyrning. Förlsag från Kodgruppen] and the subsequent handling of the formal referral process through SOU 2004, p. 130 [Svensk Kod för Bolagsstyrning. Betänkande av Kodgruppen]. The work by the Code group was done in collaboration with a number of associations for stock market issues (see SOU, 2004, pp. 46, 130; also Jonnergård & Larsson, 2007, p. 467). Today the code group has changed into the Swedish Corporate Governance Board [Kollegiet för Svensk Bolagsstyrning] which mission is to promote good corporate governance practices and administer the Swedish code of Corporate Governance [Svensk Kod för Bolagsstyrning]. In connection to the treatment of different themes and issues in this thesis we will sometimes refer to the work by this Board. To simplify we often cite this in short as SCGB.

In addition to corporate failures, changes in shareholder patterns have resulted in investors asserting power over boards and management, and have required certain board characteristics and governance arrangements. According to Williamson (1985), the classical work by Berle and Means (1932) pointed to the problems resulting from diffuse ownership whereby it was concluded that the possibility of management operating the business in its own interests could not be dismissed (Williamson, 1985, p. 299). According to Williamson the board of directors should therefore be regarded as a primary governance structure safeguard between the firm and the owners (p. 298).

Hence executive management and executive powers have traditionally been regarded as a key driver for effective corporate governance and the risk of inappropriate management behavior is also recognized in practitioner texts on the subject (see Apostolou, Hassell, & Webber, 2001, pp. 49–50; Radin, 2008, pp. 6–7) and audit standards (see IAASB, ISA 240, 2006, p. 7; or FAR SRS, RS 240, 2009, p. 232).

It is however important to point out that executive management has also been referred to as a vital component in ensuring sound governance and management. By using terms such as *tone-at-the-top* and the *control environment* both practical frameworks and professional audit standards indicate the importance of management attitudes in fostering a healthy and sound approach to risk taking and general business practice. Scientific studies have also shown the importance of top management behavior for engineering appropriate employee behavior (see Holmes, Langford, Welch, & Welch, 2002) and financial reporting decisions (see D'Aquila, 1998).

A third important driver for the increasing attention given to good corporate governance is the legal climate in some parts of the world, where legal risk appears to have increased thus contributing to the demand for improved governance practices (Hermanson & Rittenberg, 2003, p. 39).

It is undoubtedly so that corporate governance, or overseeing that firms are run appropriately, has attracted significant attention during the last 15 years and has become a key theme in corporate regulation (Power, 2007, p. 34). Perhaps we can observe a slight shift in focus: *from the importance of managing the firm to the importance of governing the firm.*

1.2 The Audit Society

The last 15 years have witnessed a significant increase in attention paid to one of the key accountability mechanisms – namely the independent audit. Michael Power, an influential British professor, has written extensively about the audit society (1997, 2000 and 2003b) and more recently about a society trying to organize its uncertainties into manageable risks (2004, 2005, 2006, 2007; Power et al., 2009). These expressions relate to the attention that audit activity has been given and the enormous *increase in audit activity* in both public and private life.

The cause of the explosion in the area of auditing can be found in two areas, according to Power (2003b). The first one relates to the way in which accounting has developed and which describes the expansion of accounting related practices driving audit. Auditing orientations focusing on arrangements that secure economy, effectiveness, efficiency and compliance are constantly growing and evolving, shaped by demand and available technologies (Power, 1997, pp. 49–51). In these cases, auditors may become change agents, *making things auditable*, rather than just a verifier (Power, 2003b, pp. 188–189).

The second area relates to the rise of new public management and its related quality assurance models of organizational control, and the increased demands for accountability and transparency, which have resulted from failure in trust of existing mechanisms of accountability. The audit explosion has been closely driven by political demands on behalf of the various stakeholders in societies and organizations – tax payers, customers and citizens. Quality assurance ideas have become blueprints for good organizational practices and the model of self-observation, inspection and external monitoring of systems of controls is fundamental today (p. 189).

As a result, there have been demands for greater accountability and transparency of organizations and institutions. Roberts and Scapens (1985, p. 447) define accountability "as the giving and demanding of reasons for conduct". Accountability and account giving is a natural part of being a member of society. Power (1997, pp. 1–4) argues that in situations characterized by doubt, conflict, uncertainty or mistrust, this account giving becomes the object of explicit checking. Statements and accounts need to be verified and evidenced. However, detailed scrutinization and verification of all social activity is neither economically viable nor reasonable. Hence, a balance is needed.

Thus the concept of trust thus becomes important for this discussion. Trust involves placing ourselves in a vulnerable position and relying on others not to take advantage of this (DesJardins & McCall, 2005, pp. 238). DesJardins and McCall (2005, p. 238) argue that trust is a vital component in all private and public activity.

> In any social setting, individuals need to rely on others, need to trust others. In modern business, trust is a fundamental requirement. I trust that drivers will stop as I enter a crosswalk, I trust that the food I eat is safe, I trust when I take my prescribed medicine that my doctor has accurately diagnosed my illness.

Even the founder of scientific economics, Adam Smith, did not exclude the importance of trust and mutual confidence (see Sen, 1993). Without this trust the cost of running the economic system would indeed be great. Placed orders could never be trusted and order execution and delivery would only be performed based on full prepayment. Too many and too costly safeguards would have to be required (p. 48) and the end result would become an inefficient economic system which ultimately, and necessarily, would break down. Evidence suggest that the growing knowledge industry in the global economy requires a greater reliance on trust (Burns & Nixon, 2005, p. 261).

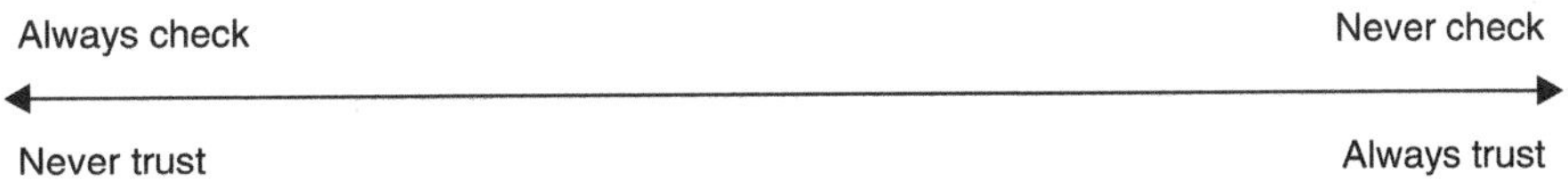

Fig. 1.2 Control versus trust as an organizing principle

Trust and mutual confidence also play a role in the classical work on transaction cost economics by Williamson (1985). Transaction cost economics, building on the work by Simon (1948), assumes that "behavior is intendedly rational but only limitedly so and is given to opportunism which is a condition of self-interest seeking with guile" (Williamson, 1985, p. 30). In a contractual relationship between parties, where the component of opportunism is non-existing, Williamson argues that "contract execution goes efficiently to completion because promises of the above-described kind are, in the absence of opportunism, self-enforcing. Contract, in this context, reduces to a world of promise." (p. 31)

Researchers such as McEvily, Perrone and Zaheer (2003) view trust as an important *organizing principle* and Skinner and Spira (2003) point to the importance of considering trust in the organization and controlling of firms. Trust releases us from checking and may accordingly function as an efficient and costless organizing principle and form of control providing, however, that people are able to place trust in others and that those people later prove to be trust*worthy*. Therein lies the dilemma.

All corporate scandals have involved violations of trust (DesJardins & McCall, 2005, p. 238), whereby trust obviously have been misplaced. Employees, investors, suppliers and consumers have all suffered great harm from these violations. As a result of the (resulting) mistrust, formal control and explicit checking have become increasingly important.

As we mentioned, trust releases us from checking, while mistrust, doubt and uncertainty force us to check. What is the appropriate balance one might ask? To a large extent this seems to be a function of what is demanded by society in general, what it is prepared to trust and the types of risk that it accepts (Power, 1997, p. 3). Accordingly, this may differ between societies, organizations and even between sub-groups within the same organization. Figure 1.2 illustrates the general relationship between checking and trusting.

Audit has become a key tool for securing accountability. According to Power (1997, pp. 10–11), the corporate actions taken by organizational members are made legitimate through examination and scrutiny. Organizastional action is in this way made into legitimate pieces of work as auditors, of various kinds, certify as to its adequacy.

1.3 Internal Control

This is a thesis about the concept of internal control. To tell any story about control appears to be a challenging task, since the term is full of nuances and has been defined in many ways. Control lies at the heart of academic fields such as organization, management control, management accounting and auditing. Academic fields which, with regard to control, exhibit significant overlap (Merchant and Otley in Chapman, Hopwood, & Shields, eds. 2007, pp. 786–787; also see Power, 2007, p. 62) but remain fragmented into their respective research domains (Maijoor, 2000, p. 102; also Merchant and Otley in Chapman, Hopwood, & Shields eds. 2007, p. 788).

To provide one single definition of the concept of control in organizational theory seems difficult since it has been defined in various ways and terms. Originally, the word control comes from the French language where it means *to check* (Tannenbaum, 1968, p. 5). Tannenbaum suggests that it is commonly used synonymously with terms such as influence and power, but that there are differences of opinion between scholars as to what these terms actually mean. Tannenbaum refers to control as "any process in which a person or group of persons or organization of persons determines, that is, intentionally affects, the behaviors of another person group or organization" (p. 5).

Accordingly, the definition of control is rather closely related to the term power, but as pointed out by Tannenbaum, many writers tend to view power as potential control, that is, a source of control but not actual control – it is an "ability and capacity to exercise control" (p. 5). Mintzberg re-enforces this view when he refers to the levers of power as means or systems of influence. These can then be used by an influencer to control decisions and actions (Mintzberg, 1983, p. 22).

This thesis will describe the accounting and auditing approach to control. Here, the concept of *internal control* has been developed along with the theory and practice of accounting and auditing and its stated objectives (Brown, 1962). In this context, internal control has traditionally been regarded as a means of ensuring reliable bookkeeping procedures as well as a way of preventing and detecting fraudulent activity (see Lee ed., 1988).

1.3.1 The Origins of Internal Control

The first slight recognition of the importance of control in accounting and auditing texts appeared in 1892, with the publication of the book *Auditing* by the English audit-specialist Lawrence Dicksee. According to Dicksee, a key task for the auditor was to review the system of controls and to look for the weakest points. The purpose of this procedure was to determine how much substantive testing was necessary.

In this book, internal control referred to as a *system of internal check, installed by the company itself,* and a matter that the financial statement auditor should consider before reviewing the annual accounts. Thus, for the outside independent auditor, control became the organization's own internal system of control.

Since internal control was first established as a concept in the accounting and auditing literature, there has been a century of debate as to its definition and content

(Heier, Dugan, & Sayers, 2005) and official definitions have often proven to be controversial (Hay, 1993). In 1992 the COSO (Committee of Sponsoring Organizations of the Treadway Commission) released their now globally accepted framework *Internal Control – Integrated Framework* – which defined internal control as:

> A process, effected by an entity's board of directors, management and other personnel, designed to provide reasonable assurances regarding the achievement of objectives in the following categories: Effectiveness and efficiency of operations, reliability of financial reporting and compliance with applicable laws and regulations. (p. 9)

The COSO differed from earlier definitions in at least two vital aspects. Firstly, it focused on *process* instead of system or structure, highlighting the loose and flexible character of internal control as opposed to it being a static and rigid system (see Kinney, 2000). Secondly, the objectives of internal control now included *other objectives in addition to the financial reporting quality* objective. Different internal control definitions exist, but COSO has been widely diffused and now serves as a reference point for both managerial practices and regulatory designs around the world (Power, 2007, p. 49).

1.3.2 The Development of Internal Control

As mentioned in Sect. 1.1 various incidents of corporate malfunction and management fraud have been a key driver behind the demands for improved organizational governance. As a result of these high-profile incidents, both the financial reporting mechanism and the independent audit – considered to be two fundamental accountability mechanisms – have been criticized. Along with the quest for better financial transparency and accountability, a *third accountability mechanism* has appeared onto the corporate governance scene – internal control.

An important joint development in the emerging audit society has namely been the *rise of internal control systems* (Power, 2007, pp. 34–65), which researchers have referred to as an internal control explosion (Maijoor, 2000), a re-invention of internal controls (Spira & Page, 2003) and an audit explosion (Power, 1997). It is difficult to overstate the growth and importance of internal controls today and Power (2007) argues that "internal control systems now lie at the very centre of governance thinking and practice; their design principles are now global" (p. 35).

Internal control, once a private matter for technical assurance specialists, has risen to become an autonomous field of expertise and a way of organizing and processing uncertainty (Power, 2007, pp. 47, 62). It is now considered to be an *extension of risk management* (Power, 2007, p. 35) and thus tied closely to the management of risk relating to strategy formulation and execution (COSO, 2004; Power, 2007; Mikes, 2009; COSO, 2009c). This is indeed an impressive development.

1.3.3 The Expansion of Internal Control

Different trends in business society have contributed to the expansion of internal control and the increased attention which it now receives. Brown argued in his essay from 1962 that there was trend towards greater reliance on internal controls. He provides four primary reasons for this: rising costs in public accounting and the consequent additional emphasis on economy and effectiveness, the increased complexity of business enterprise resulting in geometric compounding of data control problems, the development of new communications and information systems as well as the introduction of extremely reliable data processing machines, and requests received by the auditor from management, owners and other parties-at-interest for additional information (p. 696). Today however, these trends identified by Brown must today however be supplemented with other developments.

With the introduction of wider definitions of internal control such as the COSO (1992), the concept is now a process which may provide reasonable assurance that different objectives, both financial and non-financial, may be met. The traditional approaches, where controls are generally directly related to the accounting records, have been supplemented by wider approaches. Today, a significant amount of organizational activity falls under the range of internal control (Maijoor, 2000) and conceptions of the concept have broadened. It would seem that internal control has *expanded its domains* significantly to form an integral part of overall management control system, and furthermore the corporate governance system of firms (Maijoor, 2000; Merchant & Otley in Chapman, Hopwood, & Shields eds., 2007, p. 787). Today, internal control today is therefore as much an object and tool for the director and manager, as for the accountant and assurance specialist.

Internal control has always had a direct relationship with risk. After all, as long ago as in 1892 and 1905, Dicksee recommended that accountants should look for the system's weakest points where risk exposures of accounting errors were greater. Later, the COSO included risk assessment as one of five internal control components. With the release of *Enterprise Risk Management – Integrated Framework* (COSO, 2004) however, the link between risk management and internal control has been made more explicit.

Researchers have discussed this development in terms of the reinvention of internal controls and its mutation into general risk management (see Spira and Page, 2003; Power, 2007). Power observes that "the COSO approach requires that the design and operation of controls be linked to, and follow from, a prior process of risk assessment (. . .) control design is explicitly related to the assessment of risk to entity objectives and sub-objectives" (p. 49). Recent thought papers commissioned by COSO on how organizations embrace and embed enterprise risk management (COSO, 2011), the crucial role of the board of directors as they oversee risk management practices of firms (2009b, 2010a) and the way in which firms more effectively may indentify and manage emerging risks also underscore the link between risk management and internal control.

With high-profile corporate malfunctions taking place all around the world, regulatory agencies have made internal control and risk management key *regulatory objects*. The current crisis within the financial sector with high-profile organizational collapses is only the most recent example of malfunctions which put the spotlight on governance, risk and internal control (see OECD, 2009a, 2009b; Birkenshaw & Jenkins, 2009, Senior Supervisors Group, 2009; The Walker Review, 2009).

This development may also be observed in the Swedish case, where supervisory authorities, most visibly perhaps the financial supervisory authority [Finansinspektionen], increasingly seem to criticize firms for their internal control and risk management deficiencies (see Arwinge & Munkby, 2011; Finansinspektionen, 2011, Grant Thornton, 2012). Internal control now constitutes a key part of most mandatory and semi-mandatory corporate governance codes and regulations. Furthermore these corporate governance codes and regulations in addition often include internal control and risk management disclosure requirements, forcing firms to describe and disclose information which may be of use for analysts, investors and other users of financial statements and internal control reports.

In a world where internal controls have *gone on-record* it is not surprising then that the concept has become a managerial object. Managers today pay increasingly more attention to the design and operating effectiveness of controls while directors and audit committee members pay increasingly more attention to ensuring that managers do so. Failure to do this effectively has proven to have severe consequences.

Corporate reputation, defined as the outcome of the shared impressions of a firm (Bebbington, Larrinaga, & Moneva, 2008, p. 339), is today considered to be a strategic resource with the potential of having value creating properties (Dolphin, 2004). These properties may include creating premium product prices, lowering the cost of capital, improving staff loyalty, allowing greater latitude in decision making and providing a goodwill cushion when there is a crisis (Bebbington, Larrinaga, & Moneva, 2008, p. 339). In the case of the audit firm Andersen, the actions of one relatively small office resulted in the disappearance of the whole firm because its reputation was so badly damaged (Pharoah, 2003, p. 46). "Risk to reputation is tricky; like a spider's web, reputation is build strand by strand over time, is easy to damage, and difficult, if not impossible, to repair" (Holland, 2009, p. 11).

So in the ultimate defense of a company's reputational capital, strategic, operational, compliance and reporting risks need to be managed. In this way company's internal control systems have become part of the *risk response mechanisms* of firms where the internal control system is conceptualized within a broader framework that focus fully on risk from an entity-wide perspective (COSO, 2004).

We can conclude that currently, a number of stakeholders have great interest in the functioning and possible malfunctioning, of firms' systems of internal controls. Regulators, supervisory authorities, directors and audit committee members, managers as well as analysts and investors are all most likely to consider internal controls rather differently than they did only a few years ago.

The concept of internal controls has truly developed and expanded its domains during the past 15 years, ensuring its place in the spotlight but also creating substantial expectations as to what internal controls must do, or should do. And as in the case of the audit expectations gap (see Sherer & Turley, 1997, p. 13) the possibility of an internal control expectations gap cannot be neglected, which means that there may be a difference between what stakeholders want internal control to be, or assume it to be, and what internal controls really are.

1.4 Research Motive and Purpose

This section describes the overall purpose of this piece of research. We will also provide an account of the motives behind this research enterprise. This piece of research is about internal control, but why are internal controls interesting or important to research? What necessitates scientific studies into this area? Before we go into the purpose of this research, we will below discuss some of our motives behind this enterprise and also briefly discuss potential implications for scholars and practitioners.

1.4.1 Research Motives

Perhaps the most compelling reason for doing research into internal controls is that the existing body of research appears to be insufficient. Kinney (2000, p. 83) claimed a few years ago that:

> Knowledge about internal control is an essential element that affects the welfare of management, corporate directors, shareholders, trading partners of an entity, auditors and society at large – yet it is relatively unexplored by researchers. All major research methods are applicable. . .(. . .). . .In short there is an outstanding opportunity for research in internal controls for accounting and auditing professors and for Ph.D. students.

Kinney accordingly argues that internal control is *under-explored* by researchers – a fact which certainly would motivate a research enterprise into this area. Power (2007, p. 62) seemingly agrees with Kinney as he claims that the concept has hardly received any serious intellectual attention so far:

> For many years, the subject of internal controls has been a private matter for a sub-group of technical control assurance specialists. . .(....) The practice by which corporations, corner shops, clubs and churches maintain a basic level of financial and non-financial control over resources, has hardly been worthy of serious intellectual attention.

Furthermore, in a recent paper on auditing research by Humphrey (2007) the author claims that little is known about auditing in practical settings (p. 171). Considering the fact that internal control is closely associated with the practice of auditing, one may infer that little is also known about internal control in practical settings. Thus additional studies that investigate the details of the workings of internal control seem important.

Internal controls now lie at the heart of governance thinking and practice (Power, 2007, p. 35) and form part of public policy, formal law and corporate governance codes. Researchers like Maijoor (2000, p. 102) however, claim that the concept of internal control as a key corporate governance mechanism remains under-explored.

> Also, most internal control research in accounting is not conducted within the context of wider corporate governance issues. Hence, many claims about the value of internal control systems for corporate governance still need to be studied.

It seems that much of the literature on internal control has traditionally taken a technical perspective, focusing on the duties of the accountant which is not surprising since for a long time internal control has been a private matter for technical assurance specialists (Power, 2007, p. 62). The auditor's perspective of internal control however, is only one of many today. Increasingly, the regulator's, director's, manager's and investor's perspectives of internal control are important to depict and discuss. We claim that there is an emerging need for studies that *synthesize* and *integrate* different perspectives on internal control (see Maijoor, 2000; also Chapman, Hopwood, & Shields eds. 2007, p. 788).

The body of research on control is vast but also fragmented into different fields (Maijoor, 2000, p. 102; Merchant & Otley in Chapman, Hopwood, & Shields eds. 2007, p. 788). Broader approaches to internal control exhibit, significant similarities definition-wise to the way in which general management control is usually defined (p. 787) and internal control as a concept draws upon theory from other fields such as risk management, organization, strategy and general management control (Kinney, 2000, p. 88). Studies on internal control that aim at combining theoretical concepts from different academic fields may therefore be important.

Another motive and one which is perhaps of a more opportunist nature for doing research into the area of internal control, could be the increasing attention that the concept has been given during the last 15 years. As mentioned in Sects. 1.3.2 and 1.3.3 increasing attention is now given by different stakeholders to the internal control and risk management practices of firms. The fact that internal control is now a key regulatory and public policy object (Power, 2007, p. 47) and considered to be a crucial governance mechanism certainly motivates additional scientific studies on the subject.

From a local Swedish perspective, broad research into internal control is important. Just as there is a lack of research on risk management and internal controls from an international perspective (see Mikes, 2009, p. 19), so too is research on the subject from a local Swedish perspective. Studies on the subject do however exist. See for example Jonnergård and Larsson (2007) who discuss the development of corporate governance codes of conduct and therefore touch upon internal control from a regulatory perspective. Also see a recent study by Franck and Sundgren (2010) on internal control investments by Swedish noted companies. Arwinge and Munkby (2011) have also done a study on internal control deficiencies noted by the

Swedish Financial Supervisory Authority [Finansinspektionen] during 1999–2010. To the best of our knowledge, however, Swedish research studies that go into the design, application and effects of internal control are scarce.

Finally Holme and Solvang, (1991) as well as Bryman (2004) argue that an important reason for doing research into an area is that the scientist should find it interesting and thus the research may originate in personal interests and experience (Bryman, 2004, p. 32). This is certainly true in this case.

1.4.1.1 Relevance for Scholars

From a scientific perspective, it may be important to find out what we know about internal control today. We have already mentioned that it appears that literature on the subject is insufficient and fragmented. Accordingly, a study that goes into the details of the concept and takes different perspectives may be important. Studies that discuss the detailed components and aspects of internal controls could be of relevance for undergraduate students as well as PhD students and senior researchers that specialize, or are interested, in this area. What do we know so far? What do we need to know more about, and which are the crucial research questions? To know more may perhaps be even more important from a local Swedish perspective since internal control practices today are widely diffused and developed while research is scarce. Accordingly, studies which may contribute to our knowledge and understanding about internal controls but also provide directions for the futures should be of importance for scholars.

1.4.1.2 Relevance for Practitioners

Even though practice in this area may be ahead of the research, a scientific study of internal control may still be relevant for practitioners, particularly since internal control practitioners today come in different "shapes and forms" and are no longer restricted to being assurance specialists or accountants. Directors, managers, analysts, regulators and specialists such as risk- and compliance officers, may find it useful to know more about the components and features of the concept.

While a number of groups may be well trained in risk and control, others are not. Managers and directors for example may lack some of the necessary understanding and skills in this area, something that has been pointed out at times by both academic writers and other commentators. In addition, specialist functions such as risk management, legal departments, security departments and the different kinds of officers specializing in anti-fraud or anti-money laundering activities could possibly also find it useful to know more about the specifics of internal controls. Further, regulators and analysts could possibly also benefit from a study into internal control. Increasingly, internal control and risk management practices are being considered and reviewed by investors and analysts and other corporate governance report users. Regulators and supervisory authorities of different kinds may also find studies such as this useful for regulatory design purposes.

1.4.2 Research Purpose and Questions

Above, we have explained why a study into the area of internal control may be both relevant and legitimate. A study needs a purpose however, and in the case of this thesis the overall purpose is to increase our understanding of internal control. This entails providing an account that may help in deepening our understanding of the complexities of the concept (Kinney, 2000, p. 88), as well as providing some clues as to what the important aspects and features may be. More specifically, the purpose of this thesis is to achieve the following:

- To provide an account of existing research on internal controls.
- To provide an account of components and features of internal control.

Based on a literature study we will investigate some of the findings that research has generated so far within this area. When doing that we will also describe and discuss different themes and issues that occur in the existing writings on internal control. We will also describe and discuss the components and the particular features of the concept so that readers may better grasp and understand its complexities. In order to fulfill the purpose of this study, we have generated specific research questions that will guide us through this thesis. Our research questions are the following:

- What are the key components of internal control?
- What are the key features of internal control?

1.5 Research Method

How will we go about answering these questions? In this section we will briefly describe our chosen research method as well as discuss some of the methodological challenges that we faced during the course of the research process.

1.5.1 Literature Study

Research method is about organizing and interpreting information so that we better may be able to understand society (Holme & Solvang, 1991, p. 12). Different research approaches are available for social scientists based on the nature of the phenomena that they investigate. These are sometimes referred to as qualitative or quantitative techniques and the two different approaches have their respective advantages and disadvantages (p. 13). Method is not simply about the choice between different neutral investigative techniques but it is also related to different visions about how social reality should be investigated. Nor is method completely intertwined with certain views of reality however (Bryman, 2004, p. 4). Any concerns regarding the incompatibility between quantitative and qualitative research approaches appear to have subsided (Bryman, 2006).

This particular piece of research is based on a literature study. We have surveyed studies that have been published by other researchers which means that a form of secondary analysis has been applied as a research method.

Secondary type information usually includes either the analysis of information collected by other researchers which may have been published in scientific papers or books, or official statistics, which may have been produced by government agencies and the like (p. 200). Bryman (2004, pp. 202–205) argues that there are a number of advantages with doing secondary analysis. These include:

- Cost and time.
- Opportunity for longitudinal analysis.
- Sub-group analysis.
- Opportunities for cross-cultural analysis.
- More time for analysis.
- Reanalysis may offer new interpretations.
- The wider obligations of the researcher.

It is thus evident that secondary analysis offers a number of benefits for researchers. However, weaknesses such as lack of control over data quality, lack of familiarity with the data and the complexity of data have also been pointed out. It is up to the scientist to take appropriate measures to address any weaknesses in the choice of method (*see* Sect. 1.5.2).

Why have we chosen to do a literature study? In Sect. 1.4.1 on research motive, we touch upon some of the reasons behind this. Based on the fact that internal control is under-explored by researchers, it seems reasonable to start off by finding out what the basics of the concepts are and what research has found to date. A literature study is a method which could help us to discover what we know about internal controls today. A literature study may also provide an adequate basis for making suggestions about future research opportunities, even from a local Swedish perspective. We have not been able to identify any prior literature studies on the subject.

The collection of information has been made by going into different databases to identify relevant scientific texts. Most of the searches have been done online, by applying search words separately as well as in combination. The databases used include the following: *Business Source Premier*, *EconLit*, *Emerald, Science Direct, ABI/INFORM* and *Elsevier Science*. Most of the searches were done during a visiting stay as PhD student and Marie Curie Fellow in 2008 at The University of Manchester, Manchester Business School (MBS), in the United Kingdom.

Additional searches were however also made later in 2008, as well as continuously during 2009 in order to identify recently published research. The following search words have been applied:

- Auditor.
- Auditing.
- Cadbury Code.
- Combined Code.
- Control.
- Control system.
- Corporate governance.
- COSO.
- COCO.
- Enterprise Risk Management (including ERM).
- Governance.
- Internal control.
- Internal control reporting.
- Risk management.
- Sarbanes-Oxley (including SOX).

In addition to the online searches in databases, a number of scientific journals have been manually surveyed for all issues between the years 2002–2008. The primary reason for choosing year 2002 as a cut-off date is that this year saw the introduction of the SOX (2002) in the United States, following several high-profile corporate disasters and fraud cases. Even though the *internal control explosion* (Maijoor, 2000) goes back further than 2002 the Sarbanes-Oxley Act has certainly put extra spotlight on internal control, which is why it may provide a good starting point. The journals which have been manually surveyed include the following:

- Academy of Management Journal.
- Accounting Horizons.
- Accounting, Organizations and Society.
- Accounting, Auditing & Accountability Journal.
- Administrative Science Quarterly.
- Auditing: A Journal of Practice and Theory.
- Corporate Governance.
- Contemporary Accounting Research.
- European Accounting Review.
- International Journal of Auditing.
- Journal of Accounting and Organizational Change.
- Journal of Accounting, Auditing and Finance.
- Journal of Applied Accounting Research.
- Management Accounting Research.
- Management Science.
- Managerial Auditing Journal.
- Organization Science.

- Strategic Management Journal.
- The Accounting Review.
- The Internal Auditor.

The manual survey of these journals has been done in order to identify papers that may have been unintentionally missed when doing online searches through the application of search words.

When potentially relevant papers have been identified, the abstracts of the papers have been reviewed but at times also the detailed content in the papers. If we concluded, based on these brief examinations, that the paper is relevant for the purpose of this thesis, we put it aside for more in-depth examination. The scientific journals have been chosen based on discussion with peer PhD students and senior researchers at both the University of Linköping and MBS. The primary reason for choosing these journals is that they are leading and top-rated journals within the fields of accounting, organization and management.

Most of the journals noted above may be regarded as accounting and auditing journals. This was a natural choice due to the primary association of internal control with auditing (Power, 2007, p. 62). However, being a complex and comprehensive concept which exhibit considerable overlap to other concepts found in academic fields such as general management control, strategy, risk management and management accounting (Kinney, 2000, p. 88; Power, 2007, p. 62), other journals have also been included to make the survey more complete. In addition to surveying scientific journals, we have also reviewed regulatory texts as well as practical and professional and guidance on internal controls. Finally two practically oriented books on internal control have also been included.

As we mentioned above, potentially relevant scientific papers and other texts were selected for further examination. During this process, different folders were created so that texts covering similar subjects or issues could be classified into different categories. The establishment of these categories has served as a *vehicle for systemizing the many texts* identified, and thus reflects different aspects of internal control writings that have emerged throughout the survey. At some point, the existing established categories appeared to provide sufficient coverage and no further categories were needed. The categories include the following:

- Accounting scandals.
- Accountability.
- Auditing theory.
- Auditing performance.
- Auditors and internal control.
- Control systems.
- Corporate governance.
- Disclosure.
- Fraud.
- Internal control.
- Management accounting.
- Management control and contingency.

- Organization theory.
- Practical frameworks.
- Professional guidance.
- Regulatory environment.
- Risk management.
- Strategy and management control systems.
- Trust and control.

These categories have been established electronically on my computer. In total, approximately 250 texts have been identified as relevant for a thesis on internal controls and thus classified into the different folders. It should be pointed out however, that relevant texts have also been identified through discussion with peer PhD students and senior researchers both in Manchester and Linköping. Also prior dissertations on the subject have been examined for relevant literature. A neat example is the doctoral dissertation on the structure and effectiveness of internal control that I became aware of during my stay at MBS (see Jokipii, 2006). Another example is the thesis by Fagerberg (2008) on auditors' perceptions of internal control and fraud red flags. They have been useful for finding relevant literature.

Since the text collection process has been and ongoing task, this has also been the case for the deeper examination of the texts. Besides being stored electronically in different folders, all the texts were also printed and placed in binders. The texts have thereafter been examined in more detail and relevant sections have been highlighted. Notes and comments have also been made in connection with certain sections that were of special interest. Based on my continual readings of the texts, and also on my practical understanding of internal control practices, a number of different themes and issues have emerged during this process. These themes and issues *reflect the re-occurring discussions on internal control* that may be found in writings on the subject. They may as such, also be regarded as clusters of questions that have been boiled down into a number of themes which have been adjusted and refined throughout the research process. How do auditors and accountants assess and evaluate internal controls? How should internal control systems be disclosed and what type of information do users of such information value? How should we regulate internal control systems? How do managers design internal controls and how do directors and audit committee members effectively oversee and govern systems of internal control? And last but not least, what is internal control and what are its boundaries?

Even though we have not used a grounded theory approach (Strauss & Corbin, 1990) the concept of saturation may still be relevant to this discussion. Towards the end of the research process, further analysis of themes or categories did not add anything and so these categories evidently proved to be sufficiently robust. Apparently some sort of *saturation* had occurred (Parker & Roffey, 1997, p. 232). Minor updated have been made to this thesis, which was originally made as part of the degree for licentiate in economics at Linköpings University. These updates have been both verbally discussed with supervisors as well as formally reviewed. Largely, these updates consist of improving a few sentences or sections in order to clarify matters. A few references have also been updated.

1.5.2 Methodological Challenges

We mentioned earlier that different research methods have their advantages and disadvantages (Bryman, 2004, p. 5). In this section, we will briefly discuss some of the methodological challenges that were faced throughout the research process. As pointed out in Sect. 1.5.1, a literature study type of research method offers a number of advantages, such as the re-analysis of findings, the saving of cost and time and the possibility to do cross-cultural analysis. But it also has its disadvantages – one of them being lack of control over the quality of the data obtained.

One measure taken to address the lack of control over the quality of the data is that a significant portion of the papers identified (and also referred to in this research piece) have been published in top-rated scientific journals. This is also true for the scientific journals that have been manually surveyed (see Sect. 1.5.1). The fact that only high-quality papers provide the basis for this thesis's argumentation should contribute to that observations and conclusions are fair and credible. However, one practitioner journal has also been included in our manual survey – *Internal Auditor*. In a few cases we have also referred to published texts in other, more practically oriented, journals or books. In these cases, care has been taken to ensure that no key finding is based solely on such references without it being supplemented and supported by other references.

Another challenge is represented in the fact that published papers will always reflect the specific cultural, economic and regulatory settings that surround them. Papers written within the context of the United Kingdom or the United States will have their specific circumstances. North American research papers on internal controls under the SOX (2002) may have limited relevance here in Sweden. Similarly research findings on internal control reporting in Sweden or in the United Kingdom may not be completely applicable in other types of regulatory and cultural contexts.

Moreover, the research findings referred to in this thesis have been derived using different research approaches – both qualitative and quantitative techniques. In addition, the research pieces may be conceptual or more or less empirically based. All these variations in method and settings must be addressed by the researcher. Throughout the analysis process and writing-up, care has been taken to consider factors such as research method and the regulatory and cultural context. Where relevant and appropriate, we have alerted readers of the fact that a certain paper, or a stream of papers, pertain to a specific regulatory environment or cultural setting. Finally it may also be important to point out that since case-studies on internal control have been scarce, we have given those special interest (see for example case studies by Mikes, 2009; and Woods, 2009).

Yet another research challenge is related to issues of objectivity. Even though it might not be possible for social scientists to remain completely objective (Bryman, 2004, pp. 21–25), researchers must however take "measures to ensure that objectivity is not compromised" (see Strauss & Corbin, 1990, p.44–45). This is done by for example periodically taking a step back and thinking about what is going on, maintaining an attitude of skepticism and following research procedures. Care has also been taken to address any biases that the researcher might have based on prior practical experience and preferences. Reading draft versions of my thesis by peer PhD students, senior researchers and practitioners may also help address this potential problem.

A pre-understanding of the research area could however also potentially benefit the research. Strauss and Corbin (1990) argue that theoretical sensitivity, which refers to a personal quality of the researcher and goes to the awareness of the subtleties of meaning of data (p. 41), may be gained through professional experience. On the importance of professional experience for the research output they (p. 42) argue that:

> Professional experience is another source of sensitivity, if a researcher is fortunate enough to have had this experience. Throughout years of practice in a field, one acquired an understating of how things work in that field, and why, and what will happen there under certain conditions. This knowledge, even if implicit, is taken into the research situation and helps you to understand events and actions seen and heard, and to do so more quickly that if you did not bring this background into the research.

Since the author of this thesis is a practicing auditor at Grant Thornton in Stockholm, Sweden, professional experience on the subject is not insignificant, and something which could potentially also benefit this thesis.

A significant problem with doing research into internal controls relates to the complexity of the phenomena involved and the fact that it draws upon theory from fields other than accounting (Kinney, 2000; Power, 2007). Auditing and accounting researchers may have limited knowledge of organization, strategy, risk management and process management (Kinney, 2000). This could at least partially explain any shortcomings in research in this area, we might add in the passing. However, this represents a research challenge which needs to be addressed. Because the supervisors of this research enterprise (and also some fellow PhD colleagues) are knowledgeable about strategy, general management control and management accounting, this potential problem could be mitigated. And since this thesis is written as a part of the *Research program for Auditors and Consultants* in which most PhD students are practicing auditors or accountants, the auditing and accounting aspects of internal control should therefore be covered adequately.

Finally we must discuss quality criteria. How do we know if this piece of research represents a reasonable, accurate and credible view of internal controls? Different proposals have been made by methodology researchers on quality criteria (see Bryman, 2004, pp. 28, 273; Bryman, Becker, & Sempik, 2008). In this case, a literature study, we might say something about *coverage* and *relevance*. Have we been able to cover the most significant aspects of internal controls? Have we identified all the relevant research papers on the subject?

Naturally, all studies will have limitations based on time, resources and other constraints. We claim however, that the searches made for relevant texts on the subject have generated a sufficiently complete account of the key components and features of internal control. Of course, relevant texts on internal controls have been unintentionally left out, simply because no searchers are perfect. We argue however, that the body of texts on the subject, that are included within the scope of this thesis, represents a sufficiently large body of research for most of the relevant aspects of the concept to be covered.

Another concern is about whether the conclusions drawn from this piece of research are valid and relevant. Are the findings believable? On credibility, Bryman (2004) points to the importance of connecting with the social world that has been examined (p. 275). Since internal control's primary association is with accounting and auditing, we have applied the proposed technique of member validation (p. 275). We thus invited members of the audit community to read through parts of the manuscript and comment on any omissions or views on my part that caused surprise or raised their objections. Members include the following:

- Agerberg, Lars. The Legal, Financial and Administrative Services Agency [Kammarkollegiet]. Formerly Authorized Public Accountant, Certified Internal Auditor, Stockholm, Sweden.
- Fagerberg, Jesper. econ.lic. Approved Public Accountant, PriceWaterhouse-Coopers, Stockholm, Sweden.
- Munkby Tomas. Certified Information Systems Auditor and formerly Authorized Public Accountant. Partner and Head of Business Risk Services, Grant and Thornton, Stockholm, Sweden.
- Scheja, Mikael. Ph.D. (econ). Authorized Public Accountant, Director, PriceWaterhouseCoopers, Stockholm, Sweden.
- Styf, Elisabeth. Head of Audit, Swedish Police Board [Rikspolisstyrelsen], Stockholm, Sweden. Certified Internal Auditor and formerly President in the ECIIA (European Confederation of Institutes of Internal Auditing).

These members read and commented on my findings to further improve credibility of findings and conclusions. In addition, informal comments have been obtained from other practicing internal and external auditors and accountants as well as technical specialists. Since the author of this thesis is a practicing auditor at Grant Thornton in Stockholm, Sweden, such input has been accessible.

1.5.3 Thesis Structure and Reading Guidance

This thesis contains six chapters and Fig. 1.3 below illustrates how the different chapters relate to certain themes and questions.

Chapter 1 introduces the general research idea to readers. We have also described the purpose of the study and the chosen research method. Finally, we have discussed our motives for doing this research and also some of the challenges faced during the research endeavor.

Chapter 2 provides a theoretical background. Agency-theory and institutional theory is described and discussed. These theoretical perspectives may be important for readers to take note of since they explain the necessity for internal controls and

Chapters	Purpose and content
Chapter 1: Introduction	✓ **introduces and describes the research idea** ✓ **describes the research design and method**
Chapter 2: The control system of the firm	✓ **introduces theoretical perspectives on control** ✓ **explains the need for control systems**
Chapter 3: Key components of internal control	✓ **introduces and discusses a practical framework** ✓ **defines and describes internal control components**
Chapter 4: A regulatory perspective	✓ **provides a regulatory perspective** ✓ **describes different regulatory environments**
Chapter 5: Themes and issues	✓ **provides an account of common themes** ✓ **discusses issues on internal control**
Chapter 6: Conclusions and future research	✓ **makes concluding observations** ✓ **suggests opportunities for future research**

Fig. 1.3 General thesis overview and structure

also how they may adapt and evolve. These theoretical perspectives will also be applied when different themes, developments and issues on internal control are treated.

Chapter 3 goes into the details of a widely diffused and leading practical framework on internal control – The COSO-framework on internal control, including their more recent releases on Enterprise Risk Management (2004) and Monitoring (2009a). Chapter 3 describes and discusses the key components of internal control systems.

Chapter 4 provides a regulatory perspective. As mentioned earlier, today internal control is a primary regulatory object, and the various corporate governance codes and regulations influence internal control and risk management practices of firms. We have chosen to describe and discuss the SOX in the United States, the Combined Code in the United Kingdom and the Swedish code of Corporate Governance [Svensk Kod för Bolagsstyrning].

Chapter 5 represents a large portion of this piece of research and goes into the different themes and issues on internal control. These themes reflect different research questions and re-occurring discussions on internal control. We will here discuss definitions and boundaries, classification, assessment and evaluation, disclosure regimes, internal control design and also the outcomes of internal control. Issues and key questions are treated in connection to each theme.

Chapter 6, the final chapter, makes some concluding observations based on what has been discussed previously in this thesis. We argue that these observations, taken together, reflect a fair description of the modern view of internal control. In connection with each key observation we also make some suggestions for future research and conclude by proposing a future research agenda.

1.6 Summary and Concluding Remarks

Based on what we have discussed we conclude this chapter by making the following observations:

- During recent years, loud calls have been made for improved corporate governance. Corporate governance is about overseeing that the firm is run properly.
- The reasons behind the calls for improved and better organizational governance may be divided into the following drivers: changes in shareholder patterns, greater legal risk and changes in the legal climate, and finally the continuing organizational disasters and high-profile fraud cases. Taken together, these developments have put the spotlight on the governance of firms and the importance of aligning shareholder interests with managers' interests.
- This thesis is about internal control. The last 15 years have witnessed a significant increase in audit activity in both public and private life. Researchers have discussed this development in terms of an audit society. An important joint development with the emerging audit society has been the rise of the internal control systems. Internal control, previously a private matter to technical assurance specialists, has risen as an autonomous field of expertise and a mode of organizing and processing uncertainty (Power, 2007, pp. 47, 62).
- Today internal control is considered a key accountability mechanism together with the independent audit and the financial reporting process. A number of reasons have been put forward for the increased reliance on internal controls. These reasons relate to efficiency in accounting practices, the growing complexity and size of firms, and greater demands from outside stakeholders for additional information. Broader definitions and the expanding boundaries of internal control also contribute to its recent success. Regulators, supervisory authorities, directors and audit committee members, managers, analysts and credit rating agencies are most likely to consider internal control rather differently than only a few years ago.
- Researchers have, however, pointed out that internal control still remains relatively un-explored and have called for more research. Much of the existing research on control is somewhat fragmented into different fields.
- The overall purpose of this research is to increase our understanding of internal controls. More specifically, the purpose of this research enterprise is to provide an account of existing research on internal control and also of its components and features. When doing so, we will also discuss themes and issues that are frequently occurring in literature on the subject. The chosen method is literature study which may be a useful method to apply in order to find out what we know about internal control and what the major issues are.

Chapter 2
The Control System of the Firm

Abstract

Purpose: The aim of this chapter is to review the arguments for internal control systems. This will be done by providing an account of theories that explain the existence and necessity of internal control. We will also describe two contrasting theoretical perspectives that help explain the design and adoption of internal controls.

Synopsis: Why do control processes exist in organizations? The modern theory of the firm focuses on the need for cooperation to achieve common goals. In this case the organization consists of a group of consciously coordinated activities for the accomplishment of common objectives. One prerequisite however, is that the group's effort to achieve this end should be performed at the right time and in the right way, and with the right proportions. Thus people's understanding of common goals becomes a fundamental variable. Man is considered rational only to a limited extent, due to, for example cognitive limitations. Because differences among personal goals may exist, it is possible that an employee will substitute the goals of the firm with his/her own goals. Accordingly, a control system that provides incentives to reconcile differences so that efforts are coordinated toward the established objectives of the organization is needed. Agency theory provides a primarily economic explanation for the form of control systems. This theory has been controversial but has nonetheless been applied in a wide variety of fields such as finance, marketing, organization behaviour and accounting. At the heart of agency theory lies the separation between ownership and control. One person (the principal) engages another person (the agent) to perform some service. An agency problem arises if the cooperative behaviour, which would maximize the group's welfare, is not consistent with each individual's self-interest. Because owners of resources will have less information than those who manage the resources, these agents may take advantage of the situation for their own benefit. As a result, different contracting arrangements and controls need to be designed in order to mitigate agency-related problems. Institutional theory provides a contrasting explanation for adoption and form of controls. This theory suggests that controls are adopted in order to gain legitimacy, as symbolic displays and imitation of

O. Arwinge, *Internal Control*, Contributions to Management Science,
DOI 10.1007/978-3-7908-2882-5_2,

practices from the outside environment. Management looks to management fads, industry norms and firm traditions when adopting and implementing new control processes.

2.1 Introduction

The existence of, and the need for, control systems in organizations has been a rather controversial topic. Zannetos (1964, p. 862) has commented that human relations researchers have contested the necessity for control systems, especially with regards to their potential impact on human wellbeing and behaviour.

Because this thesis will deal with the internal control and changes in internal control, it is appropriate to first discuss the theory behind the existence of internal control systems and also why controls may be adopted and changed. Therefore we will start off by introducing and briefly discussing the modern theory of the firm, which puts forward a number of arguments that explain the existence and necessity for internal control systems. We will thereafter continue by describing two different and contrasting theories that help explain how control systems in organizations are formed an developed. These theoretical perspectives will be used throughout this thesis in connection with the treatment and analysis of specific issues and developments.

2.2 The Need for Control Systems

Why do control systems exist in organizations? What necessitates internal controls? In this section, we will outline the modern theory of the firm which has been used to explain the existence of control systems within firms (Zannetos, 1964). The modern theory of the firm focuses on conscious and purposeful cooperative behaviour. This is quite different from the classical microeconomic theory of the firm, or the so-called scientific view of the firm proposed by Taylor (1911). With regards to the microeconomic theory of the firm, as argued by Zannetos (1964), "the factors of production are in the end result considered as lacking will, issues of control and organizational nature do not arise" (p. 860). In the case of Taylor (1911) and his scientific view of the firm, purposeful behaviour is also absent because it has been replaced by programmed tasks, converting man into special purpose machines. Work is performed in the most efficient way and so the individual cannot effectively exercise his/hers will. Accordingly the need for internal control does not exist.

The modern theory of the firm is rather different and descends from work done by for example Barnard (1938), Simon (1948) and March and Simon (1958). These classical works focus on the need for cooperation to achieve common goals, and in these works man is often viewed as being only partly rational. The point of departure is that an organization is a group of consciously coordinated activities for the accomplishment of common objectives. From this definition, several implications arise. One stems from the fact that organizational effort comprises of more than one man. These participants can achieve more than any individual would alone, provided that their effort is timed so that efforts are performed at the right time and in the right way, and with the right proportions. And so the understanding of common goals becomes vitally important.

The view taken by the modern theory of the firm is that individuals are wilful and purposeful participants in organizations. This implies two things: first, man is only rational to a limited extent due to cognitive limitations for example (Simon, 1948; also see Zannetos, 1964, p. 864). Second, differences among personal goals may exist which is why it is possible that an employee will substitute company objectives with his/her own goals. This assumption of *bounded rationality* has been carried forward into areas such as transactional economics (Williamson, 1985) which view human nature as self-interest seeking and where problems of opportunistic behaviour may occur.

And so, due to their cognitive limitations, people make their own mental models about organizational goals and how to best achieve them. De Haas and Algera (2002) argue that chances are negligible that a group of people would construct and maintain the same mental models of the perceived reality. Thus individual visions about organizational goals within any group may very well diverge. The managerial challenge is therefore to make them converge. De Haas and Algera have proposed the concept of goal coherence as "the degree of consensus on constituency goal priorities" (p. 45).

As a result of these bounded rationalities and goal-replacement, incompatibilities may thus arise in any group action and in any organizational effort which aims to achieve common objectives. This can become manifested in disagreement or open conflict between participants, making the economic system less efficient and effective. De Haas and Algera (2002, p. 43) argue that:

> All else being equal, the larger the discrepancies between managers' and/or employees' mental models, the greater the lack of shared vision, the more the divergence in behavior and the higher the dispersion of organizational energy.

So if visions about what to achieve are shared (i.e. visions are converging) the challenge is to "produce goal congruent behaviors amongst the group members through the coordinated allocation of human resources" (p. 41). Because people are wilful and are able to make value judgements, and because they are only partially rational, a system that will manage possibly diverging interests is needed. A system which imposes limitations on the freedom of organizational members, and provides them with incentives to reconcile differences so that efforts are coordinated towards established objectives of the group is required (Zannetos, 1964,p. 863).

Thus, in any organizational activity, there must exist some form of control system that manages these issues as they occur, and makes sure that individual behaviours are consistent with the established group intent, i.e. that behaviours that are goal-congruent. A management control system that will be used to maintain or alter organizational activities based on information received (Simons, 1991, p. 49). Tannenbaum (1968, p. 3), an influential writer within the area of organizational control, argued that:

> Organization implies control. A social organization is an ordered arrangement of individual human interactions. Control processes help circumscribe idiosyncratic behaviours and keep them conformant to the rational plan of the organization. Organizations require a certain amount of conformity as well as the integration of diverse activities. It is the function of control to bring about conformance to organizational requirements and achievement of the ultimate purposes of the organizations. The coordination and order created out of the diverse interests and potentially diffuse behaviours of members are largely a function of control.

The necessity of control systems and internal controls may thus be explained by the *need for convergence, congruence and conformity* based on certain assumptions about human nature.

2.3 Adoption and Design of Controls

Having discussed the modern theory of the firm, a theory which provided a theoretical explanation of why control systems in firms exist, in the sections below we will introduce theories that help explain the shape and form of various internal control systems of organizations, including how they evolve and develop.

We will therefore introduce two contrasting, and perhaps supplementary, theoretical perspectives that may be used in order to explain certain organizational processes and control arrangements. The first theoretical orientation that we will discuss is agency theory (Jensen & Meckling, 1976; Fama & Jensen, 1983), considered by many to be a mainstream view of control. The agency theory provides a primarily economic explanation for the design and form of control systems. The second theoretical orientation that will be described, institutional theory (Meyer & Rowan, 1977; DiMaggio & Powell, 1983), offers a contrasting explanation for the development and form of control systems and uses a perhaps more sociological approach (see Eisenhardt, 1988, pp. 488–489).

2.3.1 The Need to Align Principals and Agents

Agency theory has been controversial, partly due to some of its assumptions about people (Eisenhardt, 1989a). Nonetheless, the theory has been applied in a wide variety of academic fields such as finance, marketing, political science, organizational behaviour and accounting (p. 57).

Agency theory, now consists of several different branches (Baiman, 1990), and was originally developed by Jensen and Meckling (1976) and later Fama and Jensen (1983). At the heart of the agency theory lies the separation of ownership and control.

Jensen and Meckling define an agency relationship as "a contract under which one or more persons (the principal(s)) engage another person (the agent) to perform some service on their behalf which involves delegating some decision making authority to the agent" (p. 308). In an agreed-upon contract between the parties, all rights and responsibilities such as compensation arrangements, information systems, allocation of duties and ownership rights are specified (Baiman, 1990, p. 342).

If both parties are so called utility maximizers there is "good reason to believe that the agent will not always act in the best interests of the principal" (Jensen & Meckling, 1976, p. 308). This underlying assumption, that all individuals are considered to be motivated solely by self-interest, is common to all agency models (Baiman, 1990). So the action taken by the agent may diverge from the cooperative action. And instead of taking the action that will maximize the group's welfare, another path is chosen by the agent whereby so-called *agency problems* arise. It is important to recognize however, that even if an agent tries his/her best to follow the principal's interests, his/her actions will always be coloured by his/hers interpretations of these. The agent's interpretation of the situation may still, unintentionally, lead to a diverging action thereby resulting in agency problems.

These agency problems must be addressed through contracting arrangements and other control mechanisms. Different agency models focus on, and propose, different solutions for these problems. What is common to all solutions however, is that they will try to limit the agent's divergences from the principal's interest, they will try to produce goal-congruent behaviors based on set (but perhaps not completely shared) goals.

These solutions will however not come at zero cost but different solutions are related to specific costs which will be allocated between the principal and the agent. These costs are known as agency costs and Jensen and Meckling (1976, p. 308) define these costs as the sum of:

- The monitoring expenditure by the principal, and
- The bonding expenditure by the agent, and
- The residual loss.

2.3.1.1 Control of Agency Problems

Agency costs necessarily are incurred because agency contracts are neither written nor enforced costlessly. They result from structuring, monitoring and bonding contracts, between principals and agents with conflicting interests, including the output loss from agency problems (Fama & Jensen, 1983, p. 304). The principal must therefore implement controls that will efficiently and effectively address these agency issues. It may however be both difficult and expensive for the principal to verify the agent's action.

As mentioned earlier, there are a variety of agency branches and these tend to focus on different areas (Eisenhardt, 1989; Baiman, 1990). The positivist agency theory focuses on contracting alternatives, often between the owners and managers of large-scale companies. A key question is often if contracts should be based on an agent's behaviour or the output produced by the agent. This branch is heavily influenced by the work by Jensen and Meckling (1976) and includes the positive theory of accounting (Watts & Zimmerman, 1983). Other, more general principal-agent researchers, have favoured a general theory that may be applied to any relationship, such as the manager and the employee or the buyer and the supplier. Different control solutions are generated as a result of the different characteristics of the principal-agent situation.

One problematic situation occurs when information asymmetries exist between principal and agent, as a result of which the principal is unable to observe agent performance. This situation is related to two specific issues, often referred to in the formal agency literature as *moral hazard* and *adverse selection*. Moral hazard refers to a lack of effort by the agent, i.e. the agent is shirking his/her duty and does not make the effort that was agreed upon. Adverse selection refers to misrepresentation by the agent, where he/she claims to posses certain skills or abilities (Eisenhardt, 1989, p. 61). In the case of unobservable behaviour, the principal may choose to invest in controls such as:

- Budget systems.
- Reporting and disclosure procedures.
- Board of directors and audit committees.
- Management layers.
- Internal and external audit activity.

Investments are therefore made in controls so that the information-gap between the principals and the agents may be reduced, or possibly even closed. To completely close the information-gap would in most cases however lead to unreasonable costs of control (see also Sect. 5.3.7). In which case, the principals *procure information* about the actual behaviour of the agents.

Another option for the principal is to contract the agent based on output. A known problem with this solution is of course that the output produced by the agent is only partly a result of the agent's efforts, which should then be reflected in the contract. In the end, these solutions are about balancing the costs from measuring and monitoring agent behaviour against the costs of measuring output and transferring risks to the agents (Eisenhardt, 1989, p. 61).

Agency theory has been used to explain demands for monitoring controls such as the financial statement audit, external directors on boards and committees (Watts & Zimmerman, 1983), audit committees (Fogarty & Kalbers, 1998), internal audit (Carcello, Hermanson, & Raghunandan, 2005) and compensation schemes (Eisenhardt, 1988). Agency theories have been used extensively in explaining earnings management and financial accounting policy choices, for transfer pricing and cost allocation and executive compensation (see Baiman, 1990). A major contribution of the principal-agent model is that is provides a coherent and useful framework for understanding managerial accounting procedures (p. 344).

Many of the entity-level and monitoring controls such as those mentioned above may be regarded as vehicles for reducing the information-gap between owners, through their representatives, and managers. As mentioned earlier however, agency problems may occur throughout the organization so different types of detailed internal controls may also be regarded as tools used to reduce agency costs associated with information asymmetries between managers and employees. Compensation schemes, performance reviews, policies and compliance checks are only a few examples of controls applied to reduce inherent uncertainties in relationships.

2.3.2 *Need for Legitimacy*

Another theoretical orientation, institutional theory, offers a contrasting explanation that may be used to understand the adoption and design of control practices within organizations. This theory, more sociological in character, originates from work done by Meyer and Rowan (1977) for example and DiMaggio and Powell (1983).

During recent years institutional theory has grown in popularity and offers a contrasting and different explanation to why new control structures and practices emerge in organizations. It has been said that institutional theory is becoming an important theoretical perspective in accounting and organization theory research (Dillard, Rigsby, & Goodman, 2004, p. 507).

Institutional theories question the technical and economic rationality for understanding corporate governance, and the structures that are invested in and developed within organizations. Instead, they offer a contrasting explanation which proposes that organizations develop and design structures, processes and systems not primarily based on rational economic cost-benefit analysis, but because they are more or less required to incorporate new practices and procedures. According to Meyer and Rowan (1977, p. 340) this means that:

> Organizations are driven to incorporate the practices and procedures defined by prevailing rationalized concepts of organizational work and institutionalized in society. Organizations that do so increase their legitimacy and their survival prospects, independent of the immediate efficacy of the acquired practices and procedures.

Organizational structures, including the various internal control functions, roles, processes and systems, become symbolic displays of conformity and social accountability. Organizations with the appropriate structures in place avoid in-depth investigations of their business operations. Meyer and Rowan, building on the work by Berger and Luckmann (1966), point to the importance of institutionalized rules. These are classifications built into society and may be taken for granted or supported by public opinion or even the force of law. These rules involve normative obligations which may be viewed as facts of (organizational) life which must be taken into account and considered by actors in the business community – whether they are risk management officers, compliance officers, managers, auditors, directors or other types of professionals within and outside of firms. The process of *institutionalization* is then *how social processes of different kinds come to take on a rule-like* status in everyday society (p. 341).

In this way repeated patterns of actions become institutions, or institutionalized rules, and thus institutional theory explains organizational phenomena by pointing to the environment and the formal and informal rules that are imposed on organizational activities. It seems reasonable to assume that not an insignificant part of organizational activity may be a result of such an aspiration of legitimacy. This would also include how internal control structures are designed and adopted. Hutter and Power (eds., 2005, pp. 137, 140), when discussing risk management practices and the rise of the chief risk officer, claim that:

> These positions are internal representations of externally encountered norms and rules... (...)...It signals organizational seriousness about matters and issues that need to be addressed in the current business climate, and have become a part of being legitimate organizations, together with audit committees and internal auditors.

This could be interpreted as that the environment imposes demands on the organization and expects certain organizational behaviors. This is how new roles and processes are implemented in the organization – roles and processes which may not immediately have a direct connection to the core operations of the organization but are instead rather loosely coupled (Meyer & Rowan, 1977). Using similar institutional arguments Power (2005, p. 3) claims, that "organizational responses to risk are shaped by their institutional environments". Calling new processes or institutions loosely coupled, also implies that they may have parallel or similar functions to existing controls (for instance), without there being a complete and explicit rational logic for how they relate.

2.3.2.1 Adoption of New Organizational Practices

According to the work done by Meyer and Rowan (1977), institutionalized rules have enormous impact on organizational activity. The rules, or the facts that must be taken for granted, define new organizing situations, redefine the old ones and prescribe how new organizational activities should or must be performed. New organizational practices spread rapidly in this way in modern society (p. 344).

In trying to explain why there is a startling homogeneity of organizational forms and practices, DiMaggio and Powell (1983, p. 149) explored the process of homogenization where they used the concept of isomorphism. Isomorphism refers to the adoption of an institutional practice by an organization. The authors refer to the process of isomorphism as "a constraining process that forces one unit in a population to resemble other units that face the same set of environmental conditions" (p. 149).

Building on earlier research, the authors go on to suggest that there exist two types of such a process, namely competitive and institutional. The first one relates to market competition and the process of companies adopting similar types of structures and systems based on efficiency reasons. The institutional form of isomorphism suggests that firms not only compete for clients and resources but also institutional legitimacy and social fitness (DiMaggio & Powell, 1983, p. 50).

DiMaggio and Powell hereby suggested three classifications that relate to the motivations to adopt these new institutional practices: coercive, mimetic and normative. Below we will discuss these classifications.

2.3.2.2 Coercive Isomorphic Change

This change stems from political influence and the problem of legitimacy. According to the authors, coercive change is based on pressures from other organizations and by cultural expectations in the society within which the firm operates. These pressures could be both formal and informal and include standards and regulations issued by government and authorities in various areas, forcing organizations to adopt and implement certain practices. It could also include subsidiaries in a group having to adopt specific organizational practices such as financial accounting choices, performance evaluations, human resources processes and budget reporting schemes. To conclude, this type of organizational change, resulting in harmonized organizational activities within the populations of firms, is derived from coercive authority.

2.3.2.3 Mimetic Isomorphic Change

Not all institutional change is derived from coercive authority. Uncertainty according to DiMaggio and Powell is an important driver for change and imitation between firms. In situations where technology is poorly understood, or when goals seem to be unclear or ambiguous, firms may resolve the situation by looking at peer firms and imitate their formal practices (1983, p. 151). Managers actively look at the competition, not only within their own field, in order to find easy and cheap solutions to solve organizational problems and create legitimate practices. New organizational practices are thus molded based on old ones.

2.3.2.4 Normative Isomorphic Change

This type of institutional change is related to the different professions within society and across firms. Different job roles such as accountants, auditors, physicians, teachers and lawyers strive for freedom to set their own standards for work performance. DiMaggio and Powell claim that important drivers for this institutional change process are the following: standardized formal education and the professional bodies and networks that work across organizations. These drivers speed up the effect of harmonizing work procedures in various organizational fields across organizations. Put differently, accounting, compliance, risk management, management and human resource specialists all work similarly, due to their formal education and memberships in professional bodies and networks.

Hence, it is possible to conclude that especially for a sub-population of firms, such as for example the firms within the banking industry, different activities within the organization may be performed in a rather similar manner. These activities could potentially include risk management, compliance, sales, human resources and corporate governance-related arrangements which include the duties of internal auditors and the audit committees. It follows that the *specific controls surrounding these practices, such as the controls over risk management processes or human resource practices also may be performed in a similar manner.*

2.4 Control from Different Theoretical Perspectives

As we have described in Sects. 2.2 and 2.3, both agency and institutional theory provide explanations for how controls are adopted by firms. They do it however in different ways. Agency theory explains the application of controls as being primarily based on economic cost-benefit analysis, where controls are installed in order to reduce information asymmetries between principals and owners. Institutional theory however, provides a different explanation. Here, controls are adopted and designed in order to gain legitimacy, as symbolic displays and imitation or as practices from the outside environment.

According to institutional theory, management is not only concerned with cost-benefit concerns and risk-reward trade-offs but looks to management fads, industry norms and firm traditions when adopting and designing new (control) practices (Eisenhardt, 1988, p. 489). Both perspectives appear to be valid. In a study to explain the use of compensation policies for sales staff, Eisenhardt (1988) applied both theoretical perspectives and found that "both perspectives are necessary for a good description of compensation policies" (p. 488).

In Table 2.1 below, we provide a summarizing description of how controls could be viewed according to the two perspectives which is based on a comparison made by Eisenhardt (1988, p. 491) between the two theoretical perspectives. Throughout the thesis we will refer to this table in connection to our discussion and treatment of specific issues. This table is a simplification however, and furthermore, a reflection of our understanding of how controls could potentially be viewed from the different perspectives.

To briefly conclude, based on Table 2.1, from an agency perspective controls are installed in order to reduce risk and the uncertainty arising from information asymmetries between principals (for example owners or managers) and agents (for example managers or employees). Controls exist solely because of their technical functionality and are installed as a result of rational cost-benefit analysis.

From institutional perspectives controls are installed in order to gain legitimacy and other less rational factors. The installation of certain governance arrangements and controls such as risk assessments, compensation committees, policies, self-assessments may thus be made partly in order to gain legitimacy. These controls *display seriousness about certain matters* and are adopted largely due to industry

Table 2.1 Different theoretical perspectives on controls

Internal control from an agency-perspective	Internal control from an institutional perspective
Controls installed in order to reduce risk and information-asymmetries	Controls installed in order to gain legitimacy
Controls installed based on rational economic cost-benefit analysis	Controls installed based on rules of thumb analysis, firm tradition, management fads, external norms and rules
Controls exist primarily for their technical functionality	Controls exist primarily as symbolic displays
Controls changes and develops based on changes in risk exposures and information-asymmetries between different principal-agent relationships	Controls changes and develop based on political influence, imitation of other firms and practices, professional standards and networking between professional bodies and networks
Controls are installed in order to fit the environment	The environment consist of a source of (internal control) practices to which the firm conforms
People are self-interested, rational and risk-averse	People are satisfiers and want to conform to external norms

standards, imitation of other firms, firm tradition and management fads. Even though this is not done based on economic cost-benefit analysis it may still be beneficial to the company. In these cases however, companies may run the risk of the controls not being effectively embedded into core operations, but instead rather loosely coupled. They are visible, but may not provide any "real" assurance since the operational performance of these processes is low.

Policy-makers and control professionals can be expected to find agency theory more helpful in diagnosing situations and designing controls. Observers of the revival of interest in internal control in recent years may find institutional perspectives suggestive of possible mechanisms and explanations of this development. Thus, we find both types of theories potentially useful for our continued work. Both theoretical perspectives have also been applied in the work we have surveyed.

2.5 Summary and Concluding Remarks

This chapter has described two significant, and potentially supplementary, theories that can help explain the adoption of internal control practises and developments in them. Based on the findings in this chapter we conclude by emphasizing the following observations:

- Agency theory takes its point of departure in the separation of ownership and control, through which one party (the principal) has delegated responsibility to a second party (the agent). If both parties are utility-maximizers, there are good

reasons to believe that the agent will not always act in the best interest of the principal. Because it is difficult or expensive for the principal to verify the actual actions of the agent, (cost-effective) controls must be established through various contracting and monitoring arrangements.
- Different branches of agency research propose different solutions. General principal-agency researchers point to solutions whereby agents may be effectively controlled by rewarding either agent behaviour or output. Agents may also be controlled through different monitoring arrangements where independent information is procured so that information asymmetries between principles and agents may be reduced.
- Institutional theories provide different explanations for why organizational control practices are adopted and evolve. Different pressures exist on different levels in society, and these produce harmonized practices across firms.
- Firms adopt practices in order to gain legitimacy in the public eye and controls are adopted based on pressures from governments, standard setters and professions, resulting in firms adopting generally acceptable practices in various areas. The end-product is a never-ending cycle where firms imitate one another through the adoption of similar practices.
- Like all popular theories, both agency and institutional theory have been criticized. Agency theory has been criticized for being too general, trivial, dehumanization and even dangerous. Institutional accounting research on the other hand, has been criticized for over-emphasizing the homogeneity of institutional fields and downplaying the importance of practice variations embedded in competing institutional logics. It has also been suggested that it ignores the deeply embedded nature of rationality and resistance to institutional pressures.
- In connection with our treatment of specific issues we will refer to the sections in this chapter and Table 2.1 which outlines how controls may be viewed from the different theoretical perspectives.

Chapter 3
Key Components of Internal Control

Abstract

Purpose: The aim of this chapter is to provide an account of the key components of internal control. This will be done by introducing a leading practical framework on internal control.

Synopsis: The COSO is a voluntary private sector organization in the United States dedicated to improving the financial reporting quality, internal control and corporate governance. In 1992, COSO issued a report entitled Internal Control – Integrated Framework. It provided in-depth guidance on internal control for directors, managers, auditors, regulators, investors and other concerned stakeholders. Since its release, the COSO has become a blue-print for firms that are struggling with the governance and management of internal controls. Furthermore the framework has been extensively applied by companies subject to the Sarbanes-Oxley Act in the United States and also underlies some of the professional standards on internal control. The COSO 1992 defines internal control as a process consisting of five interrelated components designed to provide reasonable assurance that organizational objectives will be met. These internal control components consist of the control environment, risk assessment, control activities, information and communication and monitoring. In 2004, the COSO released the integrated framework on Enterprise Risk Management which highlighted the importance of effective risk management practices. The COSO 2004 explicitly tied internal control even closer to risk, regarding internal control as a risk treatment for risk exposures. Through responses such as reducing, accepting, sharing and avoiding, risk exposures may be addressed through the application of controls for example. Those events which potentially have a negative impact are dealt with through a disciplined risk management process. Those events which potentially could have a positive outcome are regarded as opportunities and fed back into the strategy and objective setting process. Later, in 2007, the COSO released a draft document on Monitoring and the final

O. Arwinge, *Internal Control*, Contributions to Management Science,
DOI 10.1007/978-3-7908-2882-5_3,

guidance was released in 2009. This guidance emphasizes the importance of monitoring controls. Through an effective internal control change management process, weaknesses in the design and operating effectiveness of controls may be identified and adjusted so that internal controls remain effective over time.

3.1 Introduction

Recent developments in internal controls have been extensively shaped by a framework developed by the COSO (Committee of Sponsoring Organizations of the Treadway Commission), a US-based organization. Indeed to many practitioners, the COSO framework on internal control define desirable internal control practices. This is a scientifically interesting course of events well worth describing in itself, but it also makes it necessary to discuss the COSO version of internal control.

This chapter will therefore introduce the framework for internal control issued by COSO in 1992 (hence COSO, 1992). Besides the COSO 1992, other frameworks for internal control such as the Criteria of Control Framework (hence COCO) issued by the Canadian Institute of Chartered Accountants (1995) exist. Both the COSO 1992 and the COCO framework have pushed the boundaries of internal controls, clearly extending the definitions beyond financial reporting quality only (Spira & Page, 2003, p. 648) to also include areas such as compliance and efficiency and effectiveness in operations. This chapter will focus on the COSO 1992 including its subsequent releases on enterprise risk management (2004) and monitoring (2007/2009a). This focus is primarily due to the following reasons:

- The COSO 1992 has been widely diffused and established a baseline for directors and managers with regards to internal control practices (Power, 2007, p. 49).
- The COSO 1992 is a framework approved by the SEC (Securities and Exchange Commission) in the United States.
- The COSO 1992 has influenced definitions of internal control in professional audit standards (see IAASB, 2006, ISA 315; PCAOB, 2007, Audit Standard No. 5).
- The COSO 1992 has influenced definitions of internal control in regulatory guidance. From a local Swedish perspective, this may include guidance issued by the Financial Supervisory Authority [Finansinspektionen] and the Swedish National Financial Management Authority [Ekonomistyrningsverket].
- The COSO 1992 has been applied by a significant portion of the companies complying with the Sarbanes-Oxley Act in the United States.
- The COSO 1992 is an approved framework by the IIA (Institute of Internal Auditors) and considered to be the "most effective internal control guidance available today" (IIA, 2004, p. 234).
- The COSO 1992 represents a modern view on internal control and includes both financial and non-financial controls.

3.2 The COSO

In the mid 1980s the American Accounting Association, the Institute of Internal Auditors, the Financial Executives Institute and the Institute of Management Accountants decided to form an independent national commission on fraudulent financial reporting. This commission came to be chaired by James C. Treadway Jr. who had previously worked for the SEC. In 1987 the commission provided 11 recommendations that were to enhance the effectiveness of audit committees. According to Vinten (2001) they came to be the key stones of corporate financial governance (p. 5).

The COSO was formed in 1985 to sponsor the national commission on fraudulent financial reporting. It is a voluntary private sector organization dedicated to improving the financial reporting quality by setting standards for business ethics, effective internal controls and corporate governance.

3.3 Internal Control: Integrated Framework

In 1992 COSO issued their report entitled *Internal Control – Integrated Framework*. The report provided definitions and comprehensive guidance on internal controls for interested parties including auditors, managers, audit committees and regulators (see Vinten, 2001). The report also provided standards by which organizations could assess their internal control systems and determine their needs for development and improvement.

This codification of internal controls represented a significant step. The COSO 1992 consisted originally of four volumes: the executive summary (p. 7), framework (p. 118), reporting to external parties (p. 25) and evaluation tools (p. 203). The framework is therefore a quite comprehensive guide to internal control. Currently, in 2011, COSO has announced a project to modernize the now over 20 years old framework.

3.3.1 Worldwide Acceptance

Although the COSO 1992 has been criticized for being confusing or not providing adequate guidance for design and implementation (Shaw, 2006, p. 75; Gupta & Thomson, 2006, p. 33), it has undoubtedly received much attention all over the world and become a key conceptual and practical framework for involved stakeholders.

With the implementation of the Sarbanes-Oxley Act in the United States and its related Section 404-requirments, the SEC required that both management and auditors use an internal control framework that meets the criteria specified in

Section II.B.3a of the Section 404 Final Rules. Gupta and Thomson (2006) point out that while the SEC recognizes the existence of other frameworks and internal control guidance, the COSO 1992 also satisfies the SEC criteria (p. 28). Moreover the IIA (the Institute of Internal Auditors), the professional body for internal auditors around the world, states in their professional practices framework that it "*believes that the most effective internal control guidance available today is the report Internal Control – Integrated Framework* (2004, p. 234).

In connection with the increasing focus on risk management practices (Spira & Page, 2003; Power, 2007; Fraser & Henry, 2007; Mikes, 2009), in 2004 COSO issued a comprehensive framework on enterprise risk management (henceforth COSO, 2004). The COSO has also issued internal control guidance for smaller firms. This guidance however was directed towards the implementation of internal control over financial reporting and the specific issues facing smaller types of companies (COSO, 2006). Finally in 2009, after issuing a discussion document on monitoring controls, the COSO finalized a guidance document in this area (COSO, 2009a). More recently guidance and thought papers have also been issued on risk management oversight for board of directors (COSO, 2009b, 2010a), how firms may better identify and manage emerging risks (COSO, 2010b) and how organizations may more effectively embrace and embed entity-wide risk management practices (COSO, 2011).

COSO 1992 later became the basis for the Statement of Auditing Standard (SAS) No. 78 that subsequently amended SAS No. 55, recognizing the definition and description of internal control found in the COSO (see Heier, Dugan, & Sayers, 2005, pp. 55–61). The earlier definition of internal control, which included the control environment, the accounting system and the control procedures, were thus replaced with the internal control components defined by the COSO.

It is safe to say that COSO 1992 has been widely diffused all over the world and now constitutes a benchmark for firms struggling with designing, managing and overseeing their systems of internal controls. As we will see later in Sect. 5.2 COSO has also provided inspiration for Swedish guidance on internal control produced by regulatory bodies. Figure 3.1 below provides an illustration of the internal control process according to COSO 1992.

3.3.2 Definition of Internal Control

COSO 1992 defines internal control as a *process* consisting of *five interrelated components* designed to provide reasonable assurance that objectives will be met within three areas, as illustrated by Fig. 3.1 above. The complete definition of internal control reads:

> A process, effected by an entity's board of directors, management and other personnel, designed to provide reasonable assurances regarding the achievement of objectives in the following categories: Effectiveness and efficiency of operations, reliability of financial reporting and compliance with applicable laws and regulations. (p. 9)

Fig. 3.1 Internal Control – Integrated Framework (COSO, 1992)

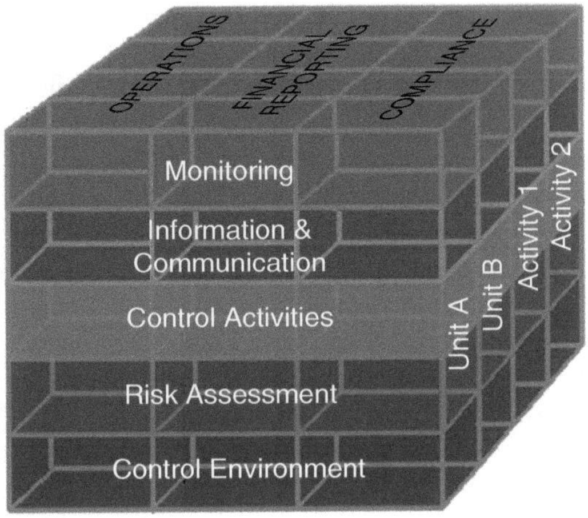

3.3.3 *The Internal Control Elements*

The definition enables us understand that internal control relates to more than just the accounting records but also contribute to efficiency in operations as well as compliance with laws and regulations. The top part of the cube illustrated in Fig. 3.1 shows these internal control objectives. From Fig. 3.1, we can also observe the means by which the internal control objectives will be met – the *five interrelated components* that managers and directors must consider. The five internal control elements are:

- Control environment.
- Risk assessment.
- Control activities.
- Information and communication.
- Monitoring.

These five components are thus necessary for effective internal control and according to Knechel (2007), they may be translated into the circumstances of the firm:

- The control environment.
- The ability to identify threats (risk assessment).
- The actions taken to mitigate those risks (control activities).
- The ability to coordinate it all through information and communication.
- The maintenance of controls (monitoring).

3.3.4 *Internal Control as a Process*

As mentioned earlier, the COSO 1992 definition of internal controls stipulates that internal control is a *process*. This is an important observation since it breaks with earlier definitions where internal control was considered to be a *system* or a *structure*. SAS 55, which was subsequently revised with the COSO-based SAS 78-defintion of internal control, applied a definition of internal control in which this type of internal control was considered to be a structure. The view of internal control as a process also contrasts with the definition of internal control provided by the FRC (Financial Reporting Council) in the United Kingdom through the guidance to the Combined Code (2005, p. 7). In this guidance, internal control is often referred to as a system of internal control. It should however be pointed out that often the terms system and process are applied more or less interchangeably.

Revisiting the work of Hammer and Champy (1993, p. 35), we find that a process is defined as a "collection of activities that takes one or more kinds of input and creates an output that is of value to the customer". Building on the definition by COSO on internal control and also on the work by Hammer and Champy we argue that the internal control process may be viewed as a *collection of control activities* that may produce assurance that financial, operational and compliance objectives can be met. Internal control should thus be viewed as a fundamental and basic process that does not solely relate to accounting, but that also produces assurance more generally regarding the reliability of information and safeguarding of firm assets (Pfister, 2009, p. 26).

3.3.5 A Means to an End

Just like control systems in general management control research (see for example Simons, 1990; Otley, 1994, 1999, 2003; Langfield-Smith, 1997; Chenhall, 2003) COSO 1992 views the internal control process as a means to an end – not as an end in itself. The internal control process namely creates output which may be of value to stakeholders, in the shape and form of *assurance*. Due to the inherent limitations of internal control, only *reasonable assurance* may be produced (see FFE, 2007, pp. 47–48; FAR SRS, RS 400, 2009, p. 259; also see Sect. 5.3.1 for a discussion). This assurance is that strategic, operational, reporting and compliance risks related to business objectives and strategies are effectively being mitigated. COSO's definition relates to three basic and broad objectives:

- Efficiency and effectiveness in operations.
- Financial reporting.
- Compliance with applicable laws and regulations.

Effectiveness and efficiency in operations relates company performance. The financial reporting objective refers to financial reporting quality, something which has traditionally been an important objective of internal control. Financial transactions should be valid, complete, authorized, valued and timely and accurately recorded so that financial reporting quality is maintained (see for example Trenerry, 1999, pp. 9–10; also see FAR SRS, RS 500, 2009, p. 274). The SOX (2002) in the United States and its related Section 404-requriements on internal controls as well as the Swedish code of Corporate Governance (Kodgruppen, 2004;

Kollegiet för Svensk Bolagsstyrning, 2008b) focus on financial reporting quality, seemingly excluding many non-financial controls.

The third internal control objective relates to compliance whereby controls should produce assurance that applicable laws and regulations are adhered to. This internal control objective seems to be increasingly important in today's business society, we might add in the passing, as the number and complexity of rules imposed on firms increases (see Ahrne & Brunsson, eds., 2004).

A final comment about the COSO definition of internal controls is that it stresses that internal controls are influenced by all the people within the organization – perhaps highlighting the importance of an appropriate organizational culture where directors and managers, those ultimately responsible for the oversight and design of controls, are supported by managers and staff on all levels. They are the people that most often operate the controls, and thus are vital for the operating effectiveness of controls.

3.3.6 The Control Environment

According to the COSO 1992 the control environment includes the following areas:

- Integrity and ethical values.
- Commitment to competence.
- Attention and direction provided by the directors or audit committee.
- Management philosophy and operation style.
- Organizational structure.
- Manner of assigning authority and responsibility.
- Human resources policies and procedures.

The control environment sets the *tone* of the company, pointing to the responsibility of directors and managers in establishing a sound control environment throughout the whole organization. It affects and instils ethical behaviour and contributes to a favourable culture of integrity and responsibility.

These controls are usually not located on a process-level but are considered to be more high-level controls with a *wide and pervasive, or important but indirect, effect* on business processes. These controls are sometimes referred to as *entity-level controls* (PCAOB, 2007, p. 403). PCAOB (Public Company Accounting Oversight Board) (2007, pp. 403–406) in the United States suggests that entity-wide controls include the following controls:

- Code of conducts.
- Controls over management override.
- Company risk assessment processes.
- Centralized processing and controls.
- Significant accounting and risk policies.
- Monitoring controls.
- Controls over the period-end financial reporting process.

3.3.7 Risk Assessment

COSO 1992 prescribes that a second important component of the internal control process comprises of the organizational *risk assessment process*. This was to highlight the importance of risk and of adopting a risk-based approach to control. Its purpose was to allow the systematic identification of risks, and to further ensure that they were appropriately governed and managed by responsible company-insiders.

As risk management practices have been made into a regulatory object by regulators and supervisory authorities, together with the fact that for many years there was no coherent and widely accepted framework for risk management (Chapman, 2003b), in 2004 the COSO (henceforth COSO, 2004) issued their framework entitled *Enterprise Risk Management – Integrated Framework*. Enterprise risk management (ERM) is defined as:

> A process, effected by an entity's board of directors, management, and other personnel, applied in a strategy setting and across the enterprise, designed to identify potential events that may affect the entity and manage risk to be within its risk appetite to provide reasonable assurance regarding the achievement of organizational objectives. (p. 8)

The COSO 2004 explicitly tied internal control even closer to risk, viewing internal control as a *risk treatment* to risk exposures. According to Chapman (2003, p. 33), this framework was designed to:

- Help management properly align risk appetite and strategy.
- Make the risk appetite of firms explicit.
- Enable better alignment between actual and desired risk exposure.
- Ensure effective risk-responses through for example internal controls.

In order to better understand this definition we may take a closer look at the key words suggested by the COSO's 2004 executive summary. Just as with the internal control process in the COSO 1992, ERM has been defined as a process and also a means to an end. Furthermore, ERM is effected by people in the organization in contrast to having an exclusive reliance on formal policies and forms.

ERM should be applied in *a strategy setting*, adopting an overall approach and a portfolio-view of risk instead of relying on a traditional intra-departmental strategy where each area manages its own risks. It follows that, according to the COSO 2004, ERM must be integrated and coordinated across the entire organization (Walker, Shenkir, & Barton, 2003, p. 52).

The event identification component of ERM should consider the organizational setting and the risk appetite, and risks should be identified, assessed and managed so that overall organizational objectives may be met (Bowling & Rieger, 2005). The concept of risk response suggests that companies should view risks as items that need to be deliberately dealt with, through a variation of risk treatments. The risk responses in COSO (2004, p. 4) include the following:

- Reduce.
- Accept.
- Share.
- Avoid.

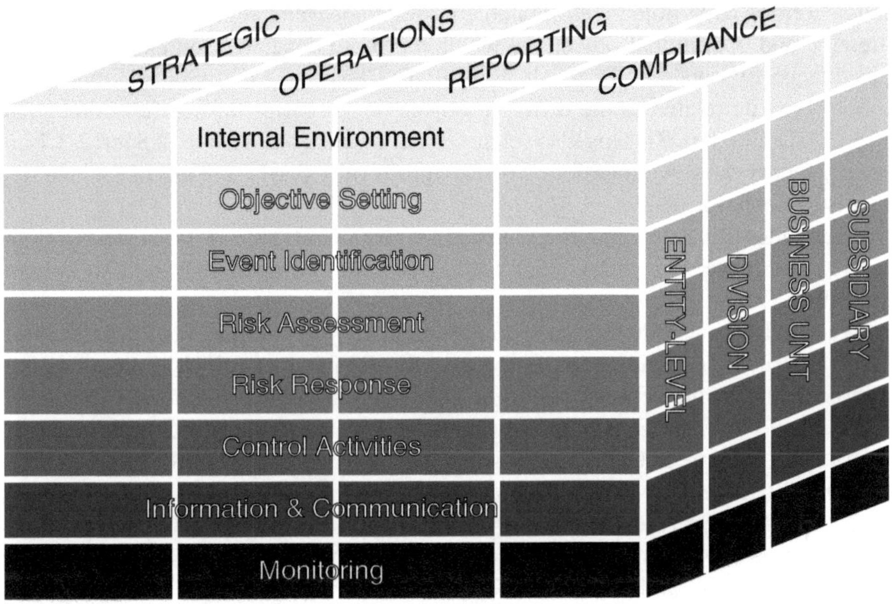

Fig. 3.2 Enterprise Risk Management – Integrated Framework (COSO, 2004)

Those events which accordingly have a potentially negative impact should be dealt with through the risk management process. However, those events which have been identified and which might have positive outcomes, should be regarded as opportunities and *fed back into the strategy and objective setting process* (Chapman, 2003, pp. 34–35).

Internal control as a part of ERM is thus regarded as one of the means for managing risks (Fraser & Henry, 2007, p. 393), and through COSO 2004, the ability of the firm to systematically and effectively identify and address risk has been acknowledged. Figure 3.2 below illustrates the COSO ERM framework of 2004.

Just like the COSO 1992, the ERM framework takes its point of departure in established company objectives – objectives related to strategic, operational, reporting and compliance capabilities (Anderson, Christ, & Sedatole, 2006, p. 48). According to the framework, the risk categories are as follows:

- Strategic risks – relate to high-level goals.
- Operational risks – relate to the effective and efficient use of resources.
- Reporting risks – relate (primarily) to financial reporting quality.
- Compliance risks – relate to laws and regulations (p. 50).

In addition to the internal control objectives given in the COSO 1992, the strategic dimension has been added. Risk management practices, and related risk treatments for example through the application of internal controls, *may however provide assurance related to these objective categories in different ways*. A firm has better control over objectives related to compliance and reporting, compared to strategic and operational objectives which are more dependent on external events and thus partly outside of a firm's control. The assurance that risk treatments are able to provide related to the different objective categories thus differs somewhat (see COSO, 2004, p. 3). This also relates to our discussion in Chap. 2 Sect. 2.3.1 on agency theory were we mentioned that output is only partly a result of the agent's efforts (Eisenhardt, 1989a, p. 61).

Event identification and the internal environment appear to correspond to control environment in the COSO 1992. The other components are also known from the COSO 1992.

We can thus conclude that important internal control components from the 1992 framework now constitute parts of the overall ERM framework. It is therefore not surprising that some researchers argue that internal control has now become an *extension of risk management* (Power, 2007, p. 35) and mutated into risk management (Spira & Page, 2003). In the passing, we may add that, as in the case with the COSO 1992, there has been some debate regarding the interpretation and usefulness of the COSO 2004 (see Quinn, 2006). Currently, in 2011 the COSO seemingly places increasingly more emphasis on the effectiveness of risk management practices of firms, and the way the board of directors oversee emerging risk exposures of firms (COSO, 2010a, 2010b, 2011). This is a result of identified risk management and oversight weaknesses following the global financial and banking crisis of 2008 (see Senior Supervisors Group, 2009).

3.3.8 Control Activities

The board of directors sets the tone at the top and establishes policies by which management and the organization are to be guided. Based on board policies, senior and lower levels of management design appropriate rules and procedures that will enable employees throughout the organization to carry out board policies.

According to COSO 1992, these *policies and procedures* represent *control activities*. It follows that control activities may be located throughout the organization, on all levels and in all business processes (Trenerry, 1999, p. 14). Control activities may for example include the following:

- Performance reviews where actual performance or output is compared to forecast, estimation and prior periods.
- Information processing controls, automated or manual, to ensure accuracy, completeness and authorization of transactions and system data.
- Physical controls such as the physical security of assets, access to assets and to computer programs and records.

- The segregation of duties, which refers to incompatible duties which should be separated if possible and performed by independent employees (p. 18). Segregation of duties is considered to be a key feature of a sound system of internal control (pp. 15–19).

From a perspective of financial reporting quality, control activities in their broadest sense, may be classified into entity-wide, or entity-level, controls and business process controls (see PCAOB, AS5, 2007, p. 401 on the top-down approach). Professional standards on internal control tend to view control activities as consisting of two parts: one policy-part that outlines the control objective and what should be done, (i.e. describing the design of the control) and one procedure-part that implements the policy (i.e. the actual performance of the control).

In general management control research these control activities are sometimes referred to as *administrative controls* to which standard operating procedures and rules for example have been included (see Langfield-Smith, 1997, p. 208). These controls are considered to be of a *feed-forward nature* (ex-ante controls) which stipulate and regulate what should be done, i.e. serve as guidance for future organizational behaviour. It may be important to realize (which we will come back to later) that feedback-controls, such as different types of monitoring controls, are often considered as being vital supplementary controls to more detailed control activities.

Through these monitoring controls and feedback systems, deficiencies in the design or operating effectiveness of more detailed controls may be identified and addressed. It is therefore of vital importance that the policies and procedures are *adequately designed and effectively operating* – two variables which are considered in auditor evaluations of controls (see IIA, PA 2130, 2009, p. 30; FAR SRS, RS 400, 2009, p. 259). Through the feedback-nature of formal and informal information systems, monitoring controls identify discrepancies and unexpected variances from targets and objectives.

Different types of control activities naturally exist in all organizations and there is evidence pointing to the importance of a balanced approach where different types of controls need to be applied (Simons, 1991). A recent case-study on the work of audit committees further highlights the importance of informal processes and controls as supplements to formal systems and controls (see Turley & Zaman, 2007). Section 5.3.3 will discuss control design in more detail.

3.3.9 Information and Communication

Information systems are naturally of vital important for managing organizational data. This is also why both companies as well as internal and external auditors allocate significant efforts towards making sure that controls over information are effectively operating. With increased complexity in operations and as information technology becomes increasingly intertwined with business processes and activities, companies are becoming ever more dependent on the reliability and accuracy of their registered data. As a result, if information is to be accurate, reliable, relevant and timely so that managers may be able to act upon it, the way information is authorized, registered, reviewed and monitored is a matter of concern. The COSO 1992 has included information as one of the five components of a sound internal control process.

The importance of information and communication in general, and the importance of producing relevant, timely and reliable information for decision-making purposes through *information-based systems* specifically, is also a core theme in the fields of management accounting and management control (see Johnson & Kaplan, 1987; Simons, 1987, 1990, 1991, 1995; Langfield-Smith, 1997; Otley, 1980, 1994, 1999, 2003, 2008; Chenhall, 2003). In this context, the control system is often described as a normative information feedback system (Simons, 1991, p. 49) where formalized control cycles have the ability to transport information so that managers are able to make informed decisions based on feedback on actual performance and the established organizational objectives. Simons (1991), an influential scholar in the field of management control, has written extensively on the subject and defines a management control system as "the formal, information-based routines and procedures managers use to maintain or alter patterns in organizational activities" (p. 49) – thus highlighting the importance of information-based routines and the communicative elements of these processes.

Internal controls are thus essential in securing assets and ensuring that management information is reliable. They constitute the foundation that ensures the integrity of the data used for management control purposes. Simons (1995, p. 181) argues that internal control prevents inefficiencies in processing and incorrect decision-making due to inaccurate data. However, he views internal control as not being *directly* related to strategy formation and implementation as it does not form part of the different control levers used by managers to control strategy formulation and implementation. Rather Simons views internal control as the basic foundation (1995, p. 177). This is seemingly also in line with the arguments made by Pfister (see 2009, pp. 22–26).

Nevertheless, appropriate internal controls must ensure that accurate management accounting information is available for effective decisions to be made. This seems to be a significant internal control challenge as data need to be *identified, captured and distributed* so that effective decisions about firm performance can be made. Through the information and communication component of the framework, the COSO shows the importance of methods for effective reporting and communication.

From a financial reporting perspective, financial transactions and other types of information need to be accurately recorded and distributed through information systems. Methods and systems used in the company need to ensure that financial data and transactions are valid, timely recorded, properly classified, valued and comply with generally accepted accounting standards (see for example Trenerry, 1999, pp. 13–14; also see FAR SRS, RS 500, 2009, p. 274 for financial assertions).

From a broader perspective however, methods and systems used should however also enable managers and staff to understand and execute other internal control components. Information needs to be identified, captured, distributed and used in the organization so that people are able to complete their internal control responsibilities. Thus various types of internal information systems and reporting methods should support the understanding of processes, controls, tasks and individual responsibilities (COSO, 2006, p. 11). It is evident from this discussion that the information systems and the communication systems are vital if relevant information is to be captured, distributed and acted upon in a cost-effective manner.

3.3.10 Monitoring

Both internal and external factors increasingly put pressure on companies to change. The explosion in rules and regulations (Ahrne & Brunsson, eds., 2004, pp. 5–6), new customer demands, increased competition and developments in information technologies are only a few of the factors that contribute to change in business models and processes. Along with these changes, risk exposures and risk treatments must accordingly adapt.

It follows that the internal control processes of the company will need to change if they are to remain effective and not grow out-of-balance. The fifth COSO 1992 internal control element constitutes of monitoring activities. These monitoring activities may be embedded in day-to-day activities and thus be performed quite frequently, or performed through separate stand-alone evaluations.

In September 2007, the COSO released a discussion document entitled *Internal Control Integrated Framework – Guidance on Monitoring Internal Control Systems*. The publication of the final guidance on the monitoring of internal control systems was in 2009. The motive behind this new guidance on monitoring is related to the challenges of appropriately and effectively implementing monitoring procedures so that internal controls will remain relevant and effective. The chairman of the COSO, Larry Rittenberg, claimed at the time that "there is a tremendous gap between the value good monitoring brings to a system of internal control and management's understanding of that value" (Whitley, 2006, p. 18). Another reason for issuing the guidance document may be that, although the monitoring component is described in COSO 1992, it does not go into much detail about how the monitoring procedures of control processes should be implemented (Cheney, 2007, p. 14).

Thus the COSO 2007 focuses on mechanisms that will provide assurance that the internal controls installed at the company remain adequate and effective over time. These mechanisms "assess the performance of the internal control systems over time. That mechanism is monitoring" (COSO, 2007, p. i). The rationale behind monitoring controls is that "unmonitored controls tend to deteriorate over time" (COSO, 2009a, p. 2). The COSO makes the following claims for the importance of monitoring:

> Over time, ineffective monitoring leads to control breakdowns which reduce the efficiency of the entire internal control system. Likewise, inefficient monitoring may limit an organization's ability of focus finite resources in the areas of greatest risk, thus reducing its effectiveness. (p. ii)

Two fundamental principles underpin the monitoring controls framework:

- Ongoing monitoring and separate evaluations enable management to determine whether the components of internal control continue to function over time.
- Internal control weaknesses should be identified and communicated in a timely manner to those parties responsible for taking corrective action and to management and the board as appropriate.

According to COSO 2007, there are three fundamental elements which will influence the effectiveness and efficiency of monitoring. Those elements will be described below and comprise of:

- The control environment in which monitoring operates.
- The effective prioritization of monitoring procedures.
- The communication structure for monitoring.

3.3.10.1 The Monitoring Control Environment

An understanding of the control environment is crucial. The tone at the top will necessarily influence monitoring activities, and there should be an organizational structure that places the right people, the evaluators, with adequate skills and authority in monitoring roles. COSO claims that:

> Organizations begin the process of meeting these expectations by placing **competent** and **objective** people in monitoring roles throughout the organization. *Competence* refers to an evaluator's knowledge of the controls and related processes, including how controls should operate and what constitutes a control weakness. *Objectivity* relates both to the way in which information is generated for use in monitoring and to the characteristics of evaluators. Objective individuals provide information and/or perform monitoring procedures with no concern about possible personal consequences and no vested interest in manipulating the information for personal benefit or self-preservation. (p. ii)

3.3.10.2 Prioritisation of Monitoring Procedures

This element concerns the organization's ability to effectively prioritize monitoring procedures so that resources are allocated to where they are most needed. This basically means the following: *monitoring should be focused on significant risks and controls* rather than the less significant areas. Since key risks and controls are usually identified in connection with the risk assessment process, another COSO-component, the establishment and prioritisation of monitoring procedures, should naturally be based on this risk assessment process.

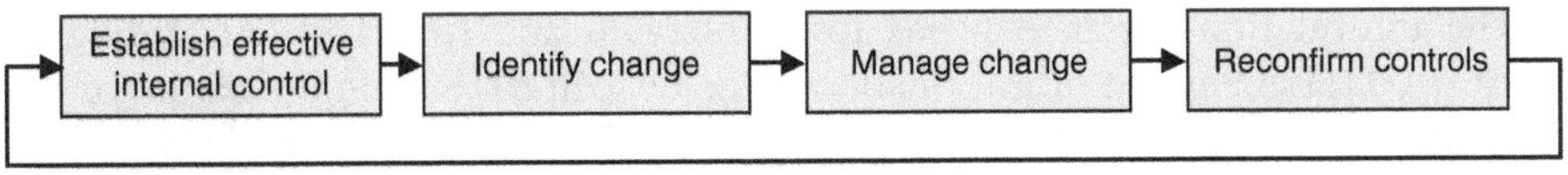

Fig. 3.3 The internal control change management process (COSO, 2007, p. 8–9)

The scope of monitoring, i.e. what is monitored, by whom and using what procedures, is based on contingency-logic which considers factors such as size and complexity of operations, the nature of the operations, the purpose of the monitoring procedures and the relative importance of the risks and controls are taken into account. COSO 2007 states that effective internal control systems loose their effectiveness when:

- Processes or risks change, and the underlying controls do not adapt, or
- Previously effective controls cease to operate as they were designed. In either case, the risk inherent in any effective internal control system is that change is not properly identified and managed (p. iii).

The COSO 2007 goes on to describe a process which enables an organization to better identify internal control weaknesses. First, there needs to be a starting-point, or a baseline, where an effective system of internal control has been established. At that point, *directors will have reasonable assurance* that the controls in place will enable the firm to meet its objectives. From this baseline, weaknesses may be identified through a change-identification process and be subsequently verified, addressed and managed through a change management process. Finally, the system of internal control is reconfirmed with regards to its design and operating effectiveness. Figure 3.3 below illustrates the internal control change management process.

Thus the entity-level controls further ensure that business process controls *remains effective*. But monitoring controls, as isolated controls, also form a vital part of the overall internal control system since they perform both ongoing and separate checks that operations are running effectively. Thus monitoring controls may be viewed as meta-controls which reviews other controls, but also as fundamental controls in themselves.

3.3.10.3 Communication Structure for Monitoring

The communication element of the monitoring component relates directly to information systems of firms, both formal and informal, and specifically to their feedback-capabilities whereby information about performance is transported and fed back to management to enable effective decision-making. This relates specifically to information about possible deficiencies in the design or operating effectiveness of controls. The firm's ability to appropriately communicate such deficiencies, or other changes with regard to risk exposures and internal controls, is crucial for a sound system of internal control and effective risk management practices.

The information obtained needs to be relevant and sufficient. According to COSO 2007, the amount of information gathered will depend on the nature of the controls. With regards to more *complex and sophisticated controls* COSO 2007 claims that "to address the variables in control operation, complex controls may warrant gathering more information than simple controls" (p. 17). The results obtained from monitoring should be reported to appropriate people, supervisors and executive management within a reasonable timeframe. COSO 2007 prescribes that:

> Identified control weaknesses, however, should be reported to the person responsible for the control's operation and to at least one level higher. Reporting at least to these two levels gives the responsible person the information necessary to correct control operation and also helps ensure that appropriately objective people are involved in the severity assessment. (p. iv)

When rating internal control weaknesses, their likelihood and significant should be considered where "*likelihood is the probability that a control will fail to detect or prevent a risk's occurrence, and significance is the potential impact of the risk if it occurs* (p. v).

3.4 Summary and Concluding Remarks

This chapter has provided an account of a globally accepted framework for internal control – *Internal Control – Integrated Framework* – issued by the COSO in 1992. Based on the findings of this chapter, we conclude by emphasizing the following observations:

- Internal control is a process and consists of five interrelated elements:
  - Control environment – the circumstances of the company.
  - Risk assessment – the ability to identify threats/risks.
  - Control activities – the actions taken to mitigate risks.
  - Information and communication – the ability to coordinate.
  - Monitoring – the ability to maintain internal controls.
- The importance of managing risks has been further highlighted through the COSO release in 2004 of *Enterprise Risk Management – Integrated Framework*. This framework was designed to:
  - Help management align risk appetite and strategy.
  - Make the risk appetite of the firm explicit.
  - Enable better alignment between actual risk and desired risk.
  - Ensure effective risk responses.
- Internal control is explicitly tied to the companies risk management practices in which controls are considered to be a risk treatment.

- The value and importance of monitoring controls were further highlighted by the COSO release in 2009 on Monitoring. Monitoring controls enable managers to ensure that internal controls remain adequate and effective over time. The internal control change management process is of vital importance as it enables weaknesses to be identified and communicated so that appropriate action may be taken.
- The COSO framework is a normative framework which seems to be based on agency theory whereby problems of moral hazard or adverse selection can be addressed through the investment in controls. Controls are applied based on rational assumptions in order to reduce agency problems. This is neither surprising nor incorrect.
- We might add however, that institutional theory provides a contrasting and complementary perspective in which control practices may be formed and installed based on developments in the institutional environment. The next chapter goes into some of the regulatory aspects of internal control, and could thus provides the reader with a better understanding of how control practices may be formed from trends in the institutional context.

Chapter 4
A Regulatory Perspective

Abstract

Purpose: The purpose of this chapter is to provide a regulatory perspective on internal control. We will therefore describe and discuss some of the internal control regulations which are imposed on firms.

Synopsis: The regulatory environment has a significant influence on the internal control practices of firms. A fundamental feature of most corporate governance regulations are their focus on transparency and disclosure. The use and usefulness of management reporting on internal control and auditor reporting on internal control have been widely debated. The Cadbury code in the United Kingdom has been a pioneer in corporate governance regulation. This code is semi-mandatory with a comply-or-explain character and has become a blueprint for other corporate codes and exported to many countries. The Cadbury code covers both financial and non-financial controls. One main controversy with the Cadbury code concerned paragraph 4.5 which prescribed that directors should report on the organization's internal control system. Later, in 1999, the Financial Reporting Council released guidance on internal control, guidance which was subsequently revised in 2005. This document is to help directors with reference to the provisions in section C.2 of the Combined Code, which relates to internal control. Following high-profile management fraud in the United States, the Sarbanes-Oxley Act of 2002 was implemented. Section 404 of this Act prescribes that managers must assess an organization's internal control over financial reporting, and that the external auditor must assess and report on both management's assessment and the effectiveness of internal controls. This unique piece of regulation has been somewhat controversial due to its relatively strict requirements and widely discussed during the last few years. In 2004 Sweden implemented its own corporate governance code. Originally, the code included strict internal control reporting requirements, but these provisions were subsequently downsized. In 2008, a revised code was released and further updates, based on the implementation of European Union directives, are expected. These changes will make mandatory the disclosure of a corporate governance report and also the existence of an audit committee for concerned listed companies. These regulations can be viewed from an agency theory perspective which explains

O. Arwinge, *Internal Control*, Contributions to Management Science,
DOI 10.1007/978-3-7908-2882-5_4, © Springer-Verlag Berlin Heidelberg 2013

how the interests of principals and agents need to be better aligned. Institutional theory however, helps understand the quick and severe responses to public and visible corporate crises.

4.1 Introduction

In a paper on the development of internal control during the last century, Heier, Dugan and Sayers (2005) suggest that the definition and application of internal control often changed as reactions to events in the environment. These events triggered debates about perceived weaknesses in the existing practices of internal control. The authors conclude that the internal control development process has been a reactive one, as may be seen *through the many laws and regulations of the twentieth century* (p. 63). Calls for stricter regulations in bad times, or for other forms of change to fix a problem and protect the investor, is neither a new nor a surprising phenomenon (Baker, Bealing, Nelson & Staley, 2006, p. 24). More importantly perhaps for the purpose of this thesis, is the point made by Heier, Dugan and Sayers (2005) on the seemingly close association between regulation and internal control.

Research done from an institutional perspective on the Sarbanes-Oxley Act has also shown the interplay between the accounting profession, law makers and regulators, thus pointing to the development of new practices based on the interaction between stakeholders in the regulatory environment (Baker et al. 2006). Other studies applying institutional concepts have provided evidence that help understand and explain the social, political and regulatory processes that prevented mandatory internal control assessments and disclosure regimes from developing prior to 2002 (Shapiro & Matson, 2008). In a paper by Kinney (2005) on audit deregulation and the re-regulation, the author shows how external events dramatically affected audit regulation activity. One of these events was the adoption of new laws and regulations, which regulated certain aspects of internal control including internal control reporting requirements (p. 92).

Further, as cross-national patterns in corporate governance practices are converging through global initiatives to standardize corporate governance (Bhasa, 2004; Davies, 2008), firms need to pay increasingly more attention to mandatory or semi-mandatory corporate governance regulations, which may often be sponsored by the governments such as in Swedish case (see Jonnergård & Larsson, 2007). New directions in corporate governance research also point to the importance of understanding the influence of regulation on the quality of corporate governance practices (Hambrick, Werder, & Zajac, 2008).

Power (2007) argues that the theme of corporate governance has dominated corporate regulation since the beginning of the 1990s (p. 34). Organizational life in the United Kingdom has undergone a *turnbullization*, by which Power means accommodation to the internal control guidance known as the Turnbull-guidance. The global *regulatory convergence on, and demand for, effective internal control* has contributed significantly to the rise of internal control (pp. 34–65) and internal control has now itself emerged as a key "regulatory and public policy object" (p. 47).

The argument which therefore motivates the existence of this chapter is this; the regulatory environment appears to have a significant impact on the practice of governance and oversight in general and, more importantly for the purpose of this thesis, also on the practice of internal controls. It is thus essential that we describe and discuss some of the regulatory requirements imposed on firm's activities with reference to internal control. In order to understand what drives and influences internal control designs, it seems necessary to provide the reader with a regulatory perspective.

Accordingly, this chapter will discuss laws and regulations on internal control. Internal control often form part of basic business regulations such as limited liability companies acts and annual account acts, as well as specific regulations provided by regulatory and supervisory agencies in regulated sectors, such as the financial sector. It is neither appropriate nor possible to go into all the relevant regulations on internal control. Instead, we will focus on but a few specific regulations that have had a significant influence on internal control practices of firms around the world. We will also provide a local Swedish perspective by describing the internal control provisions of the Swedish code of Corporate Governance. Below we provide a brief account of these regulations and reasons for why they may be important to discuss.

- In the United Kingdom, the Combined Code, especially Section C.2-requirements regarding internal controls and the related Turnbull-guidance from 1999 to 2005. The Combined Code, with its comply-or-explain approach, has had significant impact and also been exported to countries, such as Sweden Kollegiet för Svensk Bolagsstyrning, (2008b). The effect of the Turnbull-guidance on internal control practices remains extensive (Power, 2007, p. 50).
- The Sarbanes-Oxley Act in the United States, especially the section 404-requirements. These requirements, which relates to internal control over financial reporting, has had a dramatic impact on the internal control practices of firms world-wide (Gee & McVay, 2005; Rittenberg & Miller, 2005; Tacket, Wolf, & Claypool, 2006; Patterson & Smith, 2007; Krishnan, Rama, & Zhang, 2008) and also generated a substantial amount of research (see DeFond & Francis, 2005).
- The Swedish code of Corporate Governance (Kodgruppen, 2004; Kollegiet för Svensk Bolagsstyrning, 2008b), especially the provisions which relates to internal control. This code has undoubtedly received significant attention in Sweden. The original code requirements on internal control have been downsized, and comments in media testify to the important and controversial nature of these provisions (Lekvall, 2008; Brandinger, 2008a; 2008b).

In the section below, we will start discussing and commenting on the details of the Combined Code in the United Kingdom, and especially the requirements imposed on firms with reference to internal controls.

4.2 The Combined Code

4.2.1 Background

As with most developments in internal control practices, the changes in governance and internal control practices in the beginning of the 1990s in the United Kingdom were sparked by external events (see Heier, Dugan, & Sayers, 2005; Kinney, 2005; Power, 2007, p. 34) which put pressure on to further regulate executive power and reform corporate governance practices. The discussions mainly concerned executive remuneration and the membership structure of the board of directors.

Pressure for reform resulted in the establishment of the Committee on the Financial Aspects of Corporate Governance. This committee subsequently published a report which included a code of principles for good corporate governance. The committee was chaired by Sir Adrian Cadbury who gave the code its name, the *Cadbury Code*. According to Power (1997), the Cadbury Code was initiated by the accounting profession, but government supported it since it reflected the regulatory mood of the agencies (p. 54).

The report, which was issued in 1992, included a number of recommendations that were meant to strengthen corporate governance. These included non-executive directors on the board, independent audit committees and management reporting on internal controls. The committee's work is still considered to have pioneered in corporate governance standards and is considered a model for sound practice worldwide Chapman (2003a).

A key feature of the Cadbury Code was its *comply-or-explain* character, which since then has become a blueprint for corporate codes and exported to other countries. The comply-or-explain principle basically means that organizations do not have to comply with the principles or standards, and need only to provide and disclose reasons for non-compliance. This is line with the general spirit of the European accounting practices which advocates guidance through principles instead of detailed rules, as opposed to the practice in the United States (Jackson, 2004, p. 61).

Besides the comply-or-explain character of the Cadbury Code, another key feature was that it put a great deal of emphasis on board disclosure and openness. Although not an optimal governance model which works effectively for any company may be possible to identify, it considers *disclosure* to be a fundamental feature common to all corporate governance models (Chapman, 2003a).

However, one main controversy with the disclosure requirements of the Cadbury Code concerned paragraph 4.5 which prescribed that directors should report on the company's internal control system. The Cadbury Code further required that an external auditor review the statement of compliance made by executive managers and board of directors. According to Power (1997), paragraph 4.5 in the Cadbury Code related to internal control disclosures "generated fundamental problems about what internal controls really are and what one is saying in describing them as effective" (p. 55).

The exact reporting format at that time was not prescribed, as it was a principles-based system, and thus caused additional problems and debate about the mode of procedure when stating compliance with the requirements. According to Power (1997) directors were unwilling to make any statements without clear guidance. To add to the confusion, in 1995 the Auditing Practices Board (APB) in the United Kingdom issued a discussion document advising external auditors against issuing opinions on Cadbury-related statements (p. 54).

Even though disclosure regimes related to firms' internal control systems was not a new phenomenon in the business world at the time (see Wallace, 1981), the implementation of paragraph 4.5 of the Cadbury Code may represent the start of the rise of the phenomena now often referred to as *management reporting on internal control* (MRIC) and also *auditor reporting on internal control* (ARIC). Moreover, it seemed to be the start of years of debate regarding how directors and managers should, and are able to, report on the soundness of their firm's systems of internal control. As a result of new internal control requirements' being prescribed by the Swedish code of Corporate Governance, the debate continues in Sweden.

4.2.2 The Turnbull Guidance

The Cadbury Code approach of *comply-or-explain* still remains a fundamental feature of corporate governance in the United Kingdom and listing rules require United Kingdom companies listed on the main market of the stock exchange in London to state compliance, and possible non-compliance, with the Code's main principles (FRC, 2008, p. 1).

The FRC (Financial Reporting Council) in the United Kingdom is the independent regulator responsible for promoting and enforcing good corporate reporting and governance and undertakes regular reviews of the impact and implementation of the Combined Code (FRC, 2008) to ensure that it continues to work effectively. For the purpose of this thesis however, we will focus on a specific section of the Combined code – section C.2.

Section C.2 in the Combined Code (FRC, 2008) refers to the *internal control component* of corporate governance and it prescribes that "the board should maintain a sound system of internal control to safeguard shareholders' investment and the company's assets" (p. 16). More specifically, code provision C.2.1 states that:

> The directors should, at least annually, conduct a review of the effectiveness of the group's system of internal control and should report to shareholders that they have done so. The review should cover all material controls, including financial, operational and compliance controls and risk management systems (FRC, 2008, p. 16).

Thus directors are to find out, at least once a year, if the financial and non-financial internal controls within the firm are operating effectively. Undoubtedly this is a challenging task.

This may also be the reason why in 1999 the FRC published the report *Internal Control – Guidance for Directors on the Combined Code* which came to be labelled the *Turnbull-guidance*. The Turnbull-guidance sets out best practices for internal control for listed companies in the United Kingdom as well as providing guidance on how to comply with section C.2 in the Combined Code (FRC, 2008).

A few years after the first release of the Turnbull-guidance, in 2004 the FRC formed a Turnbull-Review Group which reviewed the guidance on internal control. Subsequently, the FRC issued a revised guidance in 2005 (hence FRC, 2005) which was to apply to listed companies and financial years beginning on or after January 1 2006. The FRC (2005, p. 4) states that:

> Paragraph 9.8.6 of the UK Listing Authority's Listing Rules states that in the case of a listed company incorporated in the United Kingdom, the following items must be included in its annual report and accounts:
>
> - A statement of how the listed company has applied the principles set out in Section 1 (referring to Section 1 in the Combined Cod which prescribes principles and provisions regarding directors, remuneration, accountability and audit, and also relations to shareholders) of the Combined Code, in a manner that would enable shareholders to evaluate how the principles have been applied;
> - A statement as to whether the listed company has:
>   - Complied throughout the accounting period with all relevant provisions set out in Section 1 of the Combined Code; or
>   - Not complied throughout the accounting period with all relevant provisions set out in Section 1 e of the Combined Code and if so, setting out:
>
>   I. Those provisions, if any, it has not complied with;
>   II. In the case of provisions whose requirements are of a continuing nature, the period within which, if any, it did not comply with some or all of those provisions; and
>   III. The company's reasons for non-compliance.

The SEC (Securities and Exchange Commission) in the United States has claimed that the Turnbull-guidance satisfies their criteria as an adequate internal control framework and may thus be applied for Sarbanes-Oxley purposes and internal controls over financial reporting. The Turnbull-guidance (FRC, 2005) basically consists of three key parts:[1]

- The maintenance of a sound system of controls.
- The review of the effectiveness of the system of internal controls.
- The statement made by company directors regarding the system of internal controls.

---

[1] To suggest that the FRC 2005 contains three key parts may be rather crude since both the introduction-part and the appendix are important elements. However, for the purposes of this thesis we will focus on the three parts noted above, since they together constitute the key guidance that needs to be addressed by directors in complying with the Combined Code, section C.2 – namely establishing and maintaining a system of internal control, reviewing its effectiveness, and reporting on the status of the system of internal control.

In the preface to FRC 2005, the Review Group concluded that the guidance on internal control had according to "investors and directors contributed to a marked improvement in the overall standard of risk management and internal control" (p. 1). They further concluded that the flexible, principles-based approach to internal control maintenance and reporting had proved to work effectively, thus they endorsed a continuation of such an approach. According to the statement made by the Review Group in the preface, overall the guidance was deemed as adequate and thus only minor changes were necessary.

The Review Group however pointed to the importance of ensuring ongoing monitoring in order to ensure that the system of internal control remains relevant and effective. FRC 2005 states that "no such system remains effective unless it develops to take account of new and emerging risks, control failures, market expectations or changes in the company's circumstances or business objectives" (p. 1), a statement clearly in line with the recent publication by the COSO on monitoring controls (COSO, 2009a). Below, we will briefly describe each of the three key internal control-related components in the FRC-guidance.

4.2.3 Maintain a Sound System of Internal Control

The FRC 2005 refers to internal control as a *system of internal control* and thus deviates for example from the COSO (1992) which refers to internal control as a process. According to the FRC, internal control"encompasses the policies, processes, tasks, behaviors' and other aspects of a company that, taken together" (2005, p. 7) facilitate effective and efficient operations, quality in internal and external reporting and compliance to applicable laws, regulations and policies. The FRC (2005, p. 7) defines the system of internal control as:

> A company's system of internal control will reflect its control environment which encompasses its organizational structure. The system will include: control activities; information and communications processes; and processes for monitoring the continuing effectiveness of the system of internal control.

The FRC 2005 definition includes all the COSO 1992 components of internal control, except for the risk-assessment-part. Seen alone, this would suggest that the FRC regard risk assessment and risk management as being separate from the system of internal control. The FRC 2005 however, points to the importance of risk assessment for designing a sound system of internal control (p. 7) and explicitly refers to the importance of the risk assessment process throughout the guidance-document.

In the first sections the FRC 2005 points out that it is the board of directors that are responsible for a company's internal control system. In exercising that responsibility the directors should establish appropriate internal control policies that will address and manage the risks that the company is facing. The FRC (2005, p. 6) points to a number of factors that should be considered when designing a company's policy, and which include:

- The nature of the business.
- The type or risks that the company is facing.
- The type of risk that the company accepts to bear.
- The cost-benefits aspects of the control system.

Like that of COSO the FRC thus adopts a *contingency-based logic* which suggests that internal control designs are dependent on variables such as risk, size, industry characteristics, management attitudes and objectives and strategies (see Sect. 5.3.3 for a more detailed account). It follows that no two firms should have identical internal control arrangements unless they are identical (Jokipii, 2006, p. 39).

According to the FRC 2005, it is the responsibility of management to "design, operate and monitor a suitable system of internal control which implements the policies adopted by the board" (p. 6). However, the FRC 2005 emphasize the importance of people in this process, suggesting that all staff at all levels of the organization have some responsibility for internal control "as part of their accountability for achieving objectives" (p. 6). Management should thus ensure that people are equipped with the necessary knowledge, skills, information and authority in order to be able to operate their part of the internal control systems effectively. This is similar to the approach taken by the COSO (1992) which states that internal control is effected by all organizational members, highlighting the importance of people and culture.

4.2.4 Review the Effectiveness of the System of Internal Control

Furthermore according to the FRC 2005, it is the responsibility of the board of directors to review the effectiveness of internal control and thus should be performed based on the information and assurances provided to them. Executive management is accountable to the directors for monitoring the system of internal control, and should provide assurance to the directors that they have done so (p. 9).

According to the FRC 2005, the division of labour between any board and its audit committee with reference to this work seems to be largely up to the individual company, but boards of directors as a whole remain ultimately responsible for all internal control disclosures in annual reports.

In paragraph 26, the FRC 2005 identifies three types of monitoring procedures with regards to internal control. The first monitoring procedure is *the seemingly embedded one* which operates as a part of the business-as-usual processes. Informal and formal information-based feedback-systems enable managers to address potential internal control deficiencies and take action accordingly.

The second monitoring procedure may be seen as a form *of meta-monitoring process*, operating on a level above the day-to-day monitoring activities. Managers and directors demand and receive separate internal control reports that provide them with (independent) information about the level of assurance that the current system of internal controls provide in different areas. An (increasingly) popular way of obtaining independent information is of course through the services of internal and external auditors. It is reasonable to assume that these monitoring controls will be performed less frequently than in the first type of monitoring, and perhaps be of a more formal nature.

The third type of monitoring procedure has the *explicit purpose of enabling directors to make a public statement* about the state of the firm's internal control system. According to the FRC 2005, this is an annual assessment based on a process defined by the directors, which enables them to prepare a statement based on "sound, appropriately documented, support" (p. 9). In addition to reviewing reports during the year (provided by management, internal auditors, external auditors, risk management officers and other stakeholders), the board of directors should undertake their own assessment for the purpose of making a public statement about internal control. FRC (pp. 10–11) suggest that this assessment should consider the following:

> Issues dealt with in reports reviewed by it during the year together with any additional information necessary to ensure that the board has taken account of all significant aspects of internal control for the company for the year under review and up to the date of approval of the annual report and accounts (. . .) The board's annual assessment should, in particular, consider:
>
> - the changes since the last annual assessment in the nature and extent of significant risks, and the company's ability to respond to changes in its business and the external environment;
> - the scope and quality of management's ongoing monitoring of risks and of the system of internal control, and, where applicable, the work of its internal audit function and other providers of assurance;
> - the extent and frequency of the communication of the results of the monitoring to the board (or board committee(s)) which enables it to build up a cumulative assessment of the state of control in the company and the effectiveness with which risk is being managed;
> - the incidence of significant control failings or weaknesses that have been identified at any time during the period and the extent to which they have resulted in unforeseen outcomes or contingencies that have had, could have had, or may in the future have, a material impact on the company's financial performance or conditions, and;
> - The effectiveness of the company's public reporting processes.

4.2.5 Management Reporting Requirements on Internal Control

The final and third key element of the responsibility of the board of directors relates to *public disclosure* and statements that have to be made by all companies regulated by the Combined Code. In line with the principles-based approach, FRC 2005 only sets out minimum standards that need to be considered by the directors. Paragraph 33 states that:

> The annual report and accounts should include such meaningful, high-level information as the board considers necessary to assist shareholders' understanding of the main features of the company's risk management processes and system of internal control, and should not give a misleading impression. (p. 12)

Furthermore, FRC 2005 states that in its narrative statement the company should describe how it has applied Code Principle C.2 on internal control, which as a minimum should include a disclosure that:

> There is an ongoing process for identifying, evaluating and managing the significant risks faced by the company that it has been in place for the year under review and up to the date of approval of the annual report and accounts, that it is regularly reviewed by the board and accords with the guidance in this document. (p. 12)

Further, the disclosure should include a statement regarding the directors' responsibility for the company's system of internal control and for reviewing its effectiveness. The real challenge for any board however is related to provision C.2.1 – how to obtain adequate support for effective internal controls on which they can provide necessary disclosures. Hereby FRC 2005 prescribes that:

> In relation to Code Provision C.2.1, the board should summarize the process it (where applicable, through its committees) has applied in reviewing the effectiveness of the system of internal control and confirm that necessary actions have been or are being taken to remedy any significant failings or weaknesses identified from that review. It should also disclose the process it has applied to deal with material internal control aspects of any significant problems disclosed in the annual report and accounts. (p. 12)

Thus the company should disclose through the annual report how they have gone about reviewing (and verifying) the effectiveness of the system of internal control. However, the uses of the words summarize the process suggests that such disclosures may be of a high-level nature.

The challenge for preparers to disclose useful information with regard to this is also highlighted by a recent report published by Grant Thornton (2009b) on Combined Code-compliance of companies listed on the main index of the Irish Stock Exchange. Additionally, the recent annual report published by the Swedish Corporate Governance Board (Kollegiet för Svensk Bolagsstyrning, 2009) suggests that disclosing and describing compliance, and specifically non-compliance, with the Swedish code requirements may be a difficult matter for preparers. In Sect. 5.3.5 on disclosure and reporting we will discuss this issue further.

4.3 The Sarbanes-Oxley Act

We have earlier claimed that changes in existing regulatory regimes and practices are closely associated with publicly visible disasters and crises. These crisis-situations create distrust in existing accountability structures and processes and a demand for regulating the previously unregulatable or imperfectly regulatable. This has also been the case for internal control developments and related regulations

(Heier, Dugan, & Sayers, 2005; Kinney, 2005). According to MaCahery, Picciotto and Collins (eds., 1993), imperfect market governance and the resulting market failure require new regulatory initiatives whose purpose is to iron out the imperfections and restore proper market governance (p. 103).

In the case of the United States, the SOX (2002) and the well-known events that took place prior to this legislation provide further evidence for the argument put forward above. After the largest bankruptcy in the history of the United States involving high-profile fraud (see Vinten, 2002; Zandstra, 2002), public pressure for reform was strong and a regulation was passed rather quickly in 2002 by the United States Congress – the Sarbanes-Oxley Act.

Officially this Act has the rather lengthy title "An Act to Protect Investors by Improving the Accuracy and Reliability of Corporate Disclosures made Pursuant to the Securities Laws and for other Purposes". This piece of legislation regulates all United States companies listed on the public stock exchange, including its foreign filers. Below we will provide a brief account of the Act's internal control requirements.

4.3.1 Management Assessment and Auditor Attestation Requirements

Through SOX 2002, a number of changes were implemented which were to have considerable impact on the accounting profession (see Yakhou & Dorweiler, 2004). This highlighted the individual responsibility of the chief executive officer and the chief financial officer, revealing the SEC's (Securities and Exchange Commission's) belief that the officers in charge had caused the well-known scandals (Yakhou & Dorweiler, 2004, p. 373).

One section of the Act, Section 404, however caused significant concern. First of all, Section 404 prescribes that managers must assess the entity's internal control over financial reporting (ICOFR), thus excluding controls related to other internal control objectives. Section 404 furthermore prescribes that the financial statement auditor must assess and report on both management's assessment of the ICOFR and the operating effectiveness on the ICOFR.

The Act is thus different from the Combined Code in the United Kingdom in at least three ways: it is a mandatory law, it relates only to financial reporting quality, and it explicitly requires a statement by management as to the operating effectiveness of controls and an attestation of that statement by the auditor.

A new regulatory agency, the PCAOB (Public Company Accounting Oversight Board), was created to monitor this practice for all companies and its subsidiaries filed with the SEC. The Section 404 requires each annual report of an issuer to contain an internal control report which shall:

- State the responsibility of management for establishing and maintaining an adequate internal control structure and procedures for financial reporting; and

- Contain an assessment, as at the end of the issuer's fiscal year, of the effectiveness of the internal control structure and procedures of the issuer for financial reporting.
- Each issuer's auditor shall attest to, and report on, the assessment made by the management of the issuer. An attestation made under this section shall be in accordance with standards for attestation engagements issued or adopted by the Board. An attestation engagement shall not be the subject of a separate engagement.

These were quite extensive requirements and really put the spotlight on the company's systems of internal control and whether or not those systems were operating effectively. This shift in focus, whereby the process of producing financial reports is increasingly important, is highlighted in a neat statement by Power (2007, p. 55):

> It remains to be seen whether this emphasis on reporting on the process of producing financial statements will become more significant for regulators than the financial statements themselves; internal control systems now have the potential to become the *primary* regulatory and managerial reporting object.

Since the Section 404 required auditor attestation of internal controls, new audit standards had to be produced to assist auditors in their new tasks. As directed by Sections 103 and 404 of SOX 2002, the PCAOB established a standard to guide the newly required audit by adopting the Auditing Standard No.2 (hence AS2), "*An Audit of Internal Control over Financial Reporting Performed in Conjunction with an Audit of Financial Statements*" in March 2004. The AS2 was subsequently approved by the SEC in June 2004. Since AS2 came into effect, the PCAOB has monitored the implementation of the Act and the related audit work performed.

As a result of the findings from the first years' "trials", PCAOB replaced AS2 with an updated standard and also implemented a new standard: *Considering and Using the Work of Others in an Audit*. The revised audit standard which replaced the AS2, Audit Standard No. 5 (hence AS5), was issued in November 2007 and its full name is "*An Audit of Internal Control over Financial Reporting That Is Integrated with an Audit of Financial Statements*". Conforming amendments to Statement of Audit Standards (SAS), such as SAS No.55 which specifies how auditors should consider internal control in their audits, were also made.

The AS5 provides detailed guidance for how auditors are to proceed when reviewing and testing internal controls over financial reporting in order to be able to form an opinion about their adequacy and effectiveness. AS5 also provides definitions and descriptions of the different controls that need to be identified and evaluated in connection with the audit – process controls and entity-level controls. The AS5 generally provides guidance on the following areas:

- Planning the audit.
- Identifying entity-wide controls.
- Selecting controls to test.
- Testing controls.
- Evaluating internal control deficiencies.
- Forming an opinion.

A recent report by the SEC (SEC, 2009a), entitled *study of the Sarbanes-Oxley Act of 2002 Section 404 internal control over financial reporting requirements*, suggests that compliance costs vary with firm size but are decreasing as a result from the 2007 reforms. Both direct (e.g. higher financial reporting quality) and indirect (e.g. ability to raise capital and investor confidence) benefits of compliance with section 404 rules are noted. Nevertheless, a large portion of firms still perceive that the cost of compliance outweigh the benefits (p. 96). Also PCAOB has recently released a report based their inspections on auditor compliance with AS5-standards (see PCAOB, 2009).

One important fact is that in connection to the issuance of the AS5, the SEC also issued separate interpretive guidance for managers which were to support them in designing, implementing and reviewing internal controls. No such guidance had earlier been available for companies, which is why they had to rely on external auditor support (Bannister, Engvall, & Martin, 2007, p. 2).

4.4 The Swedish Code of Corporate Governance

Following a number of both foreign and domestic high-profile corporate failures, a governmental commission was established – the *commission for trust* [Förtroendekommissionen] – where the purpose was to rebuild trust in the financial markets and the business community. The task of developing a Swedish code of corporate governance was assigned to a code group (see Jonnergård & Larsson, 2007).

The process of developing the corporate governance code was carried out through self-enforced regulation, a method where the business community produces its own standards while the state controls and accepts them (Jonnergård & Larsson, 2007, p. 482). The new code of 2004 (henceforth Code, 2004) adopted the *comply-or-explain* approach imported from the Cadbury-report in the United Kingdom (SOU, 2004a: 130, p. 5).

In the beginning of 2008, a proposal for an updated code was referred to stakeholder groups for comments and a revised code (henceforth Code, 2008) was issued in May 2008 (Kollegiet för Svensk Bolagsstyrning, 2008b). Even though the Code is primarily aimed at publicly listed companies it also applies to state-owned companies according to guidance on board responsibilities for state-owned companies [Styrelseansvaret i företag med statligt ägande] (Regeringskansliet, 2008, p. 4).

Like the corporate governance code in the United Kingdom, the Swedish code places substantial emphasis on *transparency and disclosure*. One part of the code concerns internal control and risk management. Below, we specifically discuss these internal control requirements that have been imposed on listed companies through the Codes 2004 and 2008 and also briefly touch upon some of the recent developments in public disclosure requirements on internal controls.

4.4.1 *The Code of 2004*

In section 3.7 of the Code 2004, it was stated on internal control and internal audit that "the boards of directors are responsible for the organizational internal control system, which has an overall purpose to protect owners' investments and company assets" (Kodgruppen, 2004, p. 29). In the following provisions, it was prescribed that:

> The board of directors shall ensure that the company has an adequate internal control, and continuously be kept informed about the system of internal controls and evaluate how the system of internal controls is operating (Section 3.7.1).
>
> The board of directors shall annually issue a report over the internal control over financial reporting and how it is organized and how well it is been operating during the last fiscal year. The report should be reviewed by the company auditor (Section 3.7.2).

From these provisions, we are able to derive the following:

- The directors should continuously monitor the adequacy and effectiveness of the internal control system.
- The directors should report on the operating effectiveness of the internal control system.
- Auditors should review the statements made by management with reference to the system of internal controls.

Accordingly these provisions may be regarded as being quite strict, and they did not differ substantially from the Sarbanes-Oxley, Section 404-rules, since they included a statement by both managers and auditors on the effectiveness of internal controls.

In the light of the internal control development process (Heier, Dugan, & Sayers, 2005), considering the controversial nature of internal control disclosure requirements, the debate that followed in Sweden was hardly surprising (Kollegiet för Svensk Bolagsstyrning, 2006b, p. 8). Just as in the case of the United Kingdom, these provisions about internal control in the Code 2004 caused concerns. According to guidance [Anvisning Nr.1-2005] issued by the SCGB in 2005, companies were expected to non-comply with these provisions due to the following reasons:

- Resource constraints caused by implementation of international financial reporting standards.
- Processes and controls were of an informal nature in businesses why they first needed be made formal before directors could make any public statement as to the effectiveness of internal controls.
- Adequate and effective audit guidance, related to provision 3.7.2 in the Code, was missing.

Based on the circumstances accounted for above, it was the subsequent decision of the SCGB that the provisions of 3.7.1 and 3.7.2 would temporarily (for year 2005) require only a report of how the company's internal control system was organized. It means that both the requirements regarding effectiveness review and auditor review were removed. Later through guidance [Anvisning Nr.1-2006] issued in 2006 by the SCGB, it was concluded that the provisions 3.7.2 and 3.7.3 had resulted in the following:

- They had generated much attention to internal control systems of firms.
- Significant work had been initiated by firms in order to develop their internal control and risk management practices.

Furthermore, according to this guidance, concerns had been raised whether management reporting on the effectiveness of internal controls really added value for users, i.e. if the information in those reports would improve the decision making process for users of such reports. Concerns were also raised about whether the requirement regarding auditor review of management's report on internal control was useful. With reference to ongoing work on corporate governance and internal control within the European Union, the SCGB concluded that neither the effectiveness statement nor the auditor review was necessary, and so these requirements were removed (Kollegiet för Svensk Bolagsstyrning, 2006a).

4.4.2 The Code of 2008

In the beginning of 2008, the Swedish SCGB presented a proposal for a revised Code. The opinion that the Code 2004 had contributed positively to Swedish corporate governance practices was presented, but also that adjustments were needed based on identified weaknesses, ongoing harmonization initiatives within the Nordic countries and the European Union as well as the somewhat different corporate governance practices of smaller companies. The main elements with regard to internal control that were discussed, related to the changes based on upcoming European Union's directives. These included the following: the 8th directive prescribing a mandatory requirement of audit committees and changes in the 4/7th directives regarding internal control disclosure requirements.

In May 2008 the SCGB issued their revised code which was to apply from July 1 2008 and regulate all companies trading on a regulated market, which corresponds to OMX Nordic Exchange Stockholm and NGM Equity (Kollegiet för Svensk Bolagsstyrning, 2008b, p. 4). The code now regulates about 300 publicly listed companies (Kollegiet för Svensk Bolagsstyrning, 2009, p. 3). The formal basis for the new code was also somewhat changed. Previously, this had been a part of the Stock Exchange listing requirements, but now the code forms part of what represents *generally accepted good practices on the Swedish stock exchange*, which means that the provisions are mandatory for all publicly listed companies according to stock exchange rules. As a consequence the stock exchange disciplinary committees will therefore be responsible for the monitoring of code compliance (Kollegiet för Svensk Bolagsstyrning, 2009, p. 4).

Section 3.7 of the Code 2004 on internal control and internal audit had now been superseded by Section 10 on *audit committee, financial reporting and internal control*. The opening statement on internal controls (Kollegiet för Svensk Bolagsstyrning, 2008b, p. 22) has now been adjusted to stipulate that:

> The board is responsible that the company has an adequate internal control system in place and formalized procedures that will ensure that established principles for financial reporting and internal control are complied with, and that the financial reports of the company conform with laws, applicable accounting standards and other regulations for publicly listed companies.

Based on a comparison between the opening statement of the Codes 2004 and 2008 we argue that the statement of 2008 has been adjusted in the following respects:

- The opening statement of 2008 focuses primarily on financial reporting quality.
- With reference to the quality of financial reporting, the opening statement focuses on the importance of compliance with laws, regulations and applicable accounting standards.
- With reference to compliance with internal controls and financial reporting principles, the opening statement now includes a passage that prescribes that the company should have *formal procedures* to ensure such compliance.

It would seem that there is a stronger focus on financial reporting quality. However, this is not a completely fair statement since the former section 3.6 on financial reporting and section 3.7 on internal control and internal audit have now merged into Section 10 (Kollegiet för Svensk Bolagsstyrning, 2008a, p. 21). With reference to the requirements that one must ensure compliance with principles of internal controls, there is no detailed guidance. No references to preferred internal control frameworks or standards are made.

In the detailed provisions of Section 10, the Code 2008 goes on to prescribe that companies must establish an audit committee. With regards to internal control matters, it may be relevant to acknowledge the following passages:

- Footnote 7 to Section 10.2 requires that audit committees treat internal control matters – but only internal controls over financial reporting.
- Section 10.2 requires that audit committees meet regularly with the company auditor and discuss the scope and focus of the audit engagement and also the coordination between external and internal audit engagements. They should also discuss the risks facing the company.
- Section 10.5 prescribes that the "the Board shall on an annual basis issue a report over the most important features of the company's system of internal controls and risk management, with reference to the financial reporting process" (p. 23). This report may be included in the annual reports but does not form part of the formal documents of the annual financial report (p. 23).

4.4.3 Recent Developments

Recently, in June 2009, the SCGB issued their annual report over the last year (Kollegiet för Svensk Bolagsstyrning, 2009). In this report recent developments are accounted for with reference to the harmonization of corporate governance rules within the European Union. As a result, a number of directives will be implemented as formal law in Sweden. For the purpose of this thesis, we are interested in the European Union's accounting directive [EU:s redovisningsdirektiv] and also the directive on auditors and auditing [EU:s direktiv om revisorer och revision] (Regeringens Proposition, 2008/09, p. 135; Regeringens Proposition, 2008/09, p. 71).

4.4.3.1 Focus on Governance and Internal Control Disclosures

Changes in the European Union accounting directive [EU:s redovisningsdirektiv], which prescribes that companies must publicly disclose a corporate governance report [bolagsstyrningsrapport], became a part of Swedish law during 2009 (Kollegiet för Svensk Bolagstyrning, 2009, p. 6). This report may however be disclosed as a separate report, thus not forming part of the annual financial report. This seems to lessen the auditor review requirement (p. 6). The Annual Accounts Act [årsredovisninglagen, 1995:1554], Limited Liability Companies Act [aktiebolagslagen] and the Code from 2008 have been updated accordingly based on these new requirements (Kollegiet för Svensk Bolagsstyrning, 2009, pp. 6–7, 2010, p. 5; also see Regeringens Proposition, 2008/09, p. 71).

4.4.3.2 Focus on Internal Control Oversight

With regard to the European Union directive on auditors and auditing [EU:s direktiv om revisorer och revision] and the specific concerns regarding audit committees, these new requirements were implemented through formal law in July 2009. Audit committees are now compulsory but their duties may be performed by the board of directors, providing that certain conditions are fulfilled. Based on these developments, the Limited Liability Companies Act [Aktiebolagslagen 2005, p. 551] and the Code 2008 have been updated accordingly based on these new requirements (Kollegiet för Svensk Bolagsstyrning, 2009, p. 7, 2010, pp. 5–6; also see Regeringens Proposition, 2008/09, p. 135). This means that the earlier section in the Code regarding audit committee, financial reporting and internal control has been removed. Specific regulations regarding the structure and work processes of the board still remain however, but in a different chapter. These regulations include matters such as board independence, size, structure and meetings (Kollegiet för Svensk Bolagsstyrning, 2010, p. 5). The updated Code was implemented in the beginning of 2010.

With regard to corporate governance in Sweden, the regulatory climate is quite influenced by the current work that is ongoing by the EU-commission. Specifically the Green Paper on the EU corporate governance framework (see COM/2011/164), which is currently out on review within the European countries, is of interest but also the green paper on corporate governance and remuneration policies in the financial sector (see COM/2010/284/3). Important issues, which are partly driven by the financial crisis of 2008, include the role of the board of directors, the effectiveness of risk management and board oversight and the role of auditors and supervisors.

4.5 Summary and Concluding Remarks

This chapter has provided a regulatory perspective. This is importance since the characteristics of the regulatory environment influence internal control practices. Publicly visible disasters often generate change in corporate governance regulations, which in turn, influence the internal control practices of firms. Based on the findings from this chapter we conclude by making the following observations:

- Internal control has emerged as a key regulatory object which also has contributed significantly to the rise of internal control. Reporting on the process of producing financial statements has the potential of becoming equally important for regulators as the financial statements themselves.
- Along with emerging mandatory or semi-mandatory corporate governance codes, internal control disclosure regimes seem to be receiving increasing attention. New laws and regulations on internal control also contribute to the attention that these matters today receive.
- In the United Kingdom, the Cadbury Code of 1992, a pioneer in good corporate governance practice, has had a significant influence on corporate regulation and has been adopted world-wide. The Code in the United Kingdom is not a mandatory regime but introduced the successful comply-or-explain approach.
- Requirements that directors have to report on internal controls have been highly controversial and a source of significant debate in the United Kingdom. Internal controls have gone on-record and this has "generated fundamental problems about what internal controls really are, and what one is saying in describing them as effective" (Power, 1997, p. 55). In the United Kingdom, the FRC has issued guidance to help directors in their reporting of internal control.
- In the United States, the Sarbanes-Oxley Act of 2002, with special reference to Section 404 of the Act, represents a strict internal control reporting regime requiring both a manager review and an auditor attest about the effectiveness of internal controls. In order to enforce this unique piece of regulation, the PCAOB was established.

- In Sweden, the Swedish Corporate Governance Board issued Sweden's first Code of Corporate Governance in 2004. This happened as a result from visible corporate mal-functions. The original provisions were quite strict, requiring both an effectiveness statement and an auditor attestation of that statement. The debate that followed resulted in that these original provisions were removed. The Code was updated once again in 2008, and recent developments, based on the implementation of changes in European Union directives, now stipulate a corporate governance report and an audit committee. New updates to the Swedish Code have been made in late 2009 due to European Union directives and the resulting changes to Swedish law.
- From a theoretical perspective, it seems that agency theory has been the primary basis for all regulatory developments described and discussed in this chapter. In order to better align the interests of principals and agents, existing controls have been improved and new controls developed. However, the quick responses to crises and corporate malfunctions might be better understood from an institutional perspective.

Chapter 5
Themes and Issues

Abstract

Purpose: The purpose of this chapter is to provide an account of some of the themes and issues that are frequently taken up in writings on internal control.

Synopsis: Official definitions of internal control develop, vary and are often somewhat controversial. Both broad and narrow approaches to internal control have co-existed for a long time and some scholars have argued that defining the boundaries of internal control remains problematic. Although internal control has always had a direct relationship to the concept of risk, recent writings suggest that this relationship is now more explicit and controls are closely associated with risk management practices. There have been continuous attempts to classify and distinguish different types of internal controls. As the concept of internal control has expanded into management control and corporate governance, design issues are becoming more important. It is however difficult to examine and measure internal control quality. Internal control designs seem however to be contingent upon a number of external and internal variables, including certain regulatory environment characteristics, business culture, uncertainty and risk, objectives and strategies, risk appetite, practical frameworks and standards and firm size. The specific design objectives often applied may be management's financial assertions or a stated risk appetite level. Existing writings on internal controls also suggest that controls need to be integrative, balanced, embedded, cost-effective and adaptive. Much has been written on the assessment and evaluation of internal control, which is unsurprising, since this constitutes a key part of the audit process. Findings suggest that internal control evaluation is part structure, part judgment. The disclosure of internal control is not a new phenomenon but is becoming increasingly important. Issues often examined include whether disclosure requirements should be voluntary or mandatory, whether they should address the effectiveness of internal controls, and also whether auditors should attest to a report on internal control. Today internal control is often referred to as a corporate governance mechanism, yet researchers have

O. Arwinge, *Internal Control*, Contributions to Management Science,
DOI 10.1007/978-3-7908-2882-5_5, © Springer-Verlag Berlin Heidelberg 2013

suggested that internal control from this perspective remains under-explored. Determining the outcomes of internal control may be difficult however, although prior writings on the subject not only discuss its fraud detection capabilities, risk and cost consequences but also its enabling effects on firm performance.

5.1 Introduction

This chapter will introduce and discuss some of the themes and issues in writings on internal control. In doing so, we will naturally draw upon accounting- and auditing-related papers, but journals on management accounting, general management control and strategy have also been important sources. The concept of internal control is not very different from the concept of management control and draws on theoretical concepts found in academic fields such as management control, organization, risk management and strategy (see Kinney, 2000, p. 88). Drawing upon writings from fields outside accounting and auditing therefore seems appropriate.

Summarizing a concept such as internal control is undoubtedly a challenging task. Writings on control are fragmented into the different fields (Maijoor, 2000, p. 102; Merchant and Otley in Chapman, Hopwood & Shields eds. 2007, p. 788). Many of the texts on internal controls have been done within the framework of the auditor's task of evaluating internal controls as part of the financial statements review. Increasingly however, new papers on internal controls broaden the perspective, examining the relationship with risk management, the factors associated with internal control quality, and how internal control disclosure requirements influence internal control practices and corporate governance quality. During recent years, a stream of research papers has also examined the effects of the SOX (2002) in the United States (see DeFond and Francis, 2005).

In conjunction to the different themes in this chapter, we will also discuss how certain developments and issues may be understood from the theoretical perspectives outlined in Chap. 3. Below, we will start by going into the origins and definitions of internal control before continuing with a deeper study of some of its particular themes and issues.

5.2 Internal Control

5.2.1 Background

Due to the increasing focus and attention on corporate governance and internal control during the last 15 years (Power, 2007) it could certainly seem to a person unfamiliar to the field that internal control is a recent invention. Any accountant and auditor obviously knows that this is not the case. For a long time however, internal controls remained private to firms, were undisclosed, and for the most part, only of interest for technical assurance specialists. Today this is no longer the case.

Table 5.1 Evolution of audit objective and technique (Brown in Lee ed. 1988, p. 697)

Period	Stated audit objective	Extent of verification	Importance of internal controls
Ancient–1500	Detection of fraud	Detailed	Not recognized
1500–1850	Detection of fraud	Detailed	Not recognized
1850–1905	Detection of fraud, detection of clerical errors	Some tests, primarily detailed	Not recognized
1905–1933	Determination of fairness of reported financial position	Detailed and testing	Slight recognition
1933–1940	Detection of fraud and errors Determination of fairness of reported financial position	Testing	Awakening interest, Substantial emphasis
1940–1960	Determination of fairness of reported financial position	Testing	Substantial emphasis

The origins of the concept of internal control go back over 1,100 years and originate in the fields of accounting and auditing (Dicksee, 1892, 1905; Lee, 1971, also ed. 1988). Ever since its introduction, it has evolved alongside the development of auditing theory and practice. Accordingly, the development of the concept and practice of internal control is associated with the development of audit objectives and techniques. In an early essay by Brown (Brown in Lee ed. 1988) from 1962 on the changing audit objectives and techniques, the author provided a summary of the evolution of the key aspects of audit procedure, including the extent to which internal control has been considered.

As may be observed from Table 5.1 above, up to about 1905 accounting and auditing theory did not consider the potential impact of internal controls on financial reporting quality and fraud. Before 1905, the objective of the financial statement audit was to discover fraud and the auditing techniques at that time comprised of *detailed verification of each transaction* that had taken place (p. 697).

From 1500 up until about 1850, audit objectives were primarily concerned with the detection of fraud. The separation between ownership and control (Jensen & Meckling, 1976; Fama & Jensen, 1983) resulted in increasing information asymmetries between principals (owners) and their agents (managers) and as a result, the discovery of fraud became more important.

Standardized accounting systems became important for firms, and even though it is not stated explicitly in the quotes used in the essay by Brown (Lee ed. 1988), there seems to be a clear understanding that an organized and standardized system of accounting would improve process- and accounting quality. However, the status of the accounting systems and thereby internal control still did not influence the audit process and the amount of detailed checking that was performed (p. 698).

During the second half of the nineteenth century, economic growth resulted in larger scale operations further increasing the gap between owners and the managers in charge of operations on a day-to-day basis. Managers became hired professionals, which resulted in the owners becoming increasingly concerned with the protection of assets and their investment. Governance in firms came to be influenced by the so called managerial capitalism. Internal control was considered to be a part of the standardized systems of accounting. Little attention was however paid to internal control with regards to audit procedure – complete reviews of accounts and transactions were still performed.

However, at the end of the nineteenth century, sampling techniques were introduced as a means of increasing efficiency. Organizations had become too large and the need for improvement was apparent. Still, one had to wait until the beginning of the twentieth century before the audit profession fully recognized the importance of internal control, and also let the quality of internal controls impact audit engagement performance (Brown in Lee, ed. 1988). For long there has been a rather close relationship between corporate governance of firms, and the way in which internal control may assure that assets are protected and that organizations follow the strategies charted by board of directors and senior officers (see Kirkpatrick, 1962).

5.2.2 First Account of Internal Control

With the publication of the book *Auditing* in 1905 by the English audit-specialist Lawrence Dicksee, it was made clear that the objective and scope of a financial audit was threefold: to detect fraud, detect technical errors and detect errors in accounting principles (p. 6). In the first version of his book, Dicksee (1892, p. 8) claimed:

> It is of the highest degree of necessity that the Auditor, before commencing the investigation should thoroughly acquaint himself with the general system upon which the books have been kept. . .(. . .). . .Having thoroughly made himself the master of the system, the auditor should look for its weakest points.

In 1905 he expanded his thoughts on the subject and dedicated a whole section of the book to this area, which he referred to as the *general system of internal check*. Dicksee (1905, p. 53) argued:

> This is a matter that may very profitably engage the careful attention of the Auditor, for not only will a proper system of internal check frequently obviate the necessity of a detailed audit, but further possesses the important advantage of causing any irregularities to be corrected at once, instead of continuing until the next visit of the auditor.

The statement made by Dicksee above is considered to be one of the first explicit accounts and slight recognition of the importance of internal control (Lee, ed. 1988; Heier, Dugan & Sayers, 2005).

The editor of the book by Dicksee in 1905 was the Lybrand Ross Brothers partner Robert Montgomery. In 1912, he published his own book in which he moved away from the English-focused audit practices and indicated that the purpose of an audit was primarily to ascertain the actual condition and earnings of an enterprise. He also expanded the discussions by Dicksee on internal checks further beyond a general explanation of the separation of duties in order to ensure satisfactory internal control, to detail the duties and checks to be performed by a number of different positions, from the cash handlers to the inventory personnel (Heier, Dugan & Sayers, 2005).

5.2.3 *Increased Reliance on Internal Control*

As may be further observed from Table 5.1, there is a development towards increased reliance on internal control by auditors. In his essay Brown (Lee ed. 1988, p. 696) claimed that there were four primary drivers behind this development:

- The increased complexity of the business enterprise resulting in geometric compounding of data control problems.
- The development of new communications and information systems and introduction of extremely reliable data processing machines.
- Requests received by the auditor from management, owners and other parties-at-interest for additional information.
- Rising costs in accounting and the consequent additional emphasis on economy and effectiveness.

The increased level of scale and complexity of the organizations' operations resulted in the impossibility to verify each transaction without incurring unreasonable costs. As a response, auditors began to rely increasingly on a risk-based approach, looking at the controls and checks surrounding the accounting system from which the financial reports were produced. Auditors were then able to limit their testing of financial transactions (Lee ed. 1988, p. 127).

With the emergence of the *audit society* (Power, 1997, 2003a, 2003b) and the related *internal control explosion* (Maijoor, 2000) the drivers mentioned by Brown must however be supplemented. Ongoing organizational disasters, changes in shareholder patterns and the legal climate have been pointed out as key drivers behind calls for better corporate governance (Hermanson & Rittenberg, 2003, pp. 38–39). The quest of better financial transparency, accountability and governance has transformed internal control into a primary regulatory and managerial object.

As such, we claim that this increased *internal control reliance is no longer to strictly driven by auditing related concerns*, but rather by concerns from the general public, media, regulators, supervisory authorities, financial statement and corporate governance report users, who are all demanding stronger and better internal control.

Today internal control is considered a key governance mechanism and Power (2007, p. 55) argues that the *process of producing the financial statements* through adequate and effective internal controls have the potential of becoming as significant for the regulators as the financial statements themselves.

5.2.4 Defining Internal Control

Ever since the concept of internal control was established, it seems that there has been an ongoing debate as to its definition (Hay, 1993; Heier, Dugan & Sayers, 2005). The task of defining internal control has not been a simple one. Heier, Dugan and Sayers (2005) argue that one of the first times that the term internal control was used in authoritative literature was the year 1936, in a work entitled Examination of Financial Statement by Independent Auditors. Section II of this document by the American Institute of Accountants (AIA) stipulates that:

> In determining the nature and extent of this examination, the accountant will necessarily take into consideration, among other things, (a) the purpose of the examinations, (b) the amount of the detail included in the statements to be covered by this report, (c) the type of business accounts of which are to be examined, and (d) the system of internal check and control (p. 7).

The AIA referred to internal control as the *system of internal check and control*, which closely resembled the definition of internal control provided by Dicksee in 1905. As may be observed, internal control was closely linked to the accounting procedures and the financial reporting process, as it was used as a means by which the financial statement auditor could improve audit process efficiency and effectiveness.

In response to widely known business failures in the early 1980s, the Treadway Commission's (see Sect. 3.2) primary concern was to find solutions to the causes of fraudulent financial reporting. Interestingly, even then the commission emphasized terms which are widely used today – the control environment and code of conduct (Heier, Dugan & Sayers, 2005) which highlight the importance for indirect and entity-level controls on financial reporting quality.

Soon after, in 1988, the Auditing Standards Board (ASB) issued the Statement of Auditing Standard (SAS) 55 entitled *Consideration of the Internal Control Structure in a Financial Statement Audit*. This standard defined internal control as the policies and procedures established to provide reasonable assurance that specific entity objectives will be met. SAS 55 regarded internal control as a structure which was divided into the following three parts (Heier, Dugan & Sayers, 2005, p. 57):

- The control environment.
- The accounting system.
- The control procedures.

This represents one of several attempts to classify and categorize internal control components. As we will see in the next section of this chapter, the task of adequately classifying internal control components, or different types of controls, has for a long time now been a source of debate (see Bower and Schlosser, 1965; Heier, Dugan & Sayers, 2005).

Not surprisingly, auditing standard No 55 received criticism for both its definition of internal controls and on how it was to be applied (Heier, Dugan & Sayers, 2005). Notwithstanding this criticism, SAS 55 required that an auditor would gain sufficient understanding of each of the control elements noted above so that the audit engagement could be efficiently and effectively executed.

The COSO (Committee of Sponsoring Organizations of the Treadway Commission) formed in 1985 and published their now globally accepted framework *Internal Control – Integrated Framework* in 1992. COSO defined internal control as a *process*, as compared to the earlier structure, emphasizing its loose, flexible and less static nature (Kinney, 2000; see Sect. 3.3 for more the complete COSO-definition). According to COSO, there are five interrelated internal control components that should be designed in order to achieve objectives:

- Control Environment.
- Risk Assessment.
- Control Activities.
- Information and Communication.
- Monitoring.

The COSO 1992 made no other difference between controls, such as the earlier classification between accounting and administrative controls. COSO is today a recognized world-wide blueprint for internal control (IIA 2004, p. 234; Power, 2007, p. 49) and has been a widely applied by companies for Sarbanes-Oxley purposes in the United States (Chambers, 2006, p. 45), not without difficulty however (see Gupta & Thompson, 2006).

It would seem that the COSO-framework has also influenced internal control guidance produced by the National Financial Management Authority [Ekonomistyrningsverket] and the Financial Supervisory Authority [Finansinspektionen] in Sweden. For government agencies, internal control practices are based on the Swedish regulation 2007:603 where internal control is defined as a process including components such as risk analysis, control activities, monitoring and documentation. Based on this regulation, the Swedish National Financial Management Authority has set out guidance through their release of 2008:13 [Handledning intern styrning och kontroll. Ett stöd vid myndigheters tillämpning av förordningen om intern styrning och kontroll]. The definition of internal control applied has significant similarities to the COSO-definition (p. 6) and Sect. 5.1 of this document explicitly states that the regulation on internal control is partly based on COSO (p. 23). More recently, in 2011, the authority has updated their guidance through ESV 2011:2, where the view on internal control quite resembles that of COSO. With regard to the internal control guidance produced by the Swedish Financial Supervisory Authority through FFFS 2005:1 it is obvious that the definition of internal control has been based on COSO, since it shows significant similarities (see Finansinspektionen, FFFS, 2005, p. 1, 2). The financial sector in general, with both banking and insurance-related regulations (such as those based on the Basel and Solvency regulatory initiatives) is quite influenced by the banking framework on internal control produced by the Basel Committee on Banking Supervision in 1998, which in turn is based on the COSO-framework with some slight deviations.

As concluded by Heier, Dugan and Sayers (2005), the last 100 years have witnessed a century of debate on internal control and how it should be defined.

Some researchers however, argue that the *meaning* of the concept has not changed significantly over the decades. Spira and Page (2003, pp. 646–648) claim:

> From the first authoritative definition of internal control by the American Institute of Public Accountants in 1949 to the definitions which still exist in professional pronouncements (.....)…there seems to have been no substantial change to meaning (....)…the incorporation of "effectiveness" was the first radical change to the idea of internal control in over four decades. By admitting "effectiveness" – the extent of achievement of objectives – into the ambit of internal controls, the statement recognizes for the first time the existence of business objectives other that efficiency and probity and goes some way to aligning the definition with business risk approaches to audit.

Other definitions of internal control, such as the Criteria of Control Framework (COCO) issued by the Canadian Institute of Chartered Accountants in 1995, certainly exist. Both the COSO and the COCO reflect a broader approach to risk and control, no longer strictly related to financial reporting quality alone (Spira & Page, 2003). Defining the exact boundaries of internal control remains problematic however (p. 648).

Following the diffusion of the broad internal control definition by the COSO, professional standards on internal control appear to have incorporated its definitions and principles – with some variations. The International Standard on Auditing (ISA) 315 (IAASB, 2006) on *identifying and assessing the risks of material misstatement through understanding the entity and its environment* refers to internal control as:

> The process designed, implemented and maintained by those charged with governance, management and other personnel to provide reasonable assurance about the achievement of entity's objectives with regard to reliability of financial reporting, effectiveness and efficiency of operations, and compliance with applicable laws and regulations. The term "controls" refers to any aspects of one or more of the components of internal control (p. 55).

According to ISA 315, the internal control components consist of the control environment, risk assessment process, information and communication systems, control activities and monitoring of controls (IAASB, 2006, pp. 57–59), thus building on the COSO framework.

In the audit standard issued by the PCAOB (Public Company Accounting Oversight Board) in the United States through Audit Standard No.5 (PCAOB, 2007), which relates to financial reporting quality only, the regulator provides the following definition of internal control:

> Internal control over financial reporting is a process designed by, or under the supervision of, the company's principal executive and principal financial officers, or persons performing similar functions, and effective by the company's board of directors, management, and other personnel, to provide reasonable assurance regarding the reliability of financial reporting and the preparation of financial statements for external purposes in accordance with GAAP and includes those policies and procedures that…(p. 431).

The International Standards for the Professional Practice of Internal Audit (IIA, 2004) seems to apply a wider approach, referring mostly to the term control (see for example pp. 209–214). Thus, the term internal control is not frequently used in the standards from 2004, with one notable exception however. The Practice Advisory on Auditing the Financial Reporting Process (2120.A1-4) refers explicitly to the term internal control and the COSO 1992 is recommended as the most effective guidance (p. 234). In other Practice Advisories, terms such as control, control environment and control processes are often used. To conclude, the various forms of guidance on internal control is quite similar to each other, with only slight differences in emphasis, and most seem to follow the COSO-based structure (Pfister, 2009, p. 19; Braiotta et al., 2010, p. 235).

5.3 Themes and Issues

Based on a survey of scientific papers, we have identified clusters of questions that seem important with regards to the theory and practice of internal control. This section will provide an account of these clusters of questions, which may also be referred to as frequently occurring themes in existing research on the subject. The different themes are noted below. In connection with our discussion of different developments and issues we will also at times apply the theoretical perspectives outlined in Chap. 2 where appropriate. Our aim is to provide the reader with a better understanding of some of the important discussions on internal control today, as well as to highlight the complexity of the concept. The themes that will be presented are, in order of appearance:

- Definition and boundaries.
- Classification.
- Design.
- Assessment and evaluation.
- Disclosure and reporting.
- Outcomes.

5.3.1 Definition and Boundaries

In the opening chapter of this thesis, we argued that the changing definitions of internal control have often proven to be controversial (Hay, 1993; Heier, Dugan & Sayers, 2005) and that some writers have suggested that the boundaries of internal control remain unclear (Maijoor, 2000, p. 105; also Spira and Page, 2003; also see Woods, 2009, p. 69). In the section below, we will investigate more thoroughly the details that underlie those statements and describe some of the issues that have been discussed in earlier writings on the subject. The challenge of defining and accurately drawing the boundaries of the internal control concept will be referred to as *external boundary-drawing concerns*. By external boundary-making concerns we simply refer to concerns related to what should be included and excluded from the concept.

5.3.1.1 Narrow and Broader Definitions

The century-long debate of internal controls (Heier, Dugan & Sayers, 2005) has often related to how one is to define and draw the boundaries around the concept of internal control. Naturally this has been an important issue for accountants, since definitions are often included in professional standards on how to proceed when the auditor evaluates internal controls.

Traditionally, the definition of internal control has had a fairly direct relationship to the accounting system and the financial reports. As time went by broader definitions of internal control began to appear. A good example of this development may be found in an early paper by Haun (p. 115), published in *The Accounting Review* in 1955, where he claimed that:

> It seems that there are two somewhat different concepts of internal control which we should recognize in our discussion. The narrower of these two concepts appears in the defining of the term in auditing texts. . .(. . .). . .The concept incorporated in this definition seems to approach the meaning expressed in the older term "internal check" and has a fairly direct relationship to financial records and reports. It emphasizes the safeguarding and compliance aspects of internal control. Eric L. Kohler, in his Dictionary for Accountants, describes internal controls as "the general methodology by which management is carried on within an organization; also any of the numerous devices for supervising and directing an operation or operations generally". Clearly this sets forth a broader concept of internal control.

A distinction may thus be made between the two different approaches to internal control. The traditional and narrow concept draws heavily upon accounting- and auditing theory which focuses on the auditor discharging his/her duty as prescribed by generally accepted auditing standards. Here internal control is primarily related to financial controls – controls that are in place to safeguard assets and ensure financial reporting quality (also see Swayze, 1946, for another early paper on the subject).

The broader approaches to internal control however, draw upon concepts found in other academic fields than accounting and auditing. Something which Power (2007, p. 62) has noted:

> The topic on internal control in organizations has never been part of mainstream management research, reflecting no doubt its position in the hierarchy of management knowledge and its primary association with auditing. Compared with the body of scholarship on management accounting and management control more generally, this is surprising since there is considerable overlap.

The rather close association between the concept of internal control and theory outside the academic fields of accounting and auditing is thus apparent with the introduction of broader approaches to internal control. In the paper by Haun (1955, p. 115), the author reviewed the internal control elements included in the broad approach to internal control, which included the following:

- Development and maintenance of functional lines of authority.
- Clear definitions of duties and responsibilities.
- Accounts of accurate and complete information.

- A structure of reports for presenting this information.
- Budgeting.
- Coordination of all controls to stimulate and take advantage of attributes of employees.

Based on a review of these internal control elements, Haun (p. 115) concluded that these controls:

> . . .are certainly not primarily aimed at safeguarding assets or checking compliance. Their contributions are towards getting instructions or information to the right parties at the proper time, keeping lines of authority clear and effective, creating and supplying employees with norms or standards for their activities, and providing measurements of operations useful in the control of business activities.

Controls included in the broader concepts of internal controls thus appear to be more targeted towards the coordination of organizational activities and strategy execution. A comparison between the broader concepts of internal control and the definitions of control which may be found in the management control research (e.g. Ouchi 1977, 1979 and 1980; Eisenhardt, 1985; Otley 1994, 1999, 2003 and 2008; Simons, 1990, 1991 and 1995; Langfield-Smith, 1997; Chenhall, 2003) reveals that the two are rather similar.

Lately, academics have begun to notice that definitions are similar. In a paper by Fadzil, Haron and Jantan (2005) the authors argue that "*the definition of internal control systems reveals that it is not fundamentally different from management control, which has an essential component of control such as planning, organization, staffing and directing*" (p. 846). Based on a review of the COSO-definition on internal control, the influential management control scholars Merchant and Otley conclude that "*this definition is indistinguishable from the narrower scope definition of management control. . .(. . .). . .that which is concerned with strategy implementation*" (Chapman, Hopwood & Shields eds. 2007, p. 787). In a paper on internal control quality Rae and Subramaniam (2008) however, claim that the internal control system is *a "feature of management control systems"* (p. 104). Hence there is seemingly no general agreement amongst researchers as to the exact relationship between the internal control and management control. However, although the concepts resemble each other, we claim that important differences between them do exist.

We argue that a key distinguishing feature between the two approaches seems to be internal control's focus on the concept of *reasonable assurance*. If one reviews the COSO-definition of internal control (see Sect. 3.3.2), the definitions provided by IAASB (2006) and PCAOB (2007) (see Sect. 5.2.4) and also the regulatory text on internal control provided by the Financial Reporting Council (FRC, 2005, pp. 7–8) in the United Kingdom, it can be observed that all definitions include the term reasonable assurance. This is because internal control simply produces assurances as output. Reasonable assurance refers to the fact that internal controls, due to their *inherent limitations*, may only provide reasonable assurance and not absolute assurance. Flaws in the design, implementation and maintenance of controls generally lead to a control component risk (FFE, 2007, pp. 47–48) which can never be eliminated, simply because there are no perfect information systems, control environments, control activities and monitoring controls (p. 32; see also FAR SRS, RS 400, 2009, p. 257).[1] Another distinguishing feature between the two approaches is the emphasis that internal control places on the terms *risk* and *risk assessment*. Internal control is always directly related to a risk exposure that needs to be addressed. A third difference may be that internal control generally adopts a corporate governance perspective, taking the view of the owners that are represented by the board of directors and the audit committee members. In internal control concepts, there is also traditionally an emphasis placed on the financial reporting quality perspective and the protection of firm assets. Finally, internal control may also be regarded as the basic and fundamental feature of organizational control, as most other control systems, processes and routines relies on reliability and integrity of data and information that is enabled by effective internal control (see Pfister, 2009, p. 26). In this way, internal control has an indirect, but pervasive and thorough effect on all organizational activity.

However, some of the features of the wider approaches to internal control are seemingly also important features of "any" management control system. A useful example to discuss is the COSO framework (1992) of internal control. COSO advocates the importance of the *control environment* component of internal control, which in turn, includes elements such as ethical conduct, management philosophy and operating style, human resource policies and organizational structure. Ethical conduct relates to terms such as norms, values, corporate culture, trust, honesty and loyalty. These are all related to the areas of human relations and business ethics. Ethical conduct seems to be becoming increasingly important for firms, perhaps due to corporate malfunctions and publicly visible fraud cases, as well as the growing importance of reputation as a value creating strategy (Dolphin, 2004). Scott and Walsham (2005, p. 308) claim that:

> Increasingly, organizations are not only subject to business definitions of credit worthiness (i.e. honouring contractual obligations) and measured against the aesthetic components of reputations (identity, image, culture, corporate brand), they must also find a place for social responsibility and business ethics..(. . .). . . Business people now find themselves answering to organizational "stakeholders" including staff, customers, interest groups, government, and regulators, on a burgeoning range of issues.

Nowadays the ethical component nowadays seems to permeate most aspects of business, touching upon areas such as marketing, the fair treatment of customers, product liability and safety, the natural environment, job security, equality and privacy (DesJardins & McCall, 2005).

[1] For more information, review FFE (The Federation of European Accountants) (2007) which provides a detailed account. The author is grateful to Ph.D. Gunilla Eklöv Alander (econ.) formerly at the Supervisory Board of Public Accountants in Sweden and currently at Uppsala University, for providing input to this section.

Furthermore, *human resource policies* relate to how the organization's human resources are managed. This could typically be associated with controls over the screening and recruiting of candidates, training, performance management and compensation schemes. Undoubtedly, such controls cover a wide range of the business activities and operations. *Organizational structure* implies a division of duties and specialization of tasks, which would then typically include controls related to the coordination of divisions, departments and employees, much like the writing about controls in organization theory (e.g. Ouchi 1977 and 1979; Eisenhardt, 1985, 1988 and 1989a).

An examination of the work by Simons (see 1987; 1990; 1991 and 1995), an influential writer within the field of management control and strategy, also suggests that the concepts of internal control and management control are somewhat overlapping at times. Simons seemingly views internal control somewhat differently than some of the more recent conceptions of the concept. For example, according to Simons (1995) to specify rules and enforce compliance is a managerial solution which constitutes a part of the control lever "boundary system" (p. 173). From an accounting and auditing point of view, policies and procedures are based on risk assessments to form control standards (Picket, 2001, p. 65) and most approaches to internal control tend to view at least the basic policies and procedures as important controls in themselves (see for example pp. 65–115). In addition, significant board and management policies may have an *entity-wide impact*, thus constituting a crucial part of the internal control system (PCAOB, 2007, pp. 403–405; Gerkes et al. 2007) thereby stipulating objectives and setting boundaries for practices in different areas. Simons (1995, p. 177) however suggests that the internal control system is different from the four basic levers of the control system.

> This system does not relate directly to strategy formation and implementation, but is essential in any business in order to ensure that assets are secure and management information reliable. Without this assurance, managers cannot rely on the control levers.

This is also seemingly in line with a more recent discussion on the subject, by Pfister (see 2009, pp. 22–26) and we agree with these views. Still, it is apparent that the definition of internal controls as prescribed by the broader approaches to internal controls is no longer strictly limited to specific controls over financial assets and the accounting records but stretches over most of the organizations business processes and objectives. And depending on the way you conceptualize and draw the exact boundaries of internal control, some of the basic controls that are most often form part of frameworks exhibit clear similarities to control features in other control-oriented concepts.

In different ways professional standards have adopted broader or narrower definitions of internal control. In Sect. 5.2.4 we referred to the International Standard of Auditing (ISA) 315 (IAASB, 2006) which builds on the COSO-definitions of internal control. Audit Standard No.5 (PCAOB, 2007) also builds on COSO when defining internal control but with obvious exclusions for non-financial controls. The standard applies the COSO-components on internal controls but seems to classify controls into entity-wide controls and process-related controls in the period-end financial reporting process (PCAOB, 2007, pp. 404–405).

The Swedish audit standard on risk assessment and internal control, RS 400 (FAR SRS, 2009), however differs somewhat from the COSO-definition. This standard defines internal control as a system rather than a process and divides internal control into two major components: the control environment, which exhibits similarities with the control environment component of COSO (see Sect. 3.3.6), and the control activities, or controls (pp. 255–256). The difference between the Swedish RS 400 and the international standard with reference to the internal control definition is explained by the fact that RS 400 is based on an earlier version of ISA which existed prior to 2002.[2]

5.3.1.2 Internal Control and Risk Management

Recent development in risk management practices, the realization by regulators and financial market stakeholders of the importance of proactively managing risks, coupled with the fact that no commonly accepted definition or framework for risk management existed, resulted in the issuance of the *Enterprise Risk Management – Integrated Framework* in 2004 by the COSO (Chapman, 2003b). This guidance for risk aligns with the revised definition of internal auditing issued in the professional standards by the Institute of Internal Auditors (IIA). These standards are moving away from a control-based approach to focus more on the risk management and governance processes of firms (see IIA, 2004, p. 29).

However, the link between internal control and risk management existed however before the COSO 2004. Risk assessment, after all, constitutes one of the five components of the internal control framework issued by the COSO in their 1992-framework. Risk has been defined as the possibility of an event occurring that will have an impact on the achievement of objectives (IIA, 2004, p. 29) and control as any action taken by management, the board, and other parties to manage risk and increase the likelihood that established goals will be achieved (IIA, 2004, p. 27).

With the release of COSO 2004, the link between risk and control was made more explicit, highlighting the idea that internal control is a *risk treatment* that may be deployed as a way of *managing risk exposures*. Internal control however should not be regarded as a risk reducing measure only – risk may also be increased, or better optimized (see Picket, 2001; Cheney, 2008).

Due to the fact that risk management has only recently emerged as a widespread practice (see Power, 2004; 2007; Beasely, Clune & Hermanson, 2005, p. 522; Mikes, 2009) research papers have also only recently begun to take an interest in the increasing risk management practices of firms (see for example Spira & Page,

[2] The author is grateful to Ph.D. Gunilla Eklöv Alander (Ek.dr.) at the Supervisory Board of Public Accountants in Sweden for providing input on the section related to differences between Swedish and international audit standards on internal control.

2003; Power, 2005; Fraser & Henry, 2007; Beasely, Clune & Hermanson, 2005; Sarens & Beelde, 2006; Mikes, 2009; Woods, 2009). We have earlier mentioned that some researchers have noted that the definition on internal control is indistinguishable from the definition of management control (Merchant and Otley in Chapman, Hopwood & Shields, eds. 2007, p. 787). Interestingly, Mikes (2009) makes a similar point, about the overlap between management control and enterprise risk management. Based on a review of the ERM-definition provided by COSO, Mikes (p. 20) states that:

> This description calls into mind Anthony's widely-quoted definition of management control: the process by which managers assure that resources are obtained and used effectively and efficiently in the accomplishment of the organization's objectives'(Anthony, 1965, p. 17). With the emphasis placed on the strategic role of ERM (applied in strategy setting...to provide...assurance regarding the achievement of entity objectives'), ERM is being advocated as a strategic management control system.

Although researchers are beginning to take an interest in risk management practices, Mikes' (2009) claim is that little is known about risk management practices in action (p. 19). With internal control being tied closer to risk management practices, Spira and Page (2003) argue that "*the relationship between internal control and risk management remains confused*" (p. 651) and Fraser and Henry (2007) suggest that "*the relationship between internal control and risk management has..(...)...not been clearly articulated*" (p. 393). In a recent paper, Woods (2009, p. 69) argues:

> National and international governance regulations reflect the view that corporate governance, internal control and risk management are inter-dependent. The boundaries between the concepts may appear rather blurred at times and it is not always clear whether risk management is a sub-division of internal control or vice versa, but the dominating recurring theme is that risk management is an integral part of the process of corporate governance.

Irrespective of whether boundaries between concepts are blurred or not, the concepts do in fact seem to become increasingly interdependent (see Bihmani, 2009) and internal control now is explicitly tied to the organizational risk management process and may as such, be regarded as an *extension of risk management* (Power, 2007, p. 35). This development could be seen as a second wave for internal controls. The first wave constitutes the shift from being *a private affair to going on-record*. The second wave constitutes the *shift towards enterprise risk management practices* and risk consideration in strategy formulation and execution. Recent papers by COSO also places additional importance of risk management oversight, and the way the board should better oversee and embed risk management in their organizations (COSO, 2009a, 2010b and 2011). In this context, the internal control system is regarded as a risk treatment whereby management mitigates risk exposures through the application of controls (COSO, 2009b, p. 18).

Institutional pressures and the increasing demand from stakeholders for greater accountability and transparency result in new roles and functions being established. As risk management practices are growing in popularity, the chief risk officer (see Hutter & Power eds., 2005; Power, 2007) and the risk management function have developed into full fledged management functions in large corporations, specifically within the financial sector (see Beasley, Clune & Hermanson, 2005, p. 529). The chief risk officer serves as a champion of the risk management processes and is responsible for working with other managers to establish effective risk management processes, monitor progress and report relevant risk information (De La Rosa, 2007).

Recent studies on risk management practices have taken a contingency-approach (Beasley, Clune & Hermanson, 2005; Mikes, 2009; Woods 2009). Woods (2009) suggests that risk management designs may be contingent upon variables such as policies, information and communication technologies and organizational size, while Beasley, Clune and Hermanson (2005) found that ERM-implementation seems to be associated with factors such as the presence of a chief risk officer, board independence, management support from CEO and CFO, auditor, company size and industry. Mikes (2009) demonstrates that risk management practices may arise as a result of institutional pressures and contingency variables such as size, age, technology, environment and strategy (p. 23). In the firms that Mikes studied, she found that different types of risk management practices had been developed – on the one hand ERM by the numbers and on the other holistic ERM. Mikes shows that that in the risk-based internal control approach called holistic ERM, informal and formal internal controls are applied in processes where risks related to objectives and strategies have been identified (p. 35). Here, risk management processes are used *interactively* (see Simons, 1990; 1991) by senior officers so that agendas and strategies may be shaped and adjusted (pp. 35–36).

Even though it is widely recognized that governance and effective risk management may be a driver of value, Sarens and Beelde (2006) argue however, that chief risk officers are struggling with implementation (p. 64). Recent research shows that management, and other stakeholders, are currently looking towards internal audit for help in implementing effective risk management practices (Sarens & Beelde, 2006; Fraser & Henry, 2007). Fraser and Henry however conclude that organizations should organize separate risk management functions in order to keep the different lines of defense separate (p. 407). Recent studies on risk management commissioned by the COSO (see 2010a, 2010b and 2011), for example regarding board oversight effectiveness and the level of matureness of risk management practices in organizations, suggest that there is still much room for improvement. The financial crisis of 2008 and ongoing regulatory initiatives, such as those within the European Union regarding corporate governance in public and financial companies, suggest that matters such as effectiveness of internal control and risk management, board risk oversight and disclosures of risk management practices made by companies, will be important going forward.

To sum up we may conclude that there seem to be different internal control definitions of internal control. Narrow definitions have a direct relationship to the financial records while the broader approaches incorporate concerns other than the quality of financial reporting and the protection of assets. The broader approach to internal control exhibits significant similarities to the definition of general management control. Recently, internal control has become increasingly tied to the risk management practices of firms and concepts such as risk, control and governance seem to be becoming increasingly interdependent. Internal control is now considered to be an explicit risk treatment process (Chapman, 2003b, p. 35; Matyjewicz & DÀrcangelo, 2004, p. 69) and recent studies show that risk management practices and internal controls may be contingent upon different factors external and internal to firms. Such factors may include company size, industry, management support, type of auditor, information- and communication technologies as well as policies.

5.3.2 Classification

Section 5.3.1 concerned the scope and boundaries of internal controls. This section is dedicated to what we refer to as *internal boundary-drawing concerns.* By internal boundary-drawing concerns, we refer to the labelling and classification of controls and control components included in the concept. Throughout the history of internal controls there has been an ongoing discussion related not only to the boundaries of the concept (i.e. what to include versus exclude), but also how to define and classify different control components within the concept (see Heier, Dugan & Sayers, 2005).

The classification problems of controls seem to be intimately connected to the introduction of wider definitions of internal control, which sparked debate on the subject (see Haun, 1955). In an early paper, under the title *Internal Control – Its true nature*, Bower and Schlosser (1965) argue that when compliance and efficiency were introduced as two additional internal control objectives, some people were satisfied with the new definitions whereas most auditors felt somewhat uncomfortable (p. 338). Possible discrepancies between what professionals perceive as internal control and what the definitions prescribe may represent a risk exposure with regards to professional responsibilities (Heier, Dugan & Sayers, 2005, p. 50). In order to clarify any confusion, efforts have been made to distinguish different controls from each other.

One way of categorizing controls has been to classify them either as operational controls (also sometimes referred to as administrative controls) or as accounting controls (also sometimes referred to as financial controls). It seems however that this is not done without difficulty. In 1958, the Committee on Auditing Procedure (a part of the American Institute of Accountants) issued their Statement of Auditing Procedures (SAS) No. 29 by classifying controls into *administrative controls* and *accounting controls*. According to Bower and Schlosser (1965, p. 27), the different types of controls defined as follows:

> Accounting controls comprise the plan of organization and all methods and procedures that are concerned mainly with, and relate directly to, safeguarding of assets and the reliability of the financial records. They generally include such controls as the systems of authorization and approval, separation of duties concerned with record keeping and accounting reports from those concerned with operation or asset custody, physical controls over assets, and internal auditing.
>
> Administrative controls comprise the plan of organization and all methods and procedures that are concerned mainly with operational efficiency and adherence to managerial policies and usually relate only indirectly to the financial records. They generally include such controls as statistical analysis, time motion studies, performance reports, employee training programs and quality controls.

Recommendations were given as to how the different controls should be considered for auditors. Accounting controls had to be considered in a financial statement audit but not administrative controls. However, the recommendations left room for professional judgment since administrative controls should be evaluated if the auditor believed that they had important bearing on the reliability of the financial records.

This classification scheme was an early attempt to classify and categorize different types of internal controls. At the time however, Bower and Schlosser concluded that "*the concept of internal control, however, needs still further refinement and more specific identification of its true nature. The above dichotomy of accounting and administrative controls has only clouded the issues*" (pp. 338–339). Bower and Schlosser suggested instead that controls could be classified into the following categories:

- Supervision.
- Clerical proof.
- Acknowledging performance.
- Transferring responsibility and segregating duties.
- Protective measures.
- Review- and approval procedures.
- Verification and evaluation.

In the United States under SOX (2002) both managers and auditors are charged with responsibility for reporting on the effectiveness of internal controls over financial reporting (ICOFR). The SEC (Securities and Exchange Commission) requires that both management and external auditors use an established internal control framework that meets the criteria specified in Section II.B.3a of the Section 404 Final Rules. Most companies reporting under the Section-404 of the Act seem to have been using the COSO-framework (1992) which is also a framework approved by the PCAOB (see Gupta & Thomson, 2006, p. 28).

The application of internal control frameworks such as the COSO has however been problematic for some companies when seeking to comply with Section 404 (see Bierstaker & Thibodeau, 2006, p. 879). Gupta and Thomson (2006) refer to comment letters filed with the SEC by companies implementing Sarbanes-Oxley Section 404-requirements, which suggest that registrants are struggling to implement the five components of the COSO 1992 framework. While suited for internal control development purposes in general, some argue that the COSO-framework is not effective when it comes to the design and implementation of internal controls related to financial reporting quality. According to Gupta and Thomson (2006, p. 33), the SEC observed in 2006 that:

> While the COSO framework provides an integrated framework that identifies components and objectives of internal controls, it does not set forth detailed guidance as to the steps that management must follow in assessing the effectiveness of a company's internal controls over financial reporting.

Another way of categorizing controls has been to categorize them according to whether they are more detailed versus high-level. Or put another way, by whether they have a *wide, pervasive and indirect* effect, or whether they directly influence a narrow and specific business process activity. Audit Standard No.5 (PCAOB,

2007), which relates to an audit of internal control in connection to a financial statement audit under Sarbanes-Oxley in the United States, broadly seems to classify controls into entity-level controls and process-based controls. Process-based controls are detailed and direct control activities, related mostly to the preparation of financial statements which include controls over the entering of transaction totals into the general ledger and controls over the initiation, authorization, recording and processing of journal entries in the general ledger (PCAOB, 2007, pp. 404–405).

Entity-level controls, which originate from the COSO-framework, have a *wide and pervasive* influence on business processes and thus apply to many departments, units and locations. Audit Standard No.5 provides examples of a number of key entity-wide controls which include the following:

- Controls related to the control environment.
- Controls over management override.
- The company's risk assessment process.
- Centralized processing controls, including shared service environments.
- Significant policies.
- Controls to monitor results of operations.
- Controls to monitor other controls.
- Controls over the period-end financial reporting process.

However, there seem to be a variety of opinions when it comes to entity-level controls (Gerkes, Van der Werf & Van der Wijk, 2007) and it has been suggested that "*relevant rule-making bodies have not issued detailed guidance on the topic, other than stressing the importance of these controls*" (p. 51). Accordingly, the task of identifying and evaluating the exact entity-wide controls appears to be a challenging one.

To sum up this section, we conclude that the appropriate classification of internal controls has long been a source of debate. Distinguishing accounting controls from operational, or administrative controls, has been one of the reoccurring themes in writings on the subject. More recently however, there has also been discussion about how to categorize the higher-level controls – controls which have a wider and more pervasive influence on internal control objectives, such as financial reporting quality. Undoubtedly new forms of classification schemes will emerge and the classification of controls will most probably remain a source of discussion.

5.3.3 Design

Another discussion which is reoccurring in the existing literature on internal control concerns how to design, and maintain, adequate and effective internal control. The design of controls seems to become increasingly important as a result of the growing attention from regulators, supervisory authorities, analysts, media and the general public. Today, directors and managers need to pay increasing attention to how controls are designed and operate (Power, 2007, pp. 34–63).

The overlap with other academic fields is perhaps nowhere more obvious than here. Management accounting, general management control research, organization theory and management all seem to have theoretical concepts with relevance for how internal control processes should be designed.

Basic questions that face any *internal control architect* include: what is the criterion for internal control quality? What are the factors associated with internal control design? Which are the factors associated with internal control quality? It is reasonable to assume that any control specialist must know something about the answers to such questions. The inherent complexity of the internal control process however, suggests that defining internal control quality is not without difficulty (see Kinney, 2000). Kinney claimed a few years ago that there was no adequate criterion for measuring internal control quality, something which poses both practice and research barriers (pp. 86–88). In a recent paper, Rae and Subramaniam (2008, p. 106) claim that:

> Previous studies on internal control have been largely descriptive…(…)…with little attention placed on how different aspects of a system of internal controls affect each other…(....) there is limited evidence on the factors that affect the quality of internal control procedures… (....)…there is scant empirical evidence on how the internal control environment and related organizational factors may affect the quality of internal control procedures.

It follows that much remains to discover about internal control quality. Thus in this section, we will discuss some of the key design challenges found based on a survey of literature on the subject. In doing so, we will not only draw upon research from accounting and auditing but also from research generated from other academic fields. This is appropriate since internal control and management control exhibit significant overlap (Power, 2007, p. 62; Merchant and Otley in Chapman, Hopwood & Shields, eds. 2007, p. 782) and the fact that recent control innovations may constitute a mix of different practices (see Mikes, 2009, p. 20) found in a variety of academic fields. Below, we will discuss a few areas which seem to be of importance for the appropriate design of internal controls.

5.3.3.1 Design Drivers

Providing a complete account of all the drivers that influence the internal control design of firms seems difficult. When we refer to drivers, we simply mean variables that influence the design of control in firms. Some drivers may be related to the environment of the firm while others are internal firm-specific variables. In Fig. 5.1 below, we provide an illustration of some of the factors that we argue drive the design of internal controls. This figure does not represent a complete account of all the variables that potentially influence design in internal controls. However, it is a summary of those variables that existing literature considers being important for internal control design. It may be important to point out that while Fig. 5.1 provides a rather detailed account of the more agency-related variables that drive internal control design, it says less about the variables that drive design, and that institutional theories often discuss, ideas such as the need for legitimacy (see Sect. 2.3.2 for a review of institutional theory).

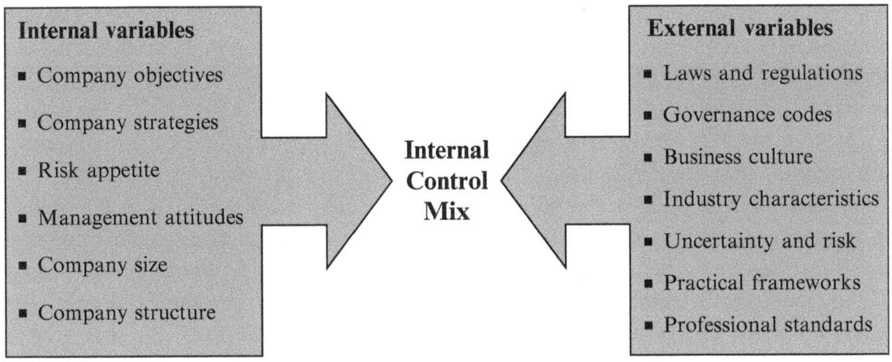

Fig. 5.1 Internal control design drivers

Let us begin by stating the following: internal control systems of firms will vary – simply because firms are different. *No two firms should have similar internal controls unless they are identical* – this follows from the COSO-framework of 1992. This statement is analogous to the *contingency approach* to control systems which states that controls are contingent on the circumstances of the specific firm (Jokipii, 2006, p. 51, also 2010).

Contingency theory (see Chapman, 1997; Langfield-Smith, 1997; Chenhall, 2003) suggests that the design of controls will depend on different contextual variables. These theories build on work done within organizational theory as early as 1960–70 (Chenhall, 2003, p. 128). These variables may include the external environment and the uncertainty facing the firm, technology, size, organizational structure, strategy and national culture (p. 128).

In any given company, the various types of internal controls that the firm applies will form an *internal control mix* contingent on the characteristics of the company and its context (based on Mikes, 2009, p. 21, where Mikes discusses a firm's constellation of risk management practices, which the author refers to as a risk management mix). Below, we provide an illustration of internal and external variables that may be derived from the existing literature on the subject and that seem to drive and influence the internal control designs of firms. We will briefly discuss these variables below, sometimes grouped into categories.

5.3.3.2 The Regulatory Environment

We have already in Chap. 4 mentioned the importance of the regulatory environment for the internal control practices of firms. In this case we are primarily concerned with the laws, regulations and corporate governance codes which prescribe and regulate internal control practices. Laws such as the SOX (2002) in the United States have obviously had a profound effect on internal control designs and practices of firms all around the world. Regulations and recommendations issued by supervisory authorities not only within the financial sector, also drive internal control design and lead to firms being expected to adopt certain practices. From a local Swedish perspective, supervisory authorities increasingly pay attention to the design and effectiveness of the systems of internal control of firms (Arwinge & Munkby, 2011; Finansinspektionen, 2011). Key regulatory initiatives such as the Basel framework in the banking sector, and Solvency in the insurance sector, significantly influence internal control practices of today.

Internal control disclosure requirements, nowadays often a fundamental part of corporate governance codes, will also influence internal control designs and practices (see Sect. 5.3.5). And as regulatory bodies such as those in the United States signal that greater disclosures by public companies about their risk management oversight practices are necessary (see COSO, 2009c, pp. 2–3), this is also likely to influence internal control designs. Greater disclosures requirements also form part of the European corporate governance discussion of 2011 (se COM/2010/284/3; COM 2011/164). Along with the increasing attention from regulatory bodies, credit rating agencies such as Standard and Poor's, increasingly take into account the risk management practices of firms when they assess and evaluate firm performance (COSO, 2009c, p. 2; Grant Thornton, 2009a, pp. 5–6). Even though credit rating agencies do not form part of the specific regulatory environment of firms, they are an increasingly crucial stakeholder for firms to consider when they adopt risk and control practices.

5.3.3.3 Professional Frameworks and Standards

In Chap. 3, we saw that practical frameworks for internal control, such as the COSO (1992, 2004), constitute important drivers, since they serve as baselines for regulatory designs and blueprints for directors, managers and other professionals as these people design, manage and oversee internal controls. We have also noted that the primary association of internal control is with the fields of auditing and accounting. It follows that professional standards for internal control for accountants and auditors will also necessarily influence internal practices of firms.

The rise of the audit society and formal monitoring mechanisms suggests that as auditing activity increases so will its influences on the internal control designs of firms. More specifically, this audit activity may influence the verifiability and auditability of controls. In these cases, audit professionals become change agents; they are *making things auditable* (see Power, 1996, 2000, 2003a, 2003b).

5.3.3.4 Business Culture

Another variable which for some time has been part of contingency-based research is culture. Culture is defined as the inherent traits such as knowledge, beliefs, morals, customs and other capabilities of those members that certain groups inhabit (Chenhall, 2003, p. 152–153). Hofstede (1984), is a widely referred to work to in this area. Culture will differ between groups and it is likely that internal control designs will be associated with business culture. Uncertainty avoidance, and an accordingly low risk-tolerance, is likely to correspond to reliance on formal controls, while the opposite corresponds to a greater reliance on trust and to informal controls. Although culture is often regarded as an independent factor that influence internal control application and outcomes, culture may also form part of control and furthermore influence the organizational culture (Pfister, 2009). This is also underscored in practically oriented texts, where the *risk culture* of firms is influenced by senior officers and that in turn influence control effectiveness. Either way, business and organizational culture will be important for internal control designs and outcomes

5.3.3.5 Industry Characteristics

Another factor, industry characteristics, will also influence the internal control designs of firms. Certain industries will have certain characteristics. The financial sector for example, is highly regulated by laws and guidelines which are enforced by supervisory authorities. Financial companies are thus required, or expected, to adopt certain internal control designs. Some reports suggest that the financial industry may be at more risk with reference to fraudulent activity (Cain, 2009, p. 15). This is likely to influence control designs related to fraud risk, including tip hotlines, fraud policies, segregation of duties and screening procedures.

Moreover, the financial sector exhibit more mature risk management practices than other firms (Beasley, Clune and Hermanson, 2005, pp. 521–522; Fraser & Henry, 2007, p. 407). This is likely to influence the design of risk management controls, such as risk appetite, risk management training programs, risk assessment processes and risk reporting to management and the board of directors.

Other industries may engage in electronic commerce or rely heavily upon outsourcing relationships with other firms (see Langfield-Smith & Smith, 2003) which in turn may influence the internal control design of firms. Newer types of organizational forms, whether called intern-organizational relationships, virtual organizations or networks, are characterized by being geographically distributed, electronically linked, functionally and culturally diverged and horizontally coordinated (DeSantis & Monge, 1999). In such cases, business processes will be more dynamic and continuously changing, something which will influence the design of controls. A recent case-study by Woods (2009) on risk management controls in the public sector also reveals that control designs in that type of environment are contingent upon certain specific public sector-related characteristics.

5.3.3.6 Uncertainty and Risk

In the revised guidance for directors on the Combined Code (FRC, 2005), Section C.2 on internal control, states that "*in determining its policies with regard to internal control*...*(*...*) the board's deliberations should include consideration of* *the following factors: the nature and extent of the risks facing the company*" (p. 6). It is furthermore stated that:

> It is the role of management to implement board policies on risk and control. In fulfilling its responsibilities management should identify and evaluate the risks faced by the company for consideration by the board and design, operate and monitor a suitable system of internal control which implements the policies adopted by the board (p. 6).

Thus, the FRC (Financial Reporting Council) of the United Kingdom sees the risk facing the firm to be an important factor which influences how the internal control system should be designed. Naturally, the risks facing firms are associated with other factors, such as firm size and industry characteristics which we discussed above. It is reasonable to assume that as firms grow bigger, the threats to the company are likely to change in scope and nature (Beasley, Clune & Hermanson, 2005, p. 524). The external environment, and specifically the uncertainty facing firms, has also been at the base of contingency-based research on control. In this case, it is regarded as a key variable which influence the design of control systems (Chenhall, 2003, pp. 137–138).

5.3.3.7 Objectives and Strategies

The internal control objectives are necessarily associated with company objectives (FRC, 2005, p. 7). From this, we may thus be able to derive that the firm's established strategic, financial, compliance and operational objectives must be an important point of departure for control design. Accordingly, the objectives established should significantly influence the control designs of firms. The modern view of internal control follows an objective setting process and the subsequent risk assessment activity which is part of the strategy formulation process (FRC; 2005, p. 13). Chenhall's (2003) review of contingency-research on strategy also suggests that the characteristics of strategies will be associated with, of best served by, specific control designs (see 150–152). A recent paper by COSO, on management and board oversight over risk, also point to the importance of risk in relation to the process of setting the objectives and the strategy selection process (2009c, p. 6).

> Risk appetite will be a key consideration in objective setting and strategy selection. If an organization is setting very aggressive goals, then it should have an appetite for a commensurate level of risk. Conversely, if the organization is very risk averse, i.e., has a low appetite for risk, the one would expect that organization to set more conservative goals. Similarly, as boards consider specific strategies, they should determine whether that strategy falls within or aligns with the organization's risk appetite.

5.3.3.8 Risk Appetite

Perhaps the most influential variable that seems to determine control designs is the risk appetite of firms. COSO (2004) prescribes that risk should be managed within risk appetite (p. 2). This means that risk exposure must be measured and aggregated so the actual risk profile may be compared to risk appetite. The risk profile may then be applied to constrain (or increase) "*the risk capacity of business initiatives and profit centers, serving as a tool for limit setting and control*" (see Mikes, 2009, p. 24). The FRC (2005) also states that "*the board's deliberations should include consideration of...(....)...the extent and categories of risk which it regards as acceptable for the company to bear*" (p. 6). According to the COSO (2004) "*the board of directors provides important oversight to enterprise risk management, and is aware of and concurs with the entity's risk appetite*" (p. 6).

In another recent paper by COSO (2009b), on the effective oversight of risk and the role of the board of directors, it is also suggested that one of the four key areas that contribute to effective oversight is the understanding of the entity's risk philosophy and concurring with the entity's risk appetite (p. 3). Risk appetite and risk acceptance seem to be somewhat connected to business culture and how different groups may approach risk (see Hofstede, 1984). Thus cultures and firms may approach risk quite differently. If a board prefers to avoid uncertainty and risk, emphasis will probably be placed on formal control arrangements and rules (Chenhall, 2003, p. 153). Risk appetite is also largely related to the risk capacity of firms, i.e. their financial and non-financial assets, and the way the balance-sheet and profit and loss statement is able to stand for the materialization of risk exposures.

The current turmoil in financial institutions, with highly visible collapses including the Lehman Brothers, has placed additional focus on board responsibilities with reference to risk appetite and risk taking. Lessons learned from the financial crisis of 2008–2009 will probably lead to changes in existing risk oversight practices, which in turn will influence control designs (see OECD, 2009a, 2009b; Senior Supervisors Group, 2009; Birkenshaw & Jenkins, 2009).

5.3.3.9 Management Attitudes

The influence of management on control design cannot be overestimated it seems. Already in the beginning of this thesis we pointed out that management have been regarded as a driver for improved corporate governance and also as crucial for instilling the right values and approach to risk and control. The importance of management for good organizational citizenship behavior has also been highlighted in a study by Holmes, Langford, Welch and Welch (2002). Beasley, Clune and Hermanson (2005) show that enterprise risk management implementation is associated with support from the CEO and CFO.

The concept of the *tone at the top* basically entails leading by example – "walking the talk" – a fundamental element which significantly influences internal control designs. Management attitudes seem to be vital for the entity's risk management philosophy. If senior executives exhibit specific attitudes towards risk taking, those attitudes will most likely be reflected in the way risks are considered in the developments of strategies and also in the daily operations to achieve those strategies (COSO, 2009c, p. 6).

5.3.3.10 Firm Size

Firm size seems to be associated with the characteristics of controls. In a case-study on the public sector by Woods (2009), the author found that controls systems were contingent on organizational size. Large-scale operations tended to have more formalized controls, characterized by a tendency to have more documented control systems (p. 80). Beasley, Clune & Hermanson (2005) also found that the extent of enterprise risk management implementation was associated with entity size. Large firms seem to have greater needs but also have greater resources available. Due to their specific nature and character, smaller types of firms faces different challenges with regard to internal control design (see Wells, 2002; COSO, 2006). According to COSO (2006, p. 3) they may include the following:

- Obtaining sufficient resources so that duties may be adequately segregated (see Taiariol, 2000, on the issue of segregating duties).
- Management's ability to dominate activities with opportunity for management override.
- Recruiting financial reporting competence for the board of directors and its committees.
- Recruiting and retaining sufficient skills with reference to financial accounting and reporting.
- Maintaining adequate and effective controls over computer processing with limited technical resources.

Smaller firms may furthermore not be regulated by laws, regulations and listing rules in the same way as larger firms are. Smaller firms may not be listed on a stock exchange, and those that are, may not be exposed to the same regulations as larger listed firms. In the United States, small listed firms have not had to comply with section 404 (b) but only filed management reports on internal control over financial reporting – a fact that potentially influence the control designs of those firms (Steffee, 2009, p. 17).

5.3.3.11 Design Objectives

In practically oriented accounting texts on internal control the point of departure is usually the organization's accounting system and its related transaction cycles (see for example Trenerry, 1999). Here *management's financial assertions* appear to be applied when internal control design is considered (pp. 9–10). The financial assertions refer to the explicit and implicit statements that are made by management regarding the information in the financial reports and include existence or occurrence, completeness, valuation or allocation, rights and obligations, and presentation and disclosure (PCAOB, 2007, p. 407; also see FAR SRS, RS 500, 2009, p. 274). Audit standard no. 5 (PCAOB, 2007, p. 433) states:

> A relevant assertion is a financial statement assertion that has a reasonable possibility of containing a misstatement or misstatements that would cause the financial statements to be materially misstated. The determination of whether an assertion is a relevant assertion is based on inherent risk, without regard to the effect of controls.

With reference to the quality of financial reporting, financial statement assertions are often applied as design objectives. It follows that adequate internal control may be designed based on these objectives. This is also stressed by Audit Standard No.5 (PCAOB, 2007, p. 431) which provides guidance on considerations of internal control design. The standard prescribes that:

> A control objective provides a specific target against which to evaluate the effectiveness of controls. A control objective for internal control over financial reporting generally relates to a relevant assertion and states a criterion for evaluating whether the company's control procedures in a specific area provide reasonable assurance that a misstatement or omission in that relevant assertion is prevented or detected by controls on a timely basis. . .(. . .). . .a deficiency in design exists when (a) a control necessary to meet the control objective is missing or (b) an existing control is not properly designed so that, even if the control operates as designed, the control objective would not be met.

With a broader approach to internal control, the system of internal control does not solely relate to the accounting system and the associated recording of financial transactions. Thus controls may include both financial and non-financial controls and refer to other internal control objectives than financial reporting quality. Even though design issues may be similar and independent of the type of control, designing a control activity that checks that all shipments billed to customers are recorded completely seems rather different from designing controls that will ensure that customers are treated fairly in the sales process.

Thus, when designing more sophisticated controls or non-financial controls, the traditional accounting objectives based on the financial assertions may not be applicable but should be *replaced*, or *supplemented*, by other design objectives. These objectives may not relate to achieving financial reporting quality but instead to risk mitigation related company objectives such efficiency or compliance. The Practice Advisory (PA) for internal auditors on control criteria 2120.A4-1 (IIA, PA2120, 2004, pp. 249–250) prescribes that:

> Before controls can be evaluated, management should determine the level of risk they want to take in the area. . .(....) this should be identified in terms of reducing the potential impact of the key threats to the achievement of the major objectives of the area (....) once the risk level is determined, the controls currently in place can be assessed to determine how successful the are expected to be in reducing the risk to the desired level.

According to PA2120, managers should stipulate what kind of risks they are willing to accept, i.e. their risk appetite. Based on a *formally approved risk appetite*, key controls should be designed so that goals may be met while significant risks are mitigated or managed. Most likely risk appetite, or the level of risk that an organization is willing to take (IIA, 2009: Standards Glossary), will become even more important in the future as a result from the lessons learned from the financial turmoil of 2008–2009 (see OECD, 2009a, 2009b; Senior Supervisory Group, 2009; Birkenshaw & Jenkins, 2009).

It may be important to point out that risk, whether being market, credit or operational, may be reduced, accepted or increased through different *risk treatments*. Too little risk may be just as bad as too much risk, and controls should enable good things to happen while stopping bad things from happening (Picket, 2001, pp. 20–21). Therefore, risk, and related controls, is not only about what can go wrong but also about what can be done better (p. 35). Besides from an explicit focus on *risk appetite* and *reasonable assurance* the internal control system is then not very different from any management control system found in literature on management control. A management control system represents a systematic use of information and feedback which enables managers to take action so that organizational objectives may be met (see Simons 1987, 1990 and 1991). According to Merchant and Otley (Chapman, Hopwood & Shields, eds. 2007) a management control system is designed to help an organization to adapt to the environment in which it is set and to deliver the key results desired by key stakeholder groups, such as the shareholders. Managers implement controls, or sets of controls, to help attain these results and to protect against threats to the achievement of good performance (p. 785).

We may conclude that controls can be designed based on the relevant financial assertions or a stated risk appetite. The financial statement assertions are often applied when considering the design effectiveness of controls related to financial reporting quality.

5.3.3.12 An Integrative Approach

Every organization consist of different types of controls, or systems of controls (see Malmi & Brown, 2008). Each system could potentially comprise of a large number of subsets which may all be interrelated (Picket, 2001, pp. 32–33). In an early paper on the contingency perspective of management accounting, Otley (1980, p. 422) claims that accounting controls are only one part of the overall control system. Otley concludes that:

> The study of the effectiveness of management accounting information systems is intimately bound up with the study of all of the many kinds of control mechanisms used by organizations in attempting to influence the behavior of their members and their relationships with the external world. It is often impossible to separate the effects of an AIS (accounting information system) from other controls; they act as a package and must be assessed jointly.

It follows that the control architecture needs to be designed from an overall perspective. If each subsystem is considered in isolation instead of jointly, it is likely that control inefficiencies will arise. This could potentially result in too much control (i.e. too little risk taking) or too little control (i.e. too much risk taking) or that controls are not optimally designed, thus incurring unnecessary costs. A recent report by Ernst & Young (2009) on risk management concludes that, although risk management practices are maturing, risk and control functions need to be better coordinated to improve efficiency, eliminate redundancies, duplication and gaps (p. 13). Evidence would therefore seem to suggest that managers need to assess and design the *enterprise-wide control package*, or *mix of controls*, jointly. An integrative approach may thus be necessary.

Since there are different internal control objectives, companies may choose to design and implement both financial and non-financial internal controls. Even though objectives related to financial reporting quality, compliance, efficiency and effectiveness may not be in conflict, it is likely that they at times are competing. Chenhall (2003) seems to recognize this when he states that "*recently many organizations have recognized the need to satisfy multiple and potentially competing goals*" (p. 136). The recognition of the importance of control conflict avoidance also calls for joint considerations where different controls, and control systems, are assessed together.

Yet another architectural challenge is related to the fact that control systems often operate both vertically and horizontally. Organizational control cycles, whether formal or more informal in character, may be embedded in processes (i.e. horizontally) and in hierarchies (i.e. vertically). The challenge here is to integrate the different control cycles so that they supplement each other as control packages (see Malmi and Brown, 2008).

However, the importance of integration is not only related to the issue of integrating different controls and sub-systems of controls so that they may effectively work together, but seems also be related to the *embedding* of controls. Many of regulatory and practical texts on internal control suggest that controls should be *embedded in the normal operations of the business* (see for example FRC, 2005, pp. 3, 7). This points to the importance of ensuring that controls operate as an integrative part of the normal day-to-day activities, as opposed to being superimposed (Picket, 2001, p. 46).

Perhaps this is related to the maturity of the control environment and the internal control process (see Hammer, 2007). Controls which are well integrated with people (control owners and performers), with information technologies and other elements of the enterprise, are potentially more embedded than those that are not, thus enabling the enterprise to meet its goals more effectively. Potentially, a control which is well integrated to the business activity may function better and also need less monitoring control since *un-embedded controls potentially deteriorate easier* (COSO, 2009, p. 2). Control arrangements which are loosely coupled (see Chap. 1, Table 1.1) with core operations will necessarily be un-embedded, and therefore probably less effective.

5.3.3.13 A Balanced Approach

Early organizational approaches to control (e.g., Ouchi 1977, 1979) suggest two underlying control strategies: control can be accomplished through performance evaluation, behavior controls or output controls, or through the use of human resources policies such as selection of candidates, training and socialization so that employees understand and internalize the firm's goals (Ouchi, 1979). Ouchi concluded that different firms and industries require different types of controls.

Behavior or output control may not be applicable to certain service industries for example, which must rely more on cultural forms of control instead (p. 845). According to Ouchi, the challenge is to "*discover that balance of socialization and measurement which most efficiently permits a particular organization to achieve cooperation among its members*" (p. 846). What Ouchi touches upon in this statement here is the following: controls need to be appropriately balanced.

In any given control process, *a set of controls* have to be designed – controls like the segregation of duties, authorization procedures, security- and system access, verification- and supervisory review (Picket, 2001, pp. 51–53). The importance of balancing different types of controls has been pointed out by scholars in general management control research (see for example Simons, 1990, 1991) and prior research has revealed a wide range of different types of controls (see Chenhall, 2003, p. 133 for a review). Most of these controls exhibit significant overlap to the controls referred to in accounting and auditing texts, using however different technical terms (Merchant & Otley in Chapman, Hopwood & Shields eds. 2007, p. 788). It appears that research on control, generated by different fields, remains fragmented and has developed rather independently of each other. Hence, there seems to be an obvious need to cross-fertilize and integrate different findings and concepts (see Maijoor, 2000, p. 102; Merchant & Otley in Chapman, Hopwood & Shields eds. 2007, p. 788).

Accounting controls highlighted in many auditing texts include the segregation of employees and functions, information-processing controls such as general processing controls and application controls, authorization, physical controls, documents, records, independent or internal checks and performance analysis (Trenerry, 1999, pp. 27–28). These controls are often directly related to the accounting system and its sub-systems, i.e. the sales and order entry, accounts receivables, accounts payables, payroll, capital expenditure and finance and treasury (p. 34). The administrative controls referred to in auditing-related texts, have been defined as:

> The organization structure and all procedures and documents that are used in management's decision-making activities that result in authorized activities and transactions. The authorization of activities is the function of management that produces approved transactions to meet their obligations to comply with policies and objectives (p. 8).

Irrespective of how one labels the different controls, the managerial task is clear: to design and apply *different types and forms of controls* that will enable the firm to effectively execute strategies and reach set objectives. This control mix will probably be contingent upon the circumstances of the firm and the situation at hand.

The importance of an appropriate and effective balance of controls is also relevant from a corporate governance perspective. Taylor (2003) argues that successful corporate governance requires a *balance between accountability and entrepreneurship*. Taylor calls for something he refers to as corporate entrepreneurship, a concept which is illustrated in Fig. 5.2 below.

> Effective board leadership requires directors to achieve a balance between "entrepreneurship", i.e. strategy, corporate renewal and innovation on one hand, and "corporate governance", which tends to emphasize holding management accountable to shareholders and imposing rigorous financial controls (p. 3).

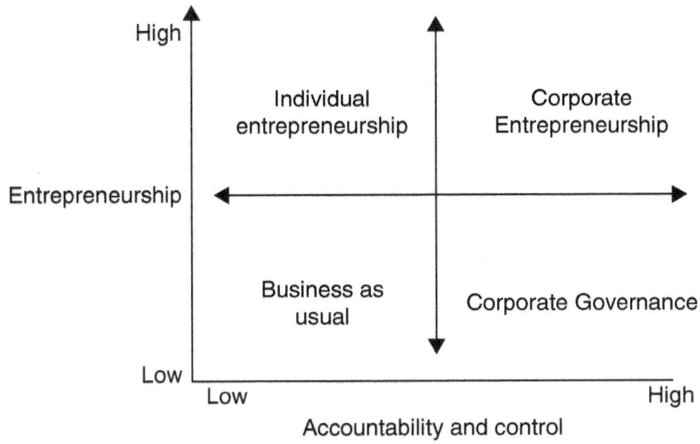

Fig. 5.2 Balancing entrepreneurship with accountability (Taylor, 2003, p. 4)

According to Taylor, the preferred governance style is neither over-dependency on charismatic leadership nor control at the expense of development. Birkenshaw and Jenkins (2009), in a report on the lessons learned from the credit crisis of 2008–2009, also discuss the importance of an appropriate balance between certain control aspects and elements. The authors argue that organizations need to strike a balance between rules and procedures, and subjective judgment and personal accountability. They conclude that in the years leading up to the crisis there was an undue focus on the formalization of risk management (p. 8).

Taylor's view of corporate entrepreneurship exhibits similarities with Simons'(1995) research on control, which recognizes *competing requirements* between freedom and constraint, empowerment and accountability, top-down direction and bottom-up creativity and experimentation and efficiency. According to Simon, increasingly businesses cannot choose between these but to be successful must have both in their organizations. Underlying this theory produced by Simons are the dynamic forces inherent in every organization, which represent different facets of the organization and produce tension. These need to be reconciled and balanced to allow an effective control of strategy. Intended strategy needs to be balanced against emergent strategy and self-interest needs to be balanced against desire to contribute. Empowerment must not lead to unlimited freedom of choice and action and control must not lead to empowerment failure with resulting lack of creativity and innovation.

Thus striking a *balance between risk and control* appears to be vital. Too much risk is just gambling while too much control will probably result in stagnation and no progress (Picket, 2001, p. 46). Therefore different controls need to be deliberately designed so that we achieve desired objectives while also making sure that we stay within our set thresh-holds for what can be accepted. Transparency and accountability underpin internal control concepts. People need to be accountable but also to be allowed to experiment and be creative when and where necessary. The purpose of controls is to provide reasonable assurance that objectives will be met. This is done by installing balanced and flexible controls that enable creativity and innovation while ensuring that key risks are managed so that they do not impair the ability to reach set targets. This may be achieved through a balanced approach which also focuses on inherent risk exposures and choice between different risk treatments – more risk, accept risk or more controls (p. 45).

Another balance that needs to be considered is cost-benefit ratios, or the *cost-effectiveness of controls*. Besides finding controls that can effectively be combined and balanced so that risks are managed, cost-benefit ratios must also be considered. All control actions namely cost money but both practical and regulatory texts point to the importance of considering costs when designing and implementing controls (Chapman, 2003b, p. 35; FRC, 2005, p. 6). Whether management chooses to design and implement certain controls is thus contingent upon the cost of operating particular controls relative to the benefit obtained (i.e. the management of risk).

This is also related to the concepts of reasonable assurance and the inherent limitations of internal control (FFE, 2007). One of inherent limitations of internal control is related to the fact that management considers cost when designing and implementing controls. Hence limitations in existing controls may have to be recognized. Nevertheless, the cost-effectiveness balance calls for a deliberate approach where controls are allocated to inherently risky and significant business activities – i.e. where controls are most needed. Furthermore, it calls for a deliberate and embedded control design where control owners and performers know what to do and when. Otherwise controls are unlikely to fulfill their purpose but still consume resources.

5.3.3.14 An Adaptive Approach

Yet another responsibility of internal control architects would be to ensure that the system of internal controls *remains effective over time*. This is also highlighted by the COSO (2009a) release on monitoring controls. In the foreword of the discussion document (COSO, 2007) the Chairman states that:

> Introduced in 1992 as one of the five fundamental components of the Framework, monitoring is designed to "ensure that internal control continues to operate effectively." COSO's 2006 internal control guidance for smaller public companies elaborates further on monitoring by emphasizing two fundamental points:
>
> - Monitoring should be designed to determine whether all components of internal control continue to operate effectively; and
> - Weaknesses in internal control should be communicated in a timely fashion to those responsible (including management and the board) such that corrective action can be taken.

What is suggested is that the internal controls must be able to *adapt in order to address changes* in the circumstances of the firm. The circumstances are represented by internal and external factors such as those highlighted in Fig. 5.1 and include objectives, strategies, risks and changes in the regulatory environment. Pathak (2005) argues that "*when internal controls and the resulting policies and*

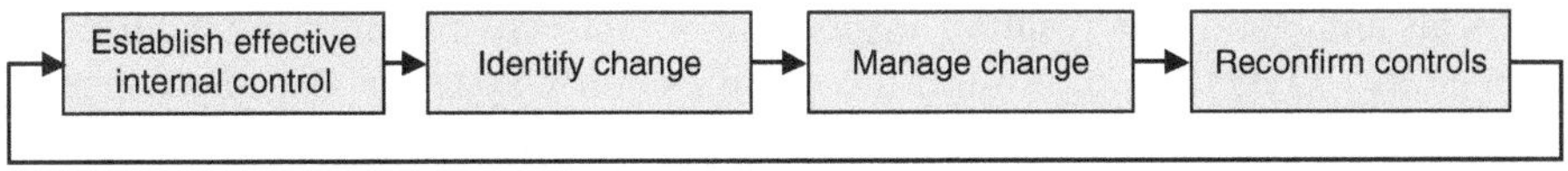

Fig. 5.3 The internal control change management process (COSO, 2007, pp. 8–9)

procedures are too rigid, dynamic systems begin to act like static systems, rigid and unchangeable; creating a gap in the protection of vulnerabilities" (p. 576).

Earlier in Sect. 3.2.10 we discussed the monitoring component of internal control and through Fig. 5.3 provided an illustration of the internal control change management process as outlined by the COSO (2007, pp. 8–9). It may be appropriate to refresh our memories here and Fig. 5.3 below repeats the illustration. This process is normative in style, much like traditional information-based feedback-systems. The objectives of existing system of controls should be continuously monitored, and based on changes in external and internal variables, action is taken to correct inadequacies or inefficiencies in the operation of existing controls.

Simons (1991) has argued that control systems should not be applied in a traditional *diagnostic* way in which the management of the system is based on exceptions, but that instead the control systems should be used actively and *interactively* in order to intervene in organizational decision making and shape formation about new strategies in different areas (p. 49). Cardinal, Sitkin and Long (2004, p. 412) also discuss the importance of re-balancing control systems and argue that research has not yet examined this area in great detail:

> Organizations operate in complex and dynamic competitive environments whereby managers are likely to find it difficult to maintain an appropriate balance among control mechanisms, or even to know what such a balance would look like..(...) despite these few and indirect references to control and the importance of balance, no attention has been paid, neither theoretically or empirically, to how control use shifts or how controls initially arise. Because balance has not been examined dynamically, we know little about efforts to establish a balanced control system or to re-establish a disrupted balance.

Developments in the field of strategy also point to the need of re-balancing existing controls. While control is about *realizing intended strategies* (Olve, Petri, Roy J. & Roy, S., 2003, p. 288) through which the established intent is fulfilled through various means of influence (Tannenbaum, 1968, p. 6; Mintzberg, 1983, p. 22), intended strategies are not always executed (Mintzberg, 1990; also Langfield-Smith, 1997, p. 210). The point is this: controls are not only dependent on intended strategies but also of realized strategies, which means that controls need to adapt to changes in intended as well as emerging strategies (Langfield-Smith, 1997, p. 210). Accordingly, the systems of internal control should be able to adapt to emerging strategies or to changes in strategy execution.

As we have noted earlier, the objectives of internal controls are to enable firms to meet established company objectives. A control system which is significantly *out-of-balance* is likely to lead to organizational problems and eventually compromise firm performance (see Cardinal, Sitkin & Long, 2004). Such an imbalance however would probably stimulate management attention because of the severity of the problems and could be a result of inadequate or ineffective monitoring controls as detailed by COSO (2007, 2009). If the internal control system is out-of-balance, it would according to COSO (2007, p. 2) constitute the following:

- Inadequacies in the design of the controls, which would translate to the existing controls, not being properly designed due to changes in either business processes or risks related to environment and strategies.
- Current controls, although being properly designed, not operating as intended.

The challenge then is to design a control system which not only identifies and manages existing inadequacies or inefficiencies in the control process, but which also allows for adaptation to changes in external and internal factors. Thus a truly adequate and effective system of internal controls should be *dynamic*, or *adaptive,* in nature. The challenge however is great. According to Whitley (2006) the Chairman of the COSO claimed "*there is a tremendous gap between the value good monitoring brings to a system of internal control and management's understanding of that value*" (p. 18), a statement which very much embodies the challenge for internal control architects in this respect.

We conclude that controls need to be flexible (Picket, 2001, p. 21). Controls are about making sure that the car goes where it is supposed to (p. 20) and if changes in roadmaps suggest alternative routes, internal controls need to adapt accordingly. An organic, and less rigid, approach to internal control seems important. Therefore the internal control change management process is vital in so far that it enables company's change initiatives by adopting controls which are able to change and thus promote overall change processes within firms (p. 223).

5.3.3.15 Design Capabilities

The task of designing internal controls is truly a challenging one. Any internal control architect must take a number of considerations into account. It is therefore necessary for a firm to ensure that is has internal control design capabilities. In a practically oriented journal, Oliviero (2002, p. 76) argued a few years ago:

> Although the responsibility for internal controls seems clear from the report, there is no reference to the specific qualification of those who create the system. . .(. . .). . .No one in the organization has been officially assigned the responsibility of viewing internal controls as an entity-wide phenomenon. No one is in charge – there is no designated expert with vision, design theory, and astute understanding of practical, effective policies and their potential behavior impact on the personnel.
>
> Internal control appears to be fragmented, and the function that should be at the beginning of the process is a missing link. Perhaps it's time for a new function – one that is headed by an expert in control processes who designed the entity's overall system and coordinated all aspects of implementation.

Oliviero (2002) concluded that "*architects are sorely missed*" (p. 76) and accordingly pointed to the importance of building internal control competence in firms. Picket (2001, p. 57) presents a similar argument:

> In one sense, the board is sold on the idea of control because they are responsible. Accountants and auditors are trained in this matter and so have no problems here. There are other people in the risk business, say, specialist staff such as insurance, health and safety, and information technology (IT) security managers, project managers and legal compliance officers who tend to appreciate the importance of risk and controls. It's all the other people who work for an organization, including managers at all levels, who are left in the dark. They get no training, no one tells them about control, and they tend to view it as a specialist subject.

The arguments presented by Oliviero (2001, 2002) and Picket (2001) suggest that firms need to invest in control competence so that internal controls may be better designed and managed throughout the organization. Recent comments made in Swedish media also suggest that these arguments may hold true. A recent comment in Swedish media by Kjellberg (2009) is relevant here. Although Kjellberg explicitly focuses on the risk management practices of firms, the findings may still relevant to this discussion. Referring to a study, Kjellberg claims that only 40 % of top executives at banks and finance firms believe that they understand risk management tools.

We conclude that the knowledge and skills required by an internal control architect are significant, and the task of appropriately designing the system of internal control should not be underestimated. The design of the internal control system is *contingent* upon a number of factors internal and external to the firm and controls should thus be based on the specific circumstances of the firm. Existing literature on internal control suggests that controls need to be integrated, balanced, adaptive and cost-effective. Controls must evolve as the business evolves and systems that are too rigid and inflexible will grow out-of-balance and cease to provide effective assurance. As a result of this, building internal control design capabilities seems crucial. Since internal control is defined as a process (COSO, 1992) it may as such be regarded as a collection of control activities[3] which transform inputs (human, financial, physical resources) to valuable output (i.e. assurance) for directors, managers, investors and other stakeholders (based on Hammer & Champy, 1993, p. 35). Every firm comprises a collection of activities (Porter, 1985, p. 36) which are the basis for cost and value creation and these are the basic units of competitive advantage (Porter, 1985, p. xv). Like all processes, design is fundamental for internal control so that cost-effective assurance may be produced. We argue that different internal control process designs lead to different internal control quality, therefore producing different levels of output, i.e. assurance. A well-managed internal control process (see Hammer, 2007) which is integrated, balanced, adaptive and cost-effective in nature, may be capable of producing stronger assurance with fewer resources. This is illustrated in Fig. 5.4.

For an organization to be able to produce such a high quality output however, it requires that the organization develop strong *internal control design capabilities*.

---

[3] Internal control activities are closely associated with what Porter (1985) refers to as *quality assurance activities*. These activities, according to Porter, ensure the quality of other primary core activities and include various monitoring, inspecting, reviewing, testing and checking activities (p. 44), which resembles internal controls.

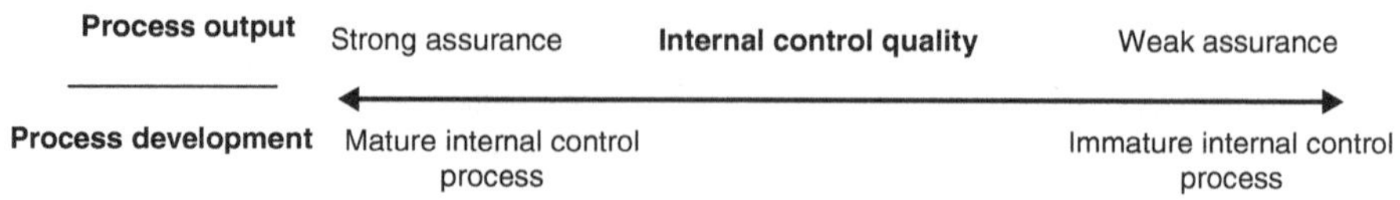

Fig. 5.4 Internal control process quality

These capabilities allow the organization to deploy and combine resources efficiently and effectively so that a high performance internal control process is created (based on Teece, Pisano & Shuen, 1997; Eisenhardt and Martin, 2000; Winter, 2003; Ethiraj, Kale, Krishnan & Singh, 2005; Hammer, 2007).

As in most writings on intentional control design, control has been viewed from a rational agency theory-like perspective. Attention to internal control design is important since it may help in mitigating agency-problems between owners and managers and also between managers and other staff. However, institutional theories provide inspiration for supplementary views such as the symbolic value of high-profile and highly visible internal control processes such as the management's attention to internal control deficiencies. Having internal control processes and procedures in place may sometimes be regarded as more important than the precise functioning of those processes and procedures.

5.3.4 Assessment and Evaluation

The evaluation and assessment of internal controls is perhaps the most frequently occurring theme in existing research on internal controls. The importance of internal control evaluation has been highlighted in philosophical texts on auditing (see Flint, 1988; Mautz & Sharaf, 1961). Flint (1988) sees three distinct stages in the audit process: obtaining evidence, evaluating evidence and drawing conclusions based on the evidence, and exercising professional judgment and reporting (p. 102). Thus, for many years, evaluation of audit evidence, including evidence of the design and effectiveness of controls, has long been an important activity for auditors and accountants. Internal control evaluation has been described as a three-phase process: documentation and learning, planning and evaluation, and re-evaluation (see Gadh, Krishnan & Peters, 1993, p. 113).

However, internal control evaluation is an inherently complex activity. Auditing researchers have examined the process and research on the subject goes back some years. This is not surprising, given the fact that auditing has received significant attention as a series of practices, procedures and techniques prior to development of any theory (Flint, 1988, p. 4). While the evaluation of internal control is an important part of the auditing process, it is also becoming increasingly important for managers and directors of firms (Changchit, Holsapple & Madden, 2001; Mock, Sun, Srivastava & Vasarhelyi, 2009, p. 65). With increasing external demands for accountability and transparency, directors and managers are paying increasing attention to the assessment of internal controls. Thus, internal control evaluation is also fundamental for management (Changchit, Holsapple & Madden, 2001, p. 437).

As it is a part of the audit process, the assessment of internal controls forms part of professional guidance for external auditors through for example international audit standard 500 (IAASB, 2006; or see FAR SRS, RS 500, 2009, pp. 272–275) and internal auditors through performance standard 2120 (IIA, 2004). The assessment of internal control is based on the identification and obtainment of information, i.e. audit evidence. Normally, such audit evidence is obtained through physical examination, inspection of documents, confirmation, inquiry, observation, re-performance, re-calculation and various analytical procedures (see for example FAR SRS, RS 500, 2009, p. 275). Inquiry alone is rarely considered conclusive evidence due to possible bias, errors, misunderstandings and the possibility of deception (Clikeman, 2009, p. 20). Other methods or tests may therefore produce greater evidence (PCAOB, 2007, p. 414).

Both quantitative and qualitative approaches are valid for internal control assessments and no required standard format requirement exists (see Bierstaker & Thibodeau, 2006, p. 878). Conventionally however, auditors have adopted more qualitative methods such as the use of questionnaires, checklists and flowcharts (Mock et al. 2009, p. 66; also see Koutoupis, 2007, on the documentation of internal controls). Different methods for documenting internal control evidence such as narratives, checklists, questionnaires or flowcharts may emphasize different aspects of the internal control system however (Bierstaker, 2003, p. 91). To avoid "check the box mentality" recent guidance suggests that auditors should not solely rely on standardized checklists when evaluating internal controls (see Bierstaker & Thibodeau, 2006, p. 878).

Irrespective of which technique is applied, for the statutory auditor its purposes is the same: it should economically and effectively assist in determining the extent of testing necessary (see Smith, 1972; also Brown, 1962, p. 50).[4] As a part of the audit process the auditor may choose to document and test certain key controls. If post-testing leads the auditor to assess that the control risk is high then substantive testing has to produce all the necessary evidence (see Smith, 1972, on the association between internal control evaluation and audit sample size; also Sherer & Turley, 1997, p. 239). For internal auditors on the other hand, sufficient, reliable, relevant and useful information should be obtained (IIA, 2004, p. 275) about the design and effectiveness of controls, so that they can form an opinion about risk management, control and governance processes (see Clikeman, 2009, p. 19; IIA, 2004, p. 161).

The assessment of internal control is a result of the testing of the effectiveness of controls, and of the auditor's professional judgment. The importance of internal

[4] From a local Swedish perspective this may not be a completely accurate statement. The Limited Liability Companies Act [SFS 2005:551 Aktibolagslagen] prescribes that the statutory audit also must include an assessment of the Board's administration of the company. Some aspects of the internal control system is hereby audited, as prescribed by Swedish audit standard RS 209 (FAR SRS, 2009, p. 205).

control evaluation appears to have increased along with the development of the risk-based approach to auditing (Sherer & Turley, 1997, p. 251; O'Leary, Iselin & Sharma, 2006, p. 71).

As mentioned earlier, the complex mode of procedure when assessing internal control together with its growing importance, has resulted in a number of studies on the subject. Here we will only touch upon a few of these studies. Since internal control evaluation is *part structure* and *part judgment*, prior studies have sometimes been categorized accordingly (see O'Leary, Iselin & Sharma 2006 for a brief summary on prior research). Research has thus been focused on both the structural elements (i.e. documentation methods) and judgmental elements (i.e. the evaluation methods) of the internal control assessment process.

In an early paper, Brown (1962) pointed to the weaknesses in subjective internal control evaluation; people may judge internal control adequacy or effectiveness differently, the evaluation mechanism may be time-consuming thus resulting in errors or mistakes, and the difficulty in assessing internal control effectiveness in different individual areas (p. 50). Brown promoted the questionnaire, which in his opinion offered five advantages: it permitted a standardized approach, it was faster and more efficient, it enabled the isolation of system weaknesses for further attention, it could be used by less experienced staff, and most importantly – it provided a standard against which to measure internal controls (pp. 50–51). Brown thus wanted a quantitative statement of the reliability of internal control, but admitted at the same time that different techniques would probably have to be combined or applied (pp. 54–55).

In another early paper, Ashton (1974) argued that there was substantial agreement about the types of evidence that need to be collected and also about the appropriate collection techniques. However, Ashton pointed out that assessing evidence is a procedure more difficult to codify, thus making professional judgment an integrated part of the assessment and evaluation activity (p. 143). Since then, different studies, including the one by Ashton have examined the extent to which judgment is consistent.

As pointed out above it is crucial for management to be able to assess and evaluate internal controls, simply because "*it is an organization's management, not auditors, who bear ultimate responsibility for maintaining an effective internal control*" (Changchit, Holsapple & Madden, 2001, p. 438). The study by Changchit, Holsapple and Madden (2001) shows that decision expert systems would in fact support and enable managers to better assess and evaluate internal controls.

Studies have also been performed on the knowledge structure of the people reviewing and assessing internal control, since studies have shown that the nature and extent of knowledge has a significant impact on the performance of internal control reviews (Borthick, Curtis & Sriram, 2006, p. 323). The results from the study by Borthick, Curtis and Sriram (2006) are consistent with previous studies on the subject, and provide support for the idea that "*the more available knowledge is, the more usable it is in a judgment task*" (p. 337). Additional studies, which build on studies which focus on the association between knowledge and experience of the preparers of internal control assessments, have also examined how auditor recall from working memory and long-term memory is associated with experience of auditors and the internal control assessments (Bierstaker, 2003). Other studies such as Bierstaker, Hunton and Thiboudau (2009) have examined how client-prepared documentation impacts on how accountants are able to identify and detect missing internal controls.

5.3.4.1 The Internal Control Environment

In the rather recent study by O'Leary, Iselin & Sharma (2006), it is suggested that for the assessment and evaluation of controls, it is necessary to know something about the following: what internal control is, the different elements of internal control, how the different elements of internal control are related, and finally, the relative importance of each element or component (p. 70).

From examining prior research, O'Leary, Iselin and Sharma suggest that, while significant research has been done on the evaluation of internal controls and more specifically, on the component control activities, "*little attention has been given to how different components of internal control may interact with each other and their relative importance*" (p. 69). Rae and Subramaniam (2008) also claim that previous studies on internal control have placed little attention on how different aspects of the internal control system affect each other (p. 106). O'Leary, Iselin and Sharma seek to address this gap and based on their findings they conclude:

> A weakness in the control environment elements appeared to have the most significant effect on overall evaluation as it impacted upon evaluations of all other elements as well (p. 85).

The evidence from their research therefore suggests that there is an order of importance between the different elements. More specifically, the evidence suggests that controls related to the internal control environment are the most important ones, as these affect all the other evaluations. The findings in a study by Fagerberg (2008) on auditors' perceptions of red flags and internal control provide corroborating support for this conclusion. Fagerberg found that certain internal control elements (based on the COSO-model) were emphasized; one of which was the *control environment*. Additional research into exactly what are the most important and significant elements of internal control evaluation and their inter-relationship to each other appears to be needed however (O'Leary, Iselin & Sharma 2006, p. 75).

The relative importance of such non-activity related controls appears to be in line with the Audit Standard No. 5 (PCAOB, 2007) which "*places greater emphasis on entity-level controls than its predecessor, Auditing Standard No.2*" (Goldberg, 2007, p. 69). Bannister, Engvall and Martin (2007, p. 5) argue that:

> In response to comments, the final form of the interpretive guidance includes more guidance about how management's evaluation of entity-level, or company-wide, control can affect, and in some cases reduce, the scope of review necessary with respect to lower-level (transaction-level) controls.

PCAOB-guidance and the new SEC interpretative guidance thus seem to adopt more of a top-down approach, emphasizing the relative importance of entity-level controls than has previous guidance (Bannister et al. 2007). According to PCAOB (2007), entity-wide controls include controls related to the internal control environment, risk assessments, centralized processing controls, monitoring controls, management override controls and significant policies. Controls related to the control environment include management's attitudes and philosophy towards controls, management's commitment to integrity and ethical values and whether the board and audit committee understand and exercise their oversight responsibility with reference to internal controls (p. 404–405). Studies on the association between internal controls and organizational citizenship also provide evidence for the vital importance of management's attitudes and behaviors (see Holmes et al. 2002).

However, assessing and evaluating non-activity related controls or more sophisticated controls is a more complex task than assessing harder controls, such as continuous account reconciliations and the segregation of duties. Entity-level controls are fundamental controls that may have a *wide, pervasive and indirect effect* on the entity's overall control over financial reporting (PCAOB, 2007). These controls are generally not found at a process-level, or transaction-related level (Gerkes, Van der Werf & Van der Wijk, 2007) and Ramos (2004) argues that:

> As opposed to an activity-level control (for example checking the mathematical accuracy of a vendor invoice) which is limited to one processing stream, the control environment has a pervasive structure that affects many business activities (....) adding to the difficulty of the testing requirement task is the fact that the control environment *is not transaction-oriented*. The test of controls auditors are accustomed to performing, such as "walk-troughs" or the re-performance of the control for a sample of items, will not be possible (pp. 75–76).

The argument put forward by Ramos (2004) is supported by Lightle, Castellano and Cutting (2007) who argue that, while the internal control environment may be the most critical component of internal controls, it is also the most difficult to assess effectively (p. 51). A recent report issued by the PCAOB (2009) on the first-year implementation of the Audit Standard No.5 also suggest that assessing and evaluating more sophisticated entity-level controls is a complex task (see pp. 6–7).

Different techniques for assessing the internal control environment have been recommended such as questionnaires targeted to employees rather than management (see Lightle, Castellano & Cutting, 2007) and using a balanced scorecard approach (see Callaghan, Savage & Mintz, 2007). The approach of Gerkes, Van der Werf and Van der Wijk (2007, p. 54) to testing entity-wide controls suggests that:

> In many cases the control description is focused on the existence of formal documentation, such as authorized policies, meeting agendas and minutes, and reports on performance... (....)...to a large extent, the test work programs will focus on the documentation already identified in the control descriptions, the implementation of relevant policies, and the actual operation of the policies and procedures.

5.3.4.2 Assessing and Classifying Internal Control Weaknesses

Internal control disclosure requirement often prescribes that companies should maintain a sound and effective system of internal control. As mentioned earlier in this thesis, the concept of an effective internal control system has been difficult for some stakeholders to grasp which is why directors in the United Kingdom for example, were unwilling to make such statements (see Power, 1997). As claimed by Raghunandan and Rama (1994), "*stating that an internal control system exists is very different from stating that such a system has been assessed to be effective*" (p. 54). As we also know from Chap. 4 on the regulatory environment, the section 404-requirements in the Sarbanes-Oxley Act in the United States prescribe an effectiveness report on internal controls by both managers and auditors. One difficulty seems to have been related to how one should accurately classify weaknesses in internal controls.

The original guidance issued by the PCAOB (2004) through Audit Standard No.2 prescribes that control weaknesses should be classified into the following categories: *control deficiency, significant deficiency and material weakness*. However, to appropriately assess and categorize different internal control issues has proven to be a challenging task (see for example Ashbaugh-Skaife, Collins & Kinney Jr., 2007; Leone, 2007 for a discussion and analysis) and there has been some confusion as to the severity of a weakness of internal control.

Partly as a response to requests for further guidance on the matter, in a coordinated action with the SEC, PCAOB (2007) released Audit Standard No.5. This means that for the first time, the SEC has provided a template for managers to consult when evaluating internal controls instead of having to rely solely on the standards and guidance from auditors (Bannister et al. 2007, p. 2). With the new SEC and PCAOB guidances, revised definitions of the terms significant deficiency and material weakness were adopted. Although they are aligned, differences do exist between the SEC and PCAOB guidances (the SEC-guidance is more principle-based) reflecting the different roles of managers and auditors (p. 3). However, with regard to the definitions of material weakness, guidance for evaluation deficiencies and the indicators of a material weakness, the guidances from SEC and PCAOB are consistent (p. 8).

The assessment of internal control is perhaps the most frequently occurring theme in writings on internal control, simply because internal control's primary association is with auditing and internal control assessment is a key part of auditing activity. Undoubtedly, both structure and judgment are important for effective internal control assessments, and factors such as documentation format, experience and available knowledge are but a few of those which have been examined by researchers and which also seem to be associated with the quality of internal control assessment. Recently, researchers have pointed out that there appears to be an order of importance with regards to the different internal control components provided by the COSO. Evaluations of control environment controls appear to have the most significant impact when evaluating different internal control components. There is also evidence that suggest that such controls may be the most difficult to assess.

5.3.5 Disclosure and Reporting

For a long time the internal control system of an organization remained a private affair. The design and effectiveness of the firm's internal control system was a matter only for the firm and any flaws in control environments or control activities remained undisclosed to the general public. Research has shown that corporate interests have been rather successful in actively resisting any proposals for stricter internal control regulations and standards (see Shapiro and Matson, 2007).

However, in the light of high-profile corporate and government scandals, crisis situations are produced where the existing corporate governance mechanisms are often deemed to be broken in one way or the other. Examples of such crisis situations from corporate United States may be the 1930s (Securities Act), the 1970s (Foreign Corrupt Practices Act) and more recently, the scandals of Enron and others, resulting in the Sarbanes Oxley Act (2002). Scandals in the United Kingdom towards the end of the 1980s and beginning of 1990s resulted in the well-known Cadbury Code (1992). In Sweden, existing corporate governance mechanisms were deemed appropriate until only a few years ago when both foreign and domestic corporate scandals shook the confidence of investors (see Kodgruppen, 2004, p. 3, also Jonnergård & Larsson, 2007, p. 462).

The answer to crisis situations has often been more regulation, either through direct state legislation such as with the Acts in the United States or a process of developing corporate governance codes of conduct as an enforced self-regulation. The latter is an effective way for the state to control the process while at the same time allowing the business community to regulate themselves, thus not hindering creativity and efficiency (Jonnergård & Larsson, 2007, p. 482).

With the introduction of corporate governance codes, such as the Cadbury Code in the United Kingdom or the Swedish Code of Corporate Governance, and regulations such as the Sarbanes-Oxley Act in the United States, the *companies' internal control systems have been turned inside out* in the quest for improved financial transparency of large corporations (see Power, 2007, pp. 34–65).

A key feature of corporate governance principles has namely been the emphasis that is put on openness and disclosure and the expectancy that both the management and board are transparent in the way they direct and control their companies (Chapman, 2003b, p. 39). More specifically, a requirement was introduced whereby organizations were obliged to maintain a sound and effective system of internal controls (Power, 2007, p. 35). In the case of the United Kingdom "*this requirement, though innocent in appearance, has generated fundamental problems about what internal controls really are and what one is saying when describing them as effective*" (Power, 1997, p. 55).

Therefore a new mechanism has been introduced into the corporate governance arena: *management reporting on internal control* (MRIC) and also the *auditor report on internal control* (ARIC). However, reporting on internal control is not a new phenomenon in corporate life (see Wallace, 1981), something which we will come back to later on in this section.

A MRIC means that executive management discloses publicly, through the annual financial reports or separate reports, how the company's internal control system is organized and possibly also its operating effectiveness. An ARIC means that the auditor reviews the MRIC and possible also reports on the assessments that the management has made based on their statements. For the first time in history, *reporting on the process of producing the financial statements has become a primary regulatory object* with the potential of becoming as important as the financial statements themselves (Power, 2007, p. 55).

With the growing interest in the importance of effective risk management practices (Power, 2007) and specifically the disclosure of *risk-related information* (Solomon et al. 2000), over the last few years management reporting on internal controls and risk management appear to have become the rule. Bronson, Carcello and Raghunandan (2006, p. 27) provide two general reasons why a company might provide the public with an MRIC:

- Stating the objectives of the internal control system and describing the various components of the internal control system.
- To indicate that management believes that internal controls are effective.

The recent implementation of the changes in the European Union accounting directive [EU:s redovisningsdirektiv] further highlight the growing interest in greater disclosures of the internal control practices of firms. An MRIC is now mandated in Swedish law through the Swedish Annual Accounts Act [Årsredovisningslagen 1995:1554].[5] Moreover, recent signals from regulatory bodies in the United States also suggest that new regulations for greater disclosures of the risk management oversight practices of firms emerge (COSO, 2009c, pp. 2–3; also see SEC, 2009b, final rule on proxy disclosure enhancements). The lessons learned from the current financial turmoil (see OECD, 2009a, 2009b; Senior Supervisory Group, 2009) will probably drive greater disclosure requirements of board risk oversight.

As mentioned earlier however an MRIC is not a new invention. Public companies in the United States, for example, have even been required by law to have effective internal controls in place since the introduction of the Foreign Corrupt Practices Act (FCPA) of 1977. This Act was adopted to deal with scandal involving illegal payments, which in turn were part of the so called Watergate

[5] As mentioned in *chapter three* these changes in Swedish law will also result in updates to the Swedish code of Corporate Governance (Kollegiet för Svensk Bolagsstyrning, 2009, p. 7). The now mandated corporate governance report [bolagsstyrningsrapport] must include information about the most important aspects of the entity´s systems for internal control and risk management, as it pertains to financial reporting quality. However, the new disclosure requirements that result from the implementation of the European Union accounting directive do not significantly deviate from the existing requirements already stipulated by the Swedish code. The SCGB has however signaled that, with reference to the content of the corporate governance report, it may be reasonable that the code requirements go beyond the minimum requirements of Swedish law (see Kollegiet för Svensk Bolagsstyrning, 2009, p. 8).

scandals in the United States (Wiesen, 2003, p. 430). Many companies have therefore reported on their internal control systems in a separate management report, attached or included in the annual report (p. 3).

The FCPA however focused only on the *maintenance* of internal controls, aiming to prevent fraud and there was no requirement on companies to report on the status and effectiveness of these internal control systems – i.e. if the controls were actually operating effectively and as intended. Further, in 1977, the American Institute of Certified Public Accountants (AICPA), and Auditing Standards Board (ASB) through Auditing Standards No. 20 required communication of material weaknesses in internal accounting controls, and additional guidance for this was issued in 1979 from AICPA. The Federal Deposit Insurance Corporation Improvement Act of 1991 also included a section requiring companies to report on internal control.

5.3.5.1 Classification of Internal Control Reporting Regimes

Different internal control disclosure regimes contain different disclosure requirements, which often however, may exhibit significant similarities. In a paper from 2003, Spira and Page classify different disclosure regimes along two axes: *scope* and *reporting requirements* (p. 651).[6]

Scope refers to the extent to which the internal control disclosure requirements cover different internal control objectives. Some regimes cover financial reporting quality only, while others include both financial and non-financial objectives. Reporting requirements seems to refer to the depth of the disclosure requirements that companies must comply with. Provisions may require firms to disclose how the internal control system is organized, or may be stricter, requiring a statement about the operating effectiveness of controls. In addition, the reporting requirements may include an auditor attestation of the MRIC. It follows that scope may be narrower or more broadly defined and that reporting requirements may vary in depth or strictness.

Figure 5.5 above is based on the classification scheme provided by Spira and Page but we have plotted in the reporting disclosure regimes in the United Kingdom (the Combined Code-requirements), the United States (the Sarbanes-Oxley, Section 404-requirements) and Sweden (the Swedish code of Corporate Governance-requirements) based on their respective reporting requirements and scope. Their appropriate positions reflect our professional judgement.[7]

[6] The requirements of Cadbury, Turnbull, Rutteman, Hampel, COSO and COCO are included in their assessment and illustration (see pp. 646–651).

[7] Their appropriate positions have been plotted based on an assessment of the following factors: whether MRICs contain a design-statement only or whether they should address the effectiveness of the internal control system as well, whether the definition of control is confined to financial reporting quality only or whether MRICs should cover other controls as well, and whether the auditors are required to attest to the MRICs or not (based on Hermanson, 2000, p. 326).

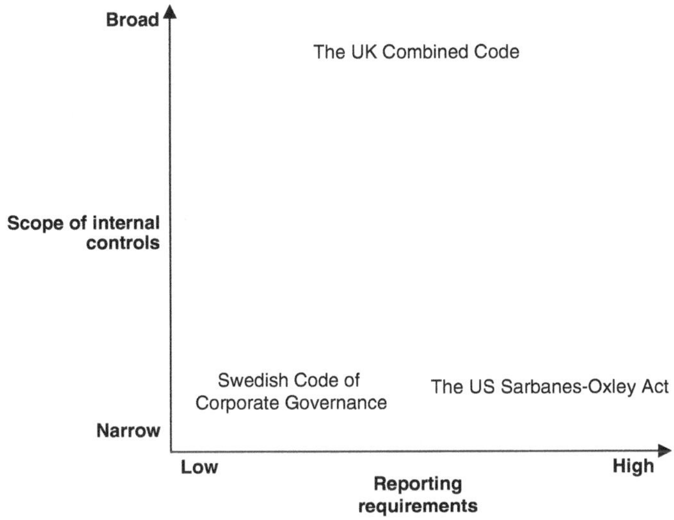

Fig. 5.5 Internal control reporting regime classification

We mentioned above that disclosure requirements vary. In an attempt to simplify one could argue that strict and broad internal control disclosure requirements include the following:

- A statement that addresses the operating effectiveness of controls.
- Coverage of both financial and non-financial controls.
- An auditor attestation of the MRIC.

A less strict and narrower regime would then include the following:

- A statement as to internal control design only.
- Coverage includes only certain types of controls.
- A non-auditor attestation of the MRIC.

A narrower scope may perhaps focus only on what is sometimes referred to as internal control over financial reporting (ICOFR), such as in the way that the scope is set under the SOX-requirements. However, recent trials in the United States have shown that such a scope actually may be rather comprehensive. Based on their assessment, Spira and Page (2003) conclude that there is a "*trend away from a narrow scope of internal controls, with a high-level of reporting requirements, towards a broader scope with less stringent reporting*" (p. 650).

The claim made by Spira and Page above appears to be relevant even in the Swedish case. The reporting requirements in Sweden have been downsized by the SCGB (Swedish Corporate Governance Board) as the original provisions concerning both the *effectiveness statement* and the *auditor review* now have been removed (Kollegiet för Svensk Bolagsstyrning, 2005; 2006a, 2006b, p. 8).

With reference to internal control, the Swedish Code primarily seems to cover financial reporting quality objectives only, thus representing a narrower regime.

What is also important to take note of is that the specific internal control reporting regime which is adopted will influence the internal control practices of firms, although the extent will vary however dependent of the nature of the regulations. A problem may occur if reporting requirements adopted is *out-of-balance* with the underlying business practices in organizations. Spira and Page (2003) conclude interestingly in their paper that "*there is a potential for significant adjustment costs as businesses are forced to implement the Turnbull Report from an inadequately prepared internal audit and control environment* "(p. 658) and recommend further (empirical) research on corporate codes and their effects on business.

Once again, the argument put forward by Spira and Page appears to be relevant in the Swedish context. In the guidance [Anvisning Nr.1-2005] issued by the SCGB, one reason stated for adjusting the internal control reporting requirements were that Swedish companies were operating on informal control processes, so that controls had first to be made formal before any meaningful public statements could be made (Kollegiet för Svensk Bolagsstyrning, 2005; also see 2006b, p. 8). From this, it would seem that the regulations in this case were out-of-balance with the underlying business practices of firms.

5.3.5.2 The Design of MRIC

As MRICs have been around for some time, they have also been the subject of research. An early paper by Wallace (1981) investigated the internal control reporting practices in the municipal sector of the United States. A detailed analysis was performed of 20 companies that were required to provide an MRIC, which should include the effectiveness of their internal control system. The study by Wallace raised concerns about the following issues:

- The scope and limitations of internal controls in the internal control reports.
- The character and format of the internal control reports (depth/length).
- The nature of the auditor's review of these controls.
- The usefulness of the information for users regarding risk exposures.
- The costs and benefits of the internal control reports.

The findings made by Wallace call attention to a number of items which are of importance if MRICs are to be designed effectively. Much of what Wallace pointed out as problematic with MRICs still remains relevant and part of the contemporary debate. See for example guidances [Anvisning Nr.1-2005, Anvisning Nr.1-2006] issued by the SCGB in 2005 and 2006 respectively (Kollegiet för Svensk Bolagsstyrning, 2005, 2006a). These guidances discuss issues related to both the usefulness of the information of internal control reports, as well as the auditor review which formed part of Swedish Code requirements at the time. Later, this discussion led to the removal of some of the stricter internal control reporting requirements in the original code from 2004.

In an interesting study by Solomon et al. (2000) performed in the United Kingdom, they inquired into the attitudes of institutional investors towards risk disclosure. They referred to the Turnbull Report (1999) and argued that although the disclosure of risk-related information appeared to be promoted by various parties, little was known about how this should be done, what form it should take and if this should remain voluntary or not (p. 448). They (Solomon et al., 2000, p. 453) claimed that:

> Turnbull provides remarkably little detail concerning the format of disclosure within the system of internal controls. However, Turnbull provides detailed guidance concerning what should be discussed in an annual assessment preceding the company's public statement on internal control....(....)...Indeed the only explicit guidance on what should be disclosed states that in their narrative statements, companies should..."as a minimum disclose that there is an ongoing process for identifying, evaluating and managing the significant risks faced by the company".

Like Wallace (1981) Solomon et al. point to the significant challenge facing preparers of internal control, and risk-related, reports to appropriately design and deliver *risk-related information that report-users value*. The results of the study suggest that the voluntary reporting framework should be kept in the United Kingdom. In addition, the results showed that a large portion of the institutional investors respond that their decision-making process would be improved with more risk-related information (p. 471).

In a subsequent study on the readability of risk-related information disclosed by companies, Linsley and Lawrence (2007) point to the challenges of designing and delivering risk-related information which users may be able to interpret and understand and builds on the study by Solomon et al. (2000). They conclude:

> One finding is that the level of readability of the risk disclosures is difficult or very difficult. In the UK, there have been suggestions that companies provide greater amounts of risk information. However, the publication of additional risk information will not necessarily lead to improved risk communication unless directors write with greater clarity when discussing risks (p. 625).

The design and content of internal control and risk disclosures seems to relate to the concept of *decision usefulness*. According to Scott (2003), the reporting of information that is useful to rational investors is called the decision usefulness approach (p. 11). The value of financial information is based on the view of accounting numbers as information on which much of the earnings management literature is based (see for example Schipper, 1989). Thus, the objective of financial reporting is decision usefulness for investors, analysts and other financial statement users. The concept of decision usefulness is associated with agency theory, see Sect. 2.3.1, where information is obtained and supplied in order to reduce asymmetries between parties. Because markets may not be characterized as ideal, individuals such as managers or directors may have information advantages over other parties such as analysts or investors (see Scott, 2003, p. 10). The solution is to obtain and supply information to help investors make better predictions about firm performance and value (see p. 11).

Solomon et al. (2000) observe that the past decade has seen a growing interest in the disclosure by of risk-related information companies in United Kingdom (p. 448). This trend seems to apply to other countries as well, including Sweden, and as we mentioned earlier, the Securities and Exchange Commission in the United States only recently in December of 2009 decided on greater disclosure requirements regarding board risk oversight (see SEC, 2009b). Even though this information does not consist of accounting numbers, the concept of decision usefulness may still be relevant. The question is: what do the internal control- and corporate governance report-users value? What kind of risk-related information can they use? It follows that if users do not value some specific information about the design and effectiveness of internal controls, then disclosures about such matters would be useless. From an institutional perspective however (see Chap. 2, Table 2.1), one might argue that forcing corporations to provide accounts of their processes will, in itself, increase the quality of these, and thus their trustworthiness. Investors may not actually consider MRICs but still consider their existence as an indication of good practices.

Hermanson (2000, p. 326) suggested a few years ago that the debate concerning management report on internal control could be broken down in three major issues: should an MRIC be voluntary or mandatory, should auditors attest to the MRIC, and should statements related to financial reporting controls only. Today, in 2011, these issues are still highly relevant. One key issue has accordingly been whether users value *mandatory* or *voluntary* internal control reporting regimes. This has been investigated in a number of different studies, see for example Raghunandan & Rama, 1994; McMullen, Ragahunandan & Rama, 1996; Hermanson, 2000; Solomon et al., 2000; O'Reilly-Allen & McMullen, 2002. In a United States-study, Hermanson (2000) examined nine different financial statement user groups: bankers, brokers, directors, executives, analysts, institutional investors, individual investors and external and internal auditors.

Hermanson found that respondents agree that voluntary MRICs improve controls, enhance oversight of controls and add information for decision making. Respondents also agree that mandatory MRICs improve controls, and enhance the oversight of controls, but are neutral as to whether mandatory MRIC would be informative for decision making. It is important to point out that overall responses were neutral on two key issues: whether the benefits of MRIC exceed the costs and whether mandatory MRIC would improve financial reporting quality (p. 340). On the basis of her research findings, Hermanson concludes that:

> The debate about MRICs has continued for over 20 years. This paper provides systematic evidence about various user groups' perceptions of MRICs. Proponents of MRICs need to clearly demonstrate how this report is going to add value. If strong demand for MRICs cannot be documented, then prescribing mandatory reports is difficult to justify (p. 340).

In another North-American study, O'Reilly and McMullen (2002) examined whether or not MRICs and ARICs affect the perceived reliability of the financial reporting (using MBA students as surrogates for financial statement users). They conclude that "*users' perceptions do not appear to be affected by the inclusion of an*

MRIC or ARIC. There was no difference between the three groups with regard to the usefulness and reliability of financial statements or the detection of fraud" (p. 106).

Most of the studies mentioned above in this section are pre-Sarbanes Oxley studies. Even though the SOX of 2002 has resulted in a mandatory disclosure regime in the United States, which includes both MRICs and ARICs, the studies referred to above remain highly relevant since most countries operate in a less strict regulatory environment than the SOX, and have less strict internal control disclosure requirements (Hoitash, Hoitash & Bedard, 2009, p. 845).

Issues related to the quality and content of risk-related disclosures and MRICs are also touched upon by the SCGB in their latest annual report (Kollegiet för Svensk Bolagsstyrning, 2009). This report addresses the attitudes of the general public and financial market stakeholders towards the Swedish corporate governance system in general and the corporate governance code requirements. According to SCGB, a number of companies did not issue corporate governance reports as stipulated. This report must also include an internal control report (p. 21), which should be an account of the most significant parts of the company's internal control and risk management systems (p. 22). According to the SCGB, such a report had been provided by 215 out of a total of 246 companies investigated (p. 22).

Following the principle-based character of the code, *describe and disclose* compliance as well as possible non-compliance is important, something which is also pointed out by SCGB when discussing the explanations for non-compliance given by firms. For information to be useful for financial statement and internal control report users, it needs to be purposeful, concrete, informative and firm-specific. The SCGB raise some concerns about this (pp. 24–25). A report by Grant Thornton (2009b) on the Combined Code-compliance of companies listed on the main index of the Irish Stock Exchange includes a similar discussion which suggests that explanations for non-compliance are typically of an insufficient nature (p. 5). An examination of the disclosures made based on the Combined Code provision C.2.1 shows that firms, unsurprisingly, are rather reluctant to discuss any internal control weaknesses and any actions taken mitigate this (Grant Thornton, 2009b, p. 31; see also thesis Sect. 4.2.4 for more details about the C.2.1 provision).

Undoubtedly, it is a challenging task for regulators, directors and managers to make sure that users get relevant and useful informational about internal control systems which adds value to the decision-making process, at a reasonable cost.

5.3.5.3 The Effects of Internal Control Reports

What type of effects do MRICs produce? This is a complex question that we will be unable to answer within the scope of this thesis. By effects however we simply refer to positive or negative outcomes from public reporting on internal controls. As we have mentioned, most of the reporting requirements on internal control and risk have the objective of improving the decision-making process of financial market stakeholders, strengthening confidence in financial markets and improve corporate governance quality. So does the public disclosure of risk-related information achieve these objectives? Below, we will highlight some of the potential effects that may arise from the public reporting on risk and internal control.

Some of the studies we discuss below relate to internal control reporting regulations in the United States under SOX (2002), and specifically, the effects of the section 404-requirements of this Act which stipulate both an MRIC and an AAIC. Wiesen (2003) argues that the enactment of the Sarbanes-Oxley covers almost every aspect of financial reporting and has significantly changed the face of corporate accountability (p. 431). Because of its significant impact all over the world, regulating also foreign registrants, it is appropriate at this point to discuss some of the effects that studies have found so far.

Critical examinations of internal control disclosure requirements under Sarbanes-Oxley suggest that costs have been substantial (see Tackett, Wolf & Claypool, 2004; Tacket et al. 2006, Foster, Ornstein & Shastri, 2007). Tacket, Wolf and Claypool conclude that "*there is little doubt that Congress made a serious error in enacting SOX under its current Section 404 configuratio*ns" (2006, p. 322). Kinney (2005) writing about the 25 years of audit de-regulation and regulation, argues that the internal control requirement through Section 404 is intended to improve the reliability of financial reporting through improved internal controls. Kinney claims however, that it may also increase the expectations gap as investor expectations rise. Kinney claims that "*Better internal controls reduce unintentional accounting errors, but are unlikely to significantly reduce intentional management misrepresentation fraud resulting management override of internal control, or collusion*" (p. 101). At the end of the paper, Kinney concludes that more research on corporate governance is needed and specifically on the stricter laws in the United States (p. 105) versus the less strict and principle-based approaches which may be found in United Kingdom or in Sweden.

Furthermore, in a paper written about the state of corporate governance in the United States, Holmström and Kaplan (2003) conclude on the subject of too much regulation that "*efforts to regulate the system so that such outrage will never again occur would be overly costly and counterproductive. It would lead to inflexibility and fear of experimentation*" (p. 20). Even though the authors are talking about the governance of firms in general, and not specifically the effects of MRICs or ARICs, it may still be relevant to this discussion. The authors suggest that too much regulation including reporting requirements which are too strict may produce unintended effects. They (2003, p. 20) claim that:

> The New Economy is moving forward and, in order to exploit the potential efficiencies inherent in the new information technologies, new business models and new organizational structures are likely to be desirable and valuable. Enron was an experiment that failed. We should take advantage of its lessons not by withdrawing into a shell, but rather by improving control structures and corporate governance so that other promising experiments can be undertaken.

In a recent study, Krishnan, Rama and Zhang (2008) on the costs to comply with SOX Section 404 conclude that costs have been high, especially for smaller firms. However, they recognize future long-term benefits which they claim are difficult to quantity (p. 184). Also the SEC (Securities and Exchange Commission) in the United

States recently issued a report on the cost and benefits related to the Sarbanes-Oxley 404-requirements. The report shows that cost of compliance is decreasing steadily after the first-year of compliance. Company insiders recognize benefits with SOX 404, especially those representing larger companies. A majority however, felt that the costs of compliance outweighed the benefits (SEC, 2009, p. 96). External users however "*tended to put a heavy premium on having high quality financial statements that are in compliance with generally accepted accounting principles, and these users felt that companies need effective ICFR to ensure this is the case*" (p. 96).

Obviously, internal control disclosure regimes produce positive effects, irrespective of their strictness. Studies such as Raghunandan & Rama (1994) also show that companies may choose to issue management reports on internal control without being obliged to do so. It is reasonable to assume that companies choose to do this because they believe that such reports add value to financial statement and internal control report users.[8] As shown by Bronson, Carcello and Raghunandan (2006) however, under voluntary disclosure regimes, a significant portion of firms will choose not disclose an internal control report and those that do will not make any statement with regards to the effectiveness of the internal controls (p. 35).

Naturally attention has been paid to the effects of Sarbanes-Oxley in the United States, and perhaps especially the Section 404 requirements. The results from these studies are too many to discuss within the scope of this thesis, but we would like to point out however that these disclosure requirements seems to have improved the quality of accruals (see Doyle, Ge & McVay, 2007 and Ashbaugh-Skaife et al. 2008). In a recent study, Shelton and Whittington (2008) show that under the mandated Sarbanes-Oxley Act the ARICs provide information to investors about investment risk and that it also impacts the likelihood of recommending stock to clients (p. 149).

These findings are also to some extent supported by an even more recent study by Ashbaugh-Skaife et al. (2009). Their results show that the 404 requirements will yield benefits through lower information risk and lower cost of equity (also see Sect. 5.3.7). However, additional studies in this area are needed to further corroborate these findings.

Other positive effects have also been examined based on the Sarbanes-Oxley requirements on internal control. As a direct result of these requirements, a number of internal control deficiencies have been disclosed by firms and it is unlikely that these deficiencies would otherwise have been disclosed to the general public. Gee and McVay (2005, pp. 153–154) found that, during the period 2002–2004, the material weaknesses in internal control were mostly made up of the following deficiency types:

---

[8] In a recent paper on the drivers of voluntary disclosures, Boessa and Kumar (2007) note on the subject that "*it has been frequently discussed that factors such as a company's effort to gain reputation, long-term value creation, market conditions, and pressures from corporate governing bodies may also be driving the voluntary disclosure practices of companies*" (p. 271). Their findings indicate that "*in addition to investors' information needs, factors such as company emphasis on stakeholder management, relevance of intangible asset, and market complexity affect both the volume as well as the quality of voluntary disclosures*" (p. 269).

- Lack of training.
- Deficiencies in the period-end reporting process and accounting policies.
- Deficient revenue-recognition policies.
- Lack of segregation of duties.
- Inappropriate account reconciliation.

These deficiencies, which were previously un-disclosed to investors, analysts and the general public, are now considered when the overall risk profile of companies is assessed. In a research paper on the benefits of Sarbanes-Oxley, Rittenberg and Miller (2005) made a survey of the assessments among internal auditors of the costs and benefits associated with Section 404-work. Results suggest that there have been significant benefits associated with the process of control identification, documentation and testing, and that future costs associated with Section 404 work will decrease. The findings in Rittenberg and Miller (2005, pp. 1–2) point to the following improvements:

- A more engaged control environment with active participation from the board, audit committee and management.
- More thoughtful analysis of monitoring controls.
- More structure to the year-end closing process and recording of journal entries.
- Implementation of anti-fraud controls with defined processes.
- Better understanding of the risks associated with general computer controls.
- Improved documentation of controls and control processes.
- Improved definition of controls, and the relationship of risks and controls.
- Improvement in audit trail.
- Control concepts more embedded in organizations.
- Re-implementation of basic controls which have been previously eroded.

From a Swedish perspective, the guidance issued by the SCGB in 2006 [Anvisning Nr.1-2006] explicitly stated that as a result of the new corporate governance code of 2004, companies had initiated ambitious work in order to improve risk management and internal control practices (Kollegiet för Svensk Bolagsstyrning, 2006a). From that statement, it is possible to deduce that the code has begun to have positive effects on the internal control systems of firms. Furthermore, in an earlier guidance issued in 2005 [Anvisning Nr.1-2005], it was suggested that internal controls in Swedish firms were of an informal nature and that directors and managers would have difficulties in making any public statement about the operating effectiveness of controls (Kollegiet för Svensk Bolagsstyrning,

---

[9] For a review of the concept and some of the effects that formalization may have on organizational performance, see for example studies such as Organ and Greene (1981), Dewar, Whetten and Boje (1980), House (1975), Podsakoff, Williams and Todor (1986), Hall, Johnson and Haas (1967), Agarwal (1993) and Michaels, Cron, Dubinsky and Joachimstahaler (1988). Building on earlier studies on formalization Hall, Johnson and Haas (1967) suggest that formalization "*is measured by the proportion of codified jobs and the range of variation that is tolerated within the rules of defining jobs. The higher the proportion of codified jobs and the less range of variation allowed the more formalized organization*" (p. 906).

2005, 2006b, p. 8). Companies thus needed to formalize their processes and controls, which could potentially correspond to another effect of the internal control requirements of the code of 2004. However, it may be important to recognize that formalization, defined as the degree to which the norms of a social system are made explicit (House, 1975, p. 22), may have both positive and negative effects on organizational performance.[9]

In order to monitor the effects of the Swedish code of Corporate Governance, the SCGB surveys the attitudes towards the corporate governance system in general and the code requirements specifically. This is done through bi-annual studies [Kodbarometern] in which two major user-groups are investigated: the general public [Allmänheten] and capital market stakeholders [Kapitalmarknaden]. The findings from the study of 2006 (Kollegiet för Svensk Bolagsstyrning, 2006c) suggest that capital market stakeholders generally display a high trust in the Swedish corporate governance system. They are also positive to how the code is associated with the quality of corporate governance. The results also show that overall the general public is positive in their attitudes towards the Swedish corporate governance, although to a somewhat lesser extent than capital market stakeholders.

In the most recent survey by the SCGB (Kollegiet för Svensk Bolagsstyrning, 2009) which was done in the midst of the financial crisis, the findings suggest that unsurprisingly the general public displays a somewhat lower confidence in the Swedish corporate governance system compared to the previous measurement. The capital market stakeholder group still exhibits strong confidence in the corporate governance system and are also fairly positive to updates made in the Swedish corporate governance code in 2008 (p. 11).

It is undoubtedly so that both mandatory and semi-mandatory internal control disclosure requirements significantly influence the internal control and risk practices of firms. Previous studies suggest that reporting requirements on internal controls will produce both costs and benefits. Research also suggests that designing competent internal control reports is difficult. Users of internal control reports need information which add value in their decision-making process – undoubtedly a challenging task for both regulators and preparers.

Different reporting regimes may be classified on the basis of the scope and requirement of the regulations. From a United Kingdom-perspective, Spira and Page (2003) suggest that the trend is to move towards a broader scope with less stringent reporting (p. 650). The authors also point to the importance of considering the control environment of firms when implementing reporting requirements – otherwise substantial adjustment costs may incur (p. 658). This can be understood as a realization that both rational (agency) and behavioural (institutional) theories can contribute to our understanding of the benefits and side-effects of reporting. The internal control disclosure requirements in the Swedish code remain a source of debate (see Lekvall 2008; Brandinger, 2008a, 2008b).

With a global move towards convergence in national corporate governance principles (see Davies, 2008) it may be appropriate to examine further the use and usefulness of internal control and risk disclosure requirements and how these are associated with corporate governance quality (see Chap. 6 for future research opportunities).

5.3.6 Corporate Governance Mechanism

Earlier we claimed that internal control has a fairly close relationship to corporate governance of firms and the way owners and directors are able to oversee and protect firm assets, through for example various internal control regimes (see Kirkpatrick, 1962). A number of actors are concerned about the internal control systems of firms. The director, the manager, the designer, the auditor, the analyst and the regulator to name only a few of the principal parties involved. In discussions about internal control, it is inevitable that the corporate governance framework of firms comes up.

A number of stakeholders, internal to the firm, undoubtedly have a say when it comes to the internal control system of the firm – the board of directors, the audit committee, the internal and external auditors and most of all management. The rather recent invention of operational risk based on Basel 2 banking regulation, and the subsequent creation of additional internal agents such as risk officers, are only the latest in the line of stakeholders involved in internal control (see Hutter & Power, eds. 2005; Power, 2005, 2006, 2007; Mikes, 2009).

Because of the many actors concerned, and also because internal control is sometimes referred to as a key corporate governance mechanism, it seems necessary to provide a brief description of the key pillars in the corporate governance structure (Cohen, Krishnamoorthy & Wright, 2004) since they are all vital for the oversight, design, management, assessment, regulation and analysis of internal control. The issues related to each of these actors are far too many and complex to provide an account of here. Instead, we will concentrate on their key duties with reference to internal controls, those key duties which are most often referred to in texts on internal controls.

5.3.6.1 The Corporate Governance Framework

Corporate governance, or organizational governance, a concept increasingly emphasized today (Netter, Poulsen & Stegemoller, 2009) has been defined in many ways. As mentioned in Chap. 1, Sect. 1.1, we refer to governance as "*overseeing that the business is run properly*" (Lazarides & Drimpetas, 2008, p. 74). In Cohen, Krishnamoorthy and Wright (2004) an illustrative figure has been provided that describes the key pillars in an effective corporate governance system (p. 89). This overview of the corporate governance system is also depicted in Fig. 5.6 and according to authors, the five *internal* corporate governance actors comprise of:

- The board of directors.
- The audit committee.
- The external auditors.
- The internal auditors.
- Executive management.

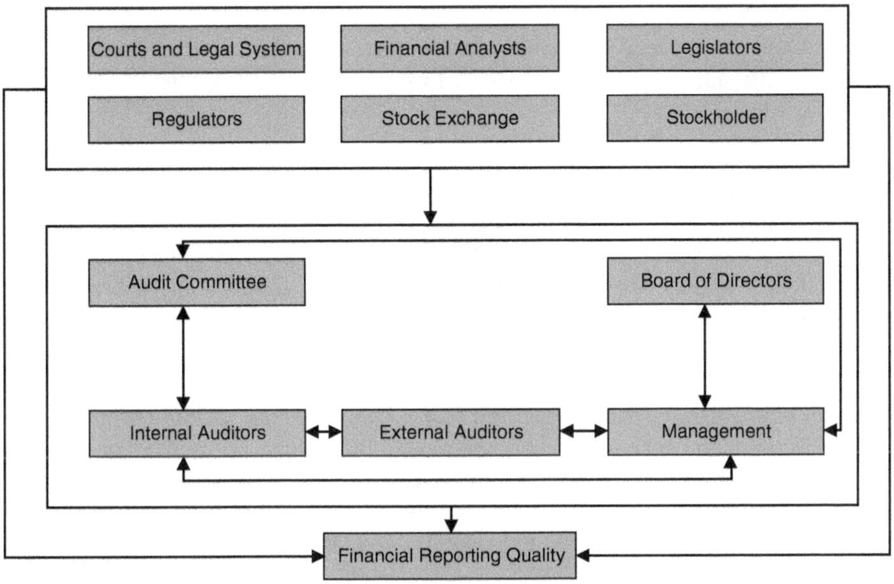

Fig. 5.6 The corporate governance system (Cohen, Krishnamoorthy & Wright, 2004, p. 89)

External actors also constitute vital parts of the corporate governance framework and include regulators, stockholders, analysts and the stock exchanges. They impose important governance rules, regulations and requirements of different sorts on firms. Regulatory bodies in particular, are important for internal control practices since they impose risk management and internal control disclosure requirements for public companies. Credit rating agencies such as Standards and Poor's should also be mentioned here, since such firms increasingly consider the effectiveness of board oversight over risk management when they asses and evaluate firm performance (COSO, 2009c, p. 3; Grant Thornton, 2009a, pp. 5–6).

The roles and responsibilities of the internal actors illustrated in Fig. 5.6 are to large extent regulated by formal law and regulations and therefore will obviously vary between countries (see Davies, 2008). According to Monks and Minow (2004) however "*the law imposes on the board a strict and absolute fiduciary duty to ensure that a company is run in the long-term interests of the owners, the shareholders*" (p. 195) and the board's primary duty is to monitor management on behalf of the shareholders (p. 195). The directors are the owner's representative whose purpose under law is to safeguard the assets of the firm (p. 196) and they constitute the crucial link between a dispersed and un-powerful group of shareholders and the small but highly powerful group of senior executives. According to Monks and Minnow (pp. 200–201) the generally accepted duties of the board of directors include:

- Select, evaluate and replace the chief executive officer.
- Oversee the conduct of the corporation's business, which include reviewing financial objectives, significant strategies and plans of the corporation.
- Review and approve major changes in accounting principles and policies.

- Provide advice and counsel to top management.
- Select and recommend to shareholder candidates for the board of directors.
- Review the adequacy of the systems to comply with all applicable laws and regulations.

Legally most jurisdictions prescribe that directors have a duty of loyalty to the firm's shareholders as well as a duty of care, which means that the directors must exercise due diligence in making decisions (p. 200). Much research exists on the board of directors and its committees. Research that has examined the composition, independence, knowledge and expertise, effectiveness, duties and responsibilities of the board as well as the association between board characteristics and earnings management and fraud (Cohen, Krishnamoorthy & Wright, 2004).

A result of the current financial crisis of 2009, there has been an even stronger focus on board risk oversight practices (see COSO, 2009b). COSO points to four vital areas that contribute to sound board oversight: understanding the risk philosophy and risk appetite, knowing about the effectiveness of the risk management or the organization, review the entity's portfolio of risk, and be up-to-date with the most significant risks and how they are treated, through internal controls (see COSO, 2009b).

The *audit committee* has gained increasingly more interest and attention during the last decade, perhaps due to recent publicly visible corporate mal-functions. In Hermanson and Rittenberg (2003) the responsibilities of the audit committee are divided into three primary duties: monitoring of the financial reporting process, *overseeing the internal controls* as well coordinating and overseeing the work by external and internal auditors (p. 50). The responsibilities of the audit committee are illustrated in Fig. 5.7. According to the combined code on corporate governance in the United Kingdom, the audit committee responsibilities spell out a similar set of responsibilities (FRC, 2008, p. 17).

The importance of an effective audit committee is widely recognized in both professional and academic writing as well as in most regulatory texts. In a Welsh study on effective working relationships between audit committees and internal audit, Davies (2009, p. 44) claims that "*the role of the audit committee has definitely evolved*".

> While the audit committee's basic function – oversight of the financial reporting process – has not changed over the years, their responsibilities have been increasing to include risk management, control, compliance and special investigations (Soltani quoted in Davies, 2009, p. 44)

Audit committee's expanded, or evolved, responsibilities are also represented in their top concerns. Responses from audit committee members and directors suggest that risk management is top concern no. 2 and maintaining internal controls is at no.4 (www.directorship.com, April/May, 2009). A recent comment in the Swedish media suggests that, while risk management is currently a major concern for board members, it is also a complex matter that board members may need to address in a more structured manner (see af Ekenstam, 2009).

Fig. 5.7 Audit committee responsibilities (Hermanson & Rittenberg, 2003, p. 50)

As mentioned earlier, the implementation of the European Union directive on auditors and auditing [EU:s direktiv om revisorer och revision] has resulted in changes to the Limited Liability Companies Act [Aktiebolagslagen, 2005, p. 551], which now regulates audit committees for publicly traded companies (Kollegiet för Svensk Bolagsstyrning, 2009, p. 7). This development further highlights the importance of audit committee duties with reference to financial reporting, risk management and internal control.

Recent studies on audit committee work point to the importance of having effective working relationship with key parties, such as with the internal audit function (Davies, 2009). Studies on audit committee work have also shown that the informal processes and structures (as opposed to the formal ones which are often specified in corporate codes and regulations) are important and may enhance audit committee effectiveness (Turley & Zaman, 2007). Today, in 2011, board oversight over the effectiveness of risk management and internal control, including the work of audit committees in this respect, represent key issues in organizational governance.

Both internal and external auditors constitute important pillars in the corporate governance framework. This is only natural perhaps, since originally internal control was primarily a matter for accountants and auditors. For the accountant employed at the firm, the task was to design and install a *system of internal checks* that would reduce the risk of mistakes, errors, fraud or other improper actions (Bower and Schlosser, 1965), while for the external auditor, the task was to appropriately consider the internal control system in the financial statement audit so that audit effort could be performed efficiently and effectively. When appropriate the external auditor made recommendations for changes in the internal control system to make it more adequate or effective. It still remains the responsibility of the statutory auditor to consider the control system of the firm when planning the audit engagement (FAR SRS, 2009: see relevant sections of RS 300, 310 and 400). The importance of external independent auditors cannot be overestimated since they "*play a crucial role in helping to promote financial reporting quality*" (Cohen, Krishnamoorthy & Wright, 2004, p. 102).

With the separation of ownership and control (Jensen & Meckling, 1976; Jensen & Fama, 1983) a gap developed between owners and those in charge of managing the firm's assets. Furthermore, as firms grew increasingly larger, the gap between policy-making management and labour widened. As we have mentioned earlier, agency-issues may occur on all levels of the organization, between managers and employees (Eisenhardt, 1989, p. 58).

As firms grew larger, it was no longer possible for a single accountant or manager to keep track of the design and operating effectiveness of the system of internal checks. Therefore the other auditing profession, that of internal auditing, with its origin in the accounting field, was established as a means for top management to establish and maintain adequate internal control.

Compared to the public accountant, the internal auditor was partial to the company which prevented him/her to *truly* represent the shareholders, in comparison to the public accountant (Garbade, 1944, p. 417). But as noted by Garbade, from a managerial view-point, this drawback becomes an asset as the internal auditor is much better informed about company policies, procedures, products, staff and company culture, thus enabling him/her to be more effective and efficient (p. 417). The company's investments in internal auditing is often perceived to be derived from principal-agent issues whereby it can be regarded either as a bonding cost incurred by the agents or as a monitoring cost incurred by the principals (Carcello, Hermanson & Raghunandan, 2005, p. 72).

The role of the internal auditor has gradually changed. Originally, internal audit was a primary tool for management to make sure that controls were in place and executed properly, as can be seen from early research papers on the subject (see Garbade, 1944; Haun, 1955). Today, this has changed dramatically and many organizations are required to have an internal audit function. This requirement is often based on guidance from supervisory authorities or stock exchange listing requirements. Subsequently its role, mandate and reporting lines have also changed. As commented by Ramamoorti (2003), there has been a gradual move from being an internal management department focused on the protection of loss of cash and other asset, to being an independent department as stipulated by recent internal audit professional practices. As Ramamoorti (2003) expressed the situation; there has been a shift from *audit for management* emphasis towards an *audit of management* approach (p. 4). Studies have also shown the importance of independent reporting structures on the perceptions of financial statement user, with regard to for example the perceptions about internal audit's fraud detection capabilities (see James, 2003).

Today, the internal audit activity is considered to be a key pillar in an effective corporate governance system. A close relationship between internal audit and the audit committee has the potential to enhance the corporate governance capabilities of firms (Cohen, Krishnamoorthy & Wright, 2004, p. 125; also see Davies, 2009). An effective relationship between external and internal auditors may also have value creating properties (see Haron, Chambers & Ismail, 2004).

Traditionally, internal auditors are considered to be experts in risk and internal controls, and the positive effect of internal auditors on the quality of internal controls has been shown by Rae and Subramaniam (2008) for example. The internal audit activity is also considered the single most successful control, or process, for detecting fraud incidents (see Fagerberg, 2008, p. 42). As risk management functions emerge and evolve as a result of new practical guidance (COSO, 2004) and banking regulation on risk (see Power, 2005), the auditors' relationship and interface to risk management functions is receiving a great deal of attention. Fraser and Henry (2007) show that existing internal audit shops work somewhat differently with regards to risk management functions, depending on the level of maturity of the company's risk management practices (Sarens & Beelde, 2006) and internal auditors' role in risk management is strongly linked with the development stage of the risk management system (p. 77). Sarens and Beelde (p. 78) conclude that:

> It should be clear that top management has to become aware of the usefulness of a formalized risk management system and their specific responsibilities in risk management. Top management has to give the right signals to the lower management levels in order to convince them of their operational responsibilities related to for example the development and implementation of internal controls.

The final pillar of the corporate governance system is represented by the executive management. The importance of management for the effectiveness of internal control cannot be overestimated. Management has been regarded as a driver for stronger governance and oversight, but also as a crucial function for instilling the right values and behaviors' (see for example Holmes et al. 2002). Practical frameworks such as the COSO (1992, 2004) as well as professional audit standards, also often refer to the importance of the *control environment* and *management's philosophy for good internal controls.* It is probable that managers are shaped by their philosophies and attitudes to risk which accordingly also shape how they consider, develop and monitor internal control systems (based on Mikes, 2009, p. 22).

If the duties of the board are to monitor and oversee management, management is concerned with the performance of the firm (Monks & Minow, 2004, pp. 254–294). Hermanson and Rittenberg (2003) argue that management is responsible for managing organizational risks and for implementing controls to mitigate such risks (p. 33). Cohen, Krishnamoorthy and Wright (2004) point out that management "*has the primary responsibility for ensuring that the company's financial reporting system, including the overall control environment, results in a high quality of financial reports*" (p. 142). Managements' installation of controls undoubtedly represents a challenging task – something we have mentioned earlier in Sect. 5.3.3 and also highlighted in a rather recent literature review of internal auditing by Allegrini et al. (2006). It is suggested in that study that internal auditors need to assume teaching roles to educate and train management in order to make them aware of their risk management responsibilities (p. 849).

In another paper on the role of internal auditors' in risk management (Sarens & De Beelde, 2006) where a comparison between United States and Belgium companies has been made, anecdotal evidence suggests that auditors are confronted by management with the question; "who is responsible for internal control? Their answer of course is; you are responsible!" (p. 71).

> They (management) should realize that an internal control is an integral part of their responsibilities, because some management levels do not realize that they are responsible for internal controls. Currently, this is one of the major stumbling blocks (p. 75).

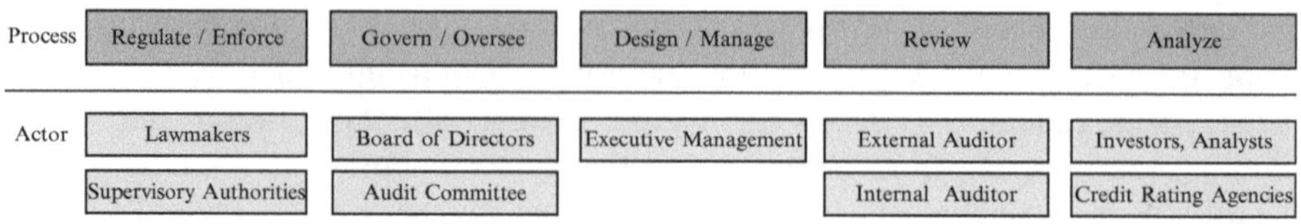

Fig. 5.8 A stakeholder-process model of internal control

Such statements appear closely associated with Oliviero's (2002, p. 76) claim that internal control architects are sorely missed (see Sect. 5.3.3). Knowledge and understanding of internal controls are of vital importance, both from an internal control oversight- and performance perspective. Any lack of knowledge and understanding is likely to result in internal control weaknesses or in failure in the way the overall organization's internal control system is coordinated, managed and governed.

We conclude that a number of actors are fundamental for the effective design, application and oversight of the internal control system. Each actor plays their own part in the *internal control framework* of firms. While the boards of directors are ultimately responsible for internal control, audit committees seem to become increasingly important with also expanding responsibilities for risk-related matters.

Below in Fig. 5.8, we end by summarizing some of the key actors in the internal control framework and how they are associated with the high-level processes of internal control. However, the figure also includes external stakeholders such as regulators, supervisory authorities, analysts and investors. We have also added credit rating agencies as stakeholders in this internal control actor-process model since they increasingly take into account the risk management and internal control systems of firms when doing their assessments. The figure is obviously a simplification however.

5.3.7 *Outcomes*

Determining the outcomes of an internal control system is not without difficulty. Reviewing earlier contingency-based management control research, Chenhall (2003) shows that prior research on management control systems has covered different types of outcomes. These include the *use and usefulness* of control systems where researchers have focused on issues such as usage of the system, or the usefulness of the information provided by the system. Another type of outcome has been the *behavioral effects* of control systems where the association between job satisfaction and stress, and the application of controls has been examined. The final, and perhaps most interesting, outcome has focused on the *organizational effects* of management control, such as unit performance (pp. 131–134).

Chenhall suggests that these outcome measures are very different, and also more or less adequate as outcome measures. There is also an implied connection between them. Better controls lead to improved use and usage which in turn would lead to better decision-making processes, thus leading to enhanced organizational performance. Such a connection is not completely straightforward to make however, as pointed out by Chenhall (2003, p. 132), and may be even more difficult to make due the basic nature of internal control and the indirect influence that internal control has on organizational decision-making quality. Higher usage of certain internal controls, such as the segregation of various duties, dual approvals of payments, various account reconciliation checks or even key entity-wide policies, will not necessarily lead to improved organizational performance.

Even though contingency-based research on control systems has achieved a great deal during the last 50 years, there is still a lot left to be known about control design and outcomes (see Chapman, Hopwood & Shields, eds. 2007). This seems to be even more true in the case of internal controls research Similar to control in contingency-based control research (see Chenhall, 2003, pp. 134–136), one problem is that determining the *criteria for control quality* is difficult (see Kinney, 2000, pp. 86–88). Kinney claims that the problem of accurately determining the criteria for internal control quality constitutes one of the biggest barriers for researching internal control (p. 86).

Contingency-based research on control systems often finds it necessary to include effectiveness as the dependent variable as this provides evidence as to the fit between the control system and the different organizational variables (Langfield-Smith, 1997, p. 226). Internal control researchers speak of both the quality (see Kinney, 2000; Rae & Subramaniam, 2008) and the effectiveness (see Jokipii, 2006) of the control of the system. In a stream of research papers following the introduction of the SOX in the United States, company practices have been examined using Sections 302 and 404 as the point of departure. In this research, internal control quality is often defined and measured as the extent of disclosed material weaknesses in internal control (Hoitash, Hoitash & Bedard, 2009, p. 840) or internal control deficiencies (Ashbaugh-Skaife et al. 2009). For each internal control deficiency, the effectiveness of the internal control system will be reduced accordingly. With no internal control deficiencies to report, the firm will have effective internal controls in place, i.e. controls will provide reasonable assurance that objectives will be met. COSO (1992) states that the system of internal control can be judged to be effective when:

> The boards of directors and management have reasonable assurance that they understand the extent to which the entity's operations objectives are being achieved, published financial statements are being prepared reliable, and the applicable laws and regulations are being complied with (COSO in Jokipii, 2006, pp. 63–64).

Since this piece of unique regulation (Hoitash, Hoitash & Bedard, 2009, p. 845) mandates public disclosures of significant internal control deficiencies, such measurements are possible. It is however, important to point out that since the requirements cover financial reporting quality only in these instances, internal control quality will only relate to financial reporting. These types of measurements require that internal control deficiencies are publicly disclosed.

In the doctoral dissertation by Jokipii (2006) on the structure and effectiveness of the internal control system, the effectiveness of internal control is defined as management perceptions of how well objectives are met. This is examined through a self-assessment questionnaire which is a method rather common in contingency-based research studies (Chenhall, 2003, p. 134).

Even though existing research on the outcomes of internal controls may be somewhat scarce, prior research on internal control provides some clues as to the outcomes of internal controls. In the following sections, we will briefly discuss some of these outcomes of internal controls. We do not apply any existing framework to categorize outcomes, although some recent studies categorize outcomes into direct and indirect benefits and costs. Usually these studies are done within the US regulatory environment of Sarbanes-Oxley.

5.3.7.1 Risk and Cost

Controls cost money. This is a fact which is also associated with the inherent limitations of internal control. A paper by Tacket, Wolf and Claypool (2006) examines the costs related to the internal control practices under Sarbanes-Oxley Act in the United States, based on the Section 404-requirements. The compliance costs here refer to the financial investments into internal controls. In the case of Section 404, these have been largely measured by calculating time spent by companies on section 404-related work (i.e. internal labor work), additional audit fees and external consulting and technology expenses (see Krishnan, Rama & Zhang, 2008). The results of the study, as mentioned earlier, suggest that monetary costs of SOX-compliance have been substantial, especially for smaller firms (p. 184).

Irrespective of the type of regulatory regime that firms are reporting under however, monetary investments need to be made in internal control. Under strict internal control disclosure requirements monetary costs may (initially) be significant. A firm which operates in a less strict regulatory environment will still have to invest in internal controls although it will be able to do so more freely perhaps. Based on the internal and external variables of the firm (see Sect. 5.3.3) the board and the executive management need to decide what type of investments they need to make.

Coletti, Sedatole and Towry (2005) state that "*control, broadly defined, comprises of the various policies and procedures that the firms use to mitigate different types of risks*" (p. 480). This would imply a relationship between control and risk, whereby controls mitigate organizational risk exposure. It follows that as control strength increases, risk will typically decrease accordingly.

If we add the element of cost to this model, the relationship between control and cost could potentially increase as financial investments are made in the internal controls, while typically risk would decrease accordingly. As financial investments are made in control systems to reduce risk, the cost of control will increase accordingly. Since the control systems of firms are likely to generate costs which are not insignificant, these basic relationships point to the importance of designing *cost-effective internal controls*, allocated to areas *where they most matter and make economic sense*.

It is however unlikely that firms are able to make an economic cost-benefit analysis for every investment in internal controls, neither does this seem reasonable. From an overall firm perspective however, it makes sense to think of cost as one of the factors to consider when analyzing internal control design options. This is also in line with practical and regulatory guidance on internal control (see for example FRC, 2005, p. 6). Value-for-money controls, which mitigate risk exposures based on the set risk appetite but which also take into account any other positive benefits that may come out of operating those controls, need to be installed.

The relationships described above are obviously simplifications since a number of factors have not been accounted for, such as dynamic effects and different periods in time. Moreover, the costs-consequences of increased control strength do not necessarily have to develop as described above. It seems perfectly possible to have informal, and less costly, controls associated with high control strength. In addition, these basic relationships do not account for the fact that risk is not only represented by a corresponding cost, but also with benefits. Nevertheless, organizational outcomes from internal control include (mitigated) risk exposures and cost consequences of controls which it would appear need to be considered in the overall design of internal controls.

5.3.7.2 Disclosure Outcomes

The effectiveness of a control system and disclosures about any internal control deficiencies are inter-related. Following the high-profile Enron-failure there has been a stream of research papers examining the design and effects of the Sarbanes-Oxley Act (see DeFond & Francis, 2005). Previous research on the economic consequences of the Sarbanes-Oxley Act has primarily focused on the costs of compliance (see Tacket, Wolf & Claypool, 2004, 2006; Raghunandan & Rama, 2006; Foster, Ornstein & Shastri, 2007; Krishnan, Rama & Zhang, 2008). Fewer studies have systematically looked at the benefits (Rittenberg & Miller, 2005, p. 1; Ashbaugh-Skaife, Collins, Kinney & Lafond, 2009, p. 2)

More recently however, researchers have begun to examine whether effective internal controls under the Sarbanes-Oxley reporting requirements have had positive effects. One study already referred to in Sect. 5.3.5 is Rittenberg and Miller (2005) who surveyed internal auditors regarding the effects of SOX. Recent papers have also examined the association between auditor's opinion of internal control and investor's evaluation (see Shelton & Whittington, 2008). The influence of internal control deficiencies on firm risk and cost of equity has also been examined (see Ashbaugh-Skaife, Collins, Kinney & Lafond, 2009).

Shelton and Wittington (2008, pp. 149–150) found for example that the auditors' report on the effectiveness of internal controls under the Sarbanes-Oxley Act provides information about investment risk, whereby adverse audit opinions regarding the effectiveness of internal controls results in higher analyst assessment of company risk. In a paper from 2009, Ashbaugh-Skaife, Collins, Kinney and Lafond explore the association between internal control quality and risk and any potential benefits in terms of cost of equity. Specifically they examined, for example, whether firms that disclosed internal control deficiencies exhibit higher cost of equity relative those firms with no disclosed deficiencies. The results from the study indicate, amongst other things that this seems to be the case (see 2009, p. 39).

It is reasonable to expect that a company that receives a less than favorable assessment of the effectiveness of their internal controls may have to pay a premium for that. A recent study by SEC (Securities and Exchange Commission) in the United States, on the Sarbanes-Oxley Section 404-requirements, also point to both direct effects (e.g. better internal control quality, financial reporting quality or financial reporting process efficiency) and indirect effects (e.g. investor confidence, ability to raise capital or costs related to risk aversion) of the Section 404-requirements (see also Krishnan, Rama & Zhang, 2008; Ahmed, McAnally, Rasmussen & Weaver, 2010). The report by SEC concludes that compliance cost resulting from the Section 404-rules are steadily decreasing but a majority of the company insiders still perceive the cost to outweigh the benefits (2009, pp. 95–97). Views often differ, however, depending on whether you are an external user (i.e. an analyst or investor) or a company insider (such as an executive).

It is probable that the future will see more research papers which examine the association between internal control disclosure requirements, the disclosure of internal control design, effectiveness and any deficiencies and the way this is associated with various costs and benefits. Understanding the effects that internal control disclosure requirements have on firms is important in any regulatory setting. Building on previous studies (see e.g. SEC, 2009; Krishnan, Rama & Zhang, 2008; Ahmed, McAnally, Rasmussen & Weaver, 2010) that examine the direct and indirect benefits and costs experienced by firms will enable us to better understand internal control disclosure outcomes.

5.3.7.3 Fraud Prevention and Financial Reporting Quality

Fraud detection and prevention capabilities represent a direct benefit, or positive outcome, of internal control. Already from the very beginning, the auditor considered the system of internal control to be a *deterrent against fraudulent behavior*. The importance of internal control to protect shareholders against company and management fraud is also represented in agency theory on control, under the term the organizational rules of the game (see Schnatterly, 2003, p. 588). In this case, effective controls are regarded as a tool for reducing information asymmetries between principals and agents so that dishonest or fraudulent behaviors may be avoided.

For a long time now, a key pillar in the internal control system has been appropriately segregated duties (see Lee, 1971). The segregation of duties generally refers to the appropriate *segregation of activities between people and functions*. The activities generally refer to authorizing, approving, recording, issuing and receiving assets, and making payments. Little and Best (2003) conclude that "*research on internal controls and external auditors judgment has indicated that the assessment of the separation of duties is a dominating factor in the auditors evaluation of the internal control structure*" (p. 420). It is assumed that adequately segregated duties will deter or detect fraudulent activity, thus having positive effects on firm performance. Other fraud controls may include fraud policies, telephone hotlines, employee reference checks, fraud vulnerability review, vendor contract reviews, analytical reviews, password protection, firewalls and digital analysis (see Bierstaker, Brody & Pacini, 2006, p. 523).

In an early paper on behavioral hypotheses of internal control, Carmichael (1970) argues that "*an effective internal control system, by threat of prompt exposure, will deter an individual from committing fraud*" (p. 237). Underlying these hypotheses are assumptions about human nature which appear to have their origins in the modern theory of the firm (see Zannetos, 1964) and which describe that individuals are willful and purposeful participants in organizations which is reflected in their behavior. Thus, organizational objectives may conflict with individual objectives, interests and behaviors (Zannetos, 1964). Carmichael (1970) claims that "*individuals have inherent mental, moral and physical weaknesses; therefore internal control methods and measures are necessary to achieve information processing system goals*" (p. 237). Zannetos (1964) argues on the subject:

> Another consequence of the assumption of purposeful behavior is the possibility of substitution of personal goals for those of the organization as a determinant of motivation. This substitution, of course, can be either unintentional, because of the lack of proper information as to what the individuals are expected to do and on how their activities contribute toward the overall goals of the organization, or else intentional. The information and control systems of the firm have a vital role to play in both cases, although the nature and difficulty of this role is different, depending on the condition that necessitates it. If we assume, however, that human nature is inherently good and it is only through ignorance or corruptive influence by the operational environment that misdirection occurs, then the two cases merge essentially into one, and result in unified information-control system requirements. And thus, because preventive, guiding as well as corrective characteristics are the essential elements of any managerial control system (p. 864).

Coleman (2001) suggests that there are three factors which explain the occurrence of fraud: *motive/incentive, neutralisation/attitude and opportunity*. Employee incentives are a strong driving force for committing fraud, and that employees may act as a result of a crisis or an opportunity. The attitude-element involves how individuals are able to rationalize their behaviours in order to justify them. The final element relates to the circumstance of the situation. Is there is an opportunity to commit fraud, and if so, how significant is it? Obviously this final element is closely associated with the status of the internal control system – a weaker system of controls will create greater possibilities for fraud than a stronger one.

Unsurprisingly, inadequate internal controls have often been found in companies exposed to fraud (Fagerberg, 2008, p. 58) underscoring the crucial role that good internal controls play in deterring and preventing occupational fraud. Opportunity-related reasons for committing fraud include insufficient controls, external collaboration, management override, internal collaboration, anonymity within the company and foreign business customers (Fagerberg, 2008, p. 45). Signs of weak internal controls include lack of integrity and ignoring ethical values, a weak control environment, failure to link top-level objectives with objectives for the operating and support units, poor communication within the organization and an inability to understand and react to changing conditions (Fagerberg, 2008, p. 46). If internal controls are to have a fully deterrent effect it seems to be important that people are aware of the organizational rules and of the fact that controls are in place to hinder inappropriate behaviours. Basically let them know that someone is watching (Wells, 2002). People should also have an understanding of the consequences of possible violations (based on BRÅ, p. 21).

One of the aims behind the SOX in the United States has been to improve the likelihood that internal controls detect fraudulent activity (Foster, Ornstein & Shastri, 2007). Foster, Ornstein and Shastri (2007) suggest that SOX, and its Section 404-requirments regarding reporting on internal control effectiveness, appears to have improved financial reporting quality in such a way that material internal control weaknesses have been identified, reported and consequently addressed. In their evaluation of the Sarbanes-Oxley Act in the United States, Tacket, Wolf and Claypool (2006) conclude about its mitigating effect on fraud risk that:

> There will be some modest deterrence to corporate fraud and financial statement misrepresentation because fraud methods will need to become more sophisticated to succeed. More specifically, future financial statement frauds will likely be based on collusion between senior management and selected members of the audit committee or board of directors (p. 322).

Further, in a recent paper on the association between the quality of internal control procedures and the perceptions of organizational justice and fraud, performed on companies regulated under the Sarbanes-Oxley Act in the United States, Rae and Subramaniam (2008, p. 119) state that:

> The incidence of fraud appears to be higher when both internal control procedure quality and employee perceptions of organizational justice are poor. As such, management control strategies for minimizing employee fraud need to consider both the quality of internal control procedures and the perceived fairness of organizational rules and policies.

Another traditional type of internal control outcome refers to the output of the financial reporting process, namely the quality of financial reports. Along with fraud prevention and protection of assets, fair and accurate financial reports have for long been a driver for the importance of internal control. Financial reporting quality in this way refers to one of the direct benefits of internal control. High-quality financial report may in turn be able to drive more indirect effects of internal control, such as the views and perceptions of investors and analysts. In this context, adequate and effective internal control (over financial reporting) is said to have a direct relationship to the quality of accounting and financial reporting (Ashbaugh-Skaife, Collins, Kinney & LaFond, 2008, p. 218). Since the introduction of the Sarbanes-Oxley act in the United States, a number of academic studies have investigated the relationship between internal control effectiveness (measured for example by disclosed internal control deficiencies) and financial reporting quality (measured for example by the quality of accruals, or misstatements etc.). A study that examines the way in which internal control effectiveness influences financial reporting quality is Ashbaugh-Skaife, Collins, Kinney and LaFond, (2008). In that study, they find strong support for that the quality of internal control affects the quality of accruals.

5.3.7.4 Efficiency and Effectiveness in Operations

Achieving (financial) reporting quality and compliance with laws and regulations is largely within the control of the organisation (COSO, 2004, p. 39). To some extent, this is also true for the protection of firm assets. The safeguarding of firm resources, however, is also part of the efficient and effective use or resources – i.e. the operations objective category according to the COSO frameworks (see COSO, 2004, p. 21). A number of variables may enable or hinder the organization in using their resources efficiency and effectively, many of which is external to the firm and thus partly outside its control (COSO, 2004, p. 39). Related to strategic and operational type of objectives, internal controls thus produce assurance that management and directors receives adequate and reliable information about the progress towards such objectives.

We have earlier pointed out that controls should not only make sure that bad things do not happen – they should also make sure that good things do happen. Too much risk is just gambling and most likely things will go bad – too little risk means no progress, only stagnation (Picket, 2001, p. 46). Accordingly, internal control may function both as an enabler and as a barrier for organizational performance, thus potentially impacting on the profit and loss statement of firms. Earlier, we mentioned the cost consequences of control, the ability of internal control to mitigate fraud risk and also the possible effects of strict disclosure requirements on internal control under the Sarbanes-Oxley Act in the United States. These outcomes will be related to firm performance, in one way or the other.

However, as we briefly mentioned in connection to Fig. 5.16, controls are not only associated with corresponding costs but also associated with benefits, since controls also enable things to go right. Thus controls and risk have benefits which may be positively associated with firm performance. This is related to internal controls over efficiency and effectiveness in operations and the manner in which internal controls provide assurance that firm objectives are met with regard to this. The implied connection is that stronger internal controls will provide better assurance that firms are efficient and effective in their operations, i.e. that they are resource-effective while also achieving established performance-related objectives. Weaker internal controls will instead disable than enable such firm performance. However, associating internal controls over efficiency and effectiveness in operations with firm performance is not without difficulty. One question for example is to appropriately define organizational performance (Chenhall, 2003, p. 135).

In Sect. 5.3.3 we pointed to the importance of building internal control design capabilities. The basis of this argument is that internal control capabilities may be a source of competitive advantage. Strong capabilities would translate into better designed, better balanced, better integrated controls, which in turn, could have positive impact on organizational performance, and vice versa. Controls need to be installed in a cost-effective manner, and take into consideration the circumstances of the firm and be allocated to significant risk areas (Picket, 2001, pp. 44–45). To install strict controls in low risk areas would be neither an efficient nor effective use of firm resources. Thus a less than dynamic, or unfocused, system of internal controls could potentially impact negatively on organizational performance and vice versa. Writers on internal control appear to be in agreement here, but limited empirical evidence seems to be available on the association between internal control practices and different levels of organizational performance.

What appears to be important from a firm performance perspective is that internal control should not only *contain activity* – it should also *allow for innovation and creativity* (Picket, 2001, pp. 219–220). Picket argues that if internal controls focus too much on restraining and containing business activity, it will have a negative impact on firm performance. Picket states that:

> At first it seems that controls work in conflict with these creative energies; they pin people down and lead to excessive paperwork. Rigid rules on accountability may mean people refuse to make decisions for fear of reprimand. Where these decisions are confined to a narrow frame... (...) we lose accountability...(...)...In the end, we lose this accountability by enforcing it too rigidly. We take no chances but make no progress (pp. 221–222).

Instead, Picket argues for pursuing a state which he labels structured innovation "*where controls keep pace with change, driven by change, sets direction and where there is measurement and review*" (p. 224). Change but also control. The overall control framework of the firm, or the management control system, should therefore allow for different types of internal controls. These controls should be precise and set standards for generally accepted ways of work – but there should also be controls which function as drivers as opposed to restrainers. The managerial task is thus to identify the different areas which require the different types of controls. Allowing deviation and initiative that is based on the firm's need (based on Picket, 2001, pp. 250–251). This is much in line with the theories developed by Simons (1987, 1990, 1991 and 1995) on the "levers of control". Picket (2001) suggests a push-pull strategy for internal controls which allows for restraint and accountability as well as drive and initiative (p. 251).

In our view, there generally seem to be two ways in which internal control quality may enable or disable the efficient and effective use of resources. The system of internal control represents a basic and fundamental feature of the overall organizational control system that produces assurances regarding reliability of information at large (Pfister, 2009, p. 26). As such, it may prevent data and information inaccuracies and irregularities throughout the business processes of firms. Firstly, installing to many checks will simply hinder performance. You control much, but you gain little. Secondly, adequate and effective controls will enable decision-making quality in firms. Internal control work indirectly to assure that the data which is identified, transported, presented and communicated through organizational decision-making processes are correct and accordingly can be trusted. In this way, internal control may produce better decision-making quality, which in turn enables better use of firm resources.

Few research papers seem to be available on the association between internal control practices and firm performance. The paper by Chenhall (2003) shows that associating control system features with organizational performance is a challenging task (p. 134). Often, these studies include self-assessments where individuals provide indications about how controls contribute to their or their unit's performance. This method was also applied by Jokipii (2006), who investigated managers' perceptions of the extent to which internal control objectives are met. Another issue however is making a connection between weak or strong internal controls and firm performance for example through share price or returns. Extracting how the functioning of different elements of internal control and statements about their effectiveness impact on such measures is not done without difficulty. Nevertheless, increased understanding of these connections seems to be crucial.

Theoretical and empirically based studies point to a number of outcomes that internal controls may have. These include fraud prevention capabilities (a sort of behaviour outcome following the categorization by Chenhall, 2003, p. 132), fraud detection capabilities, outcomes from reporting and disclosure requirements on internal controls and cost and risk consequences. Building on the findings from contingency-based management control research, (Chenhall, 2003) outcomes may be classified into the use and usefulness of the system, behavioural outcomes and organizational outcomes.

From an organizational point of view internal controls will necessarily restrain or promote risk. Controls are therefore applied as a means of tackling risk, whether this is too much or too little risk. Naturally there will be monetary cost consequences of control investments which points to the importance of implementing cost-effective controls in the right areas. Recent studies done within the context of Sarbanes-Oxley (2002) in the United States suggest that internal control deficiencies will impact on investors' assessment of risk and also on the cost of equity. More studies are necessary however.

One of the frequently occurring themes in writings on internal control refers to fraud (see Fagerberg, 2008) and financial reporting. For a long time internal control has been considered a fundamental component for combating occupational fraud. With regard to financial reporting, there is an acclaimed direct relationship between the quality of internal control and financial reporting quality. Finally, a great deal of both the practical and the regulatory writings suggests that internal control may facilitate firm performance. It seems reasonable that a well-balanced, dynamic and cost-effective system of internal control will have a positive impact on firm performance. We claim that the evidence available in this area is however limited.

5.4 Summary and Concluding Remarks

The present chapter is made up of two major sections. The first Sect. 5.2 introduces the concept and definition of internal control and the second Sect. 5.3 discusses a number of themes on internal control that frequently occurs in writings on the subject. Based on the findings from Sect. 5.2 we conclude that:

- Internal control is no recent invention but goes back over 1,100 years. It was introduced by the English audit-specialist Dicksee as a "system of internal check". This system was internally installed by the company and the financial statement auditor was to consider this system since this would enable a more efficient and effective audit process.
- The increasing reliance on internal control is explained by the following factors: rising costs in public accounting and the consequent additional emphasis on economy and effectiveness; the increased complexity of the business enterprise resulting in geometric compounding of data control problems; the development of new communications and information systems and the introduction of extremely reliable data processing machines; requests received by the auditor from management, owners and other parties-at-interest for additional information. Today, however, reliance on internal control and attention to this is no longer strictly driven by auditing related concerns. Regulators, supervisory authorities, financial statement users and media all want and demand better internal controls today.
- There has been a century of debate about the definition of internal controls, and usually changes to existing definitions have been controversial. Different definitions for internal control exist but the framework of internal control issued by the COSO in 1992 has become the world-wide blueprint.

Based on the findings from Sect. 5.3 we conclude that:

- There are different definitions on internal control. Definitions may be narrow with a fairly direct relationship to the financial records or significantly broader. The broader definitions of internal control are not very different from the definitions of management control systems found in management control research. The internal control concept however, takes a corporate governance perspective and focuses on terms such as reasonable assurance and risk appetite. The exact relationship between internal control and management control has not been clearly articulated however. During recent years, internal controls have developed into an extension of risk management and are now considered to be a risk treatment.
- Ever since the introduction of the concept, internal controls have been classified into different categories. As time goes by, categories develop and new ones are established. Control categories are tied closely to both practical frameworks and professional audit standards. Prior studies suggest that classifying controls may be both difficult and controversial.

- Financial assertions and stated risk appetites may be applied as internal control design objectives. Previous studies, regulatory guidance and practical frameworks suggest that control designs are contingent upon internal and external variables. These include company objectives and strategies, business culture, industry characteristics, firm size, uncertainty, the risk appetite and the regulatory environment.
- Design of controls is a challenging task for any internal control internal control architect. Previous findings suggest that controls need to be integrative, balanced, dynamic and adaptive, cost-effective and embedded in the daily operations rather than super-imposed or loosely coupled. Building internal control design capabilities seems important.
- The assessment and evaluation of controls is perhaps the most frequently occurring theme on internal controls. This is only natural since for a long time internal control evaluation has been a key part of the audit process. A significant body of research exists on the subject, and previous studies have examined the role of format, structure and judgment with regards to the evaluation of internal control. Some findings suggest that control environment controls are relatively more important than other controls, but also more difficult to assess. Internal control evaluation is an inherently complex process that is made up of both structure and judgment.
- Internal controls have gone from being off-record to going on-record. Internal controls have become a regulatory object and reporting on the process of producing the financial reports has the potential of becoming as important as the financial reports themselves.
- The public disclosures of internal controls represent a key feature of corporate governance laws, regulations and codes. Public disclosure requirements for internal control vary in scope and depth. Previous research has been concerned with the following key issues: whether management reports on internal controls should be voluntary or mandatory, whether statements should address the effectiveness of the system and whether auditors should attest to reports provided by management.
- Control practices may produce outcomes related to the use and usefulness of the system, behavior outcomes and organizational outcomes. The concept of internal control quality is however complex and for researchers it is difficult to examine and determine. Previous writings suggest however that internal control quality may prevent fraud and facilitate better firm performance. Obviously controls will cost money but also yield benefits such as mitigated risk. Recent studies have also examined disclosure outcomes under SOX-404 in the United States. These studies suggest that cost of compliance has been substantial but recent studies also suggest that internal control quality may yield benefits related to investment risk evaluation and cost of equity.

Chapter 6
Conclusions and Future Research

Abstract

Purpose: The aim of this chapter is to make concluding observations based on what we have discussed in other previous chapters as well as to describe future research opportunities within the area of internal control.

Synopsis: Internal control seems to be an all-encompassing process. The wider approaches to internal control have expanded its boundaries significantly, far beyond the financial reports and the duties of the accountant. Financial reporting quality objectives have been supplemented with other internal control objectives which are related to compliance, efficiency and effectiveness. Today internal controls may be dispersed and embedded in most of the company's business activities. Furthermore, internal control has transformed into an extension of risk management and thus tied closer to the strategy formulation and execution process. Internal control is considered to be a form of risk treatment through which inherent risk may be increased or decreased through the design and application of controls. Furthermore, it is today a regulatory object. Lawmakers and supervisory authorities are increasingly concerned with the design and operating effectiveness of internal controls. Disclosure requirements imposed on firms are forcing them to provide public disclosures about their internal control systems, which were previously private to firms. Today internal control is also considered to be a key corporate governance mechanism and corporate governance rating systems and credit rating agencies increasingly take into account the internal control and risk management practices of firms. Some researchers however have pointed out that there is still much to learn about internal control quality, and how internal control is associated with corporate governance quality. The fact that internal control is an inherently complex concept poses a significant research barrier, and while all research methods are valid, it is unlikely that archival studies or experiments are able to capture measures of internal control quality. Finally, practical, regulatory and academic texts suggest that internal control designs are contingent upon certain variables. These variables include company objectives, strategy, regulatory characteristics, risk and risk appetite, management attitudes and firm size. Prior research also points to the challenge facing any internal control architect. Building

O. Arwinge, *Internal Control*, Contributions to Management Science,
DOI 10.1007/978-3-7908-2882-5_6,

internal control capabilities would seem to be of great importance if firms are to be able to design internal controls which are balanced, integrated, dynamic and cost-effective.

6.1 Introduction

The previous chapters have looked at many of the elements and aspects of internal control. In this final chapter, we will make some concluding observations based on these earlier discussions. We will also recommend areas for future research. However it is first appropriate to revisit the purpose of this research and the research questions proposed in the first chapter, Sect. 1.4.2. The purpose has been to account for existing research on internal control including the concept's key components and features. In doing that we also presented certain themes and issues frequently discussed in writings on the subject. Hopefully this will provide readers with a deeper understanding of the complexity of the concept.

Previous chapters have discussed theories that explain the necessity for controls and also how controls may develop and change. We have also discussed the components of internal control using a practical framework. Since internal control is associated with regulatory and institutional developments, we also found it necessary to provide a regulatory perspective in Chap. 4. In Chap. 5 we described some of the frequently occurring themes and issues on internal controls that are discussed in prior research. This final chapter will make some concluding observations derived from findings in previous chapters. As such, they may be regarded as overall conclusions.

We argue that these concluding observations show the distinguishing features of the modern view of internal control and thus provide an adequate description of the concept. We further argue that all six observations are quite concept-specific and necessary for the understanding of the modern view of internal control.

6.2 Concluding Observations

6.2.1 An All Encompassing Process

More than a century of debate over internal control demonstrates the importance as well as the complexity of the concept (see Kinney, 2000; Heier, Dugan, & Sayers, 2005). For a long time, internal control remained unfamiliar to most people outside of accounting community. This is unlikely to be the case today and the concept has expanded its boundaries significantly, far beyond the financial reports and the duties of the accountant (Maijoor, 2000, p. 102; Merchant & Otley in Chapman, Hopwood, & Shields eds., 2007, p. 787).

Both broad and narrow approaches to internal control have, however, for a long time co-existed (Haun, 1955). The traditional, narrow approach has a fairly direct relationship to financial reporting quality (p. 114). This seems largely unchanged and the *process of producing the financial statements* in this way is sometimes referred to as internal control over financial reporting, a term applied for example by the PCAOB (Public Company Accounting Oversight Board) in the United States following the introduction of the SOX in 2002. With the introduction of frameworks such as the COSO (1992, 2004) the broader approach to internal control has gained significant ground. COSO is now established as a leading guidance on internal control for directors and managers world-wide (Power, 2007, p. 49).

A key feature of the COSO-framework is that it does not only encompass financial reporting quality but also covers objectives related to compliance and efficiency and effectiveness in operations. Definition wise this is then not very different from some other control concepts, such as the management control system referred to in management control research (see Merchant and Otley in Chapman, Hopwood, & Shields eds., 2007, p. 787). The internal control concept, however, emphasizes terms such as *risk assessment*, *reasonable assurance*, *financial reporting* and *safeguarding of assets* and furthermore adopts a *governance perspective*. In this way, internal control is a basic system that produces assurances about information quality and the protection of firm resources.

Another key feature of the COSO is that it defines internal control as a process, rather than a system or a structure. The fact that it does this is most likely to highlight its loose and dynamic character, as opposed to being a static and fixed system (see Kinney, 2000). If we build on the writings on process management (Hammer & Champy, 1993, p. 33), internal control could be regarded as a collection of control activities designed to convey valuable output (i.e. assurance) to its "customers", such as the board of directors, audit committee members and executive managers.

Taken together these two features suggest that internal control is a vast and comprehensive concept which encompasses most parts of the company's business activities (Maijoor, 2000, p. 105). Today internal control is considered to be a co-extensive with risk management (Power, 2007, p. 35) and controls are applied as ways of dealing with strategic, reporting, compliance and operational risk exposures. It follows that controls may be applied in most business- and support processes of firms, wherever risk exposures need to be dealt with. Hence *internal control is an all-encompassing process.*

Revisiting the ideas behind process management (Hammer & Champy, 1993; Hammer, 2007), the internal control process appears to differ from other processes in one important aspect. The end-to-end concept, where processes start and end, appears to be rather different for the internal control process. Compared to conventional processes (see for example the value chain by Porter, 1985) clear-cut beginnings or endings are more difficult to identify in this case. This is perhaps due to the fact that internal control should be regarded as a collection of control activities that are (more or less) embedded into normal operations and business processes. This claim would again point to the challenge facing the internal control architect (see Oliviero, 2002) or the internal control process manager (see Hammer, 2007).

6.2.1.1 Future Research Opportunities

The key research questions in this area are associated with the *management of the internal control process*. How do firms go about managing the internal control process from an overall organizational perspective? We have already concluded that the process is far-reaching and that furthermore it may comprise different sub-systems and controls. Future research in this area would certainly be beneficial to increase our understanding of how the internal control process is designed and managed by firms. Specific research questions include:

- How do firms manage the internal control process of the organization?
- How are different control systems and internal controls coordinated and integrated from an overall organizational perspective? How do controls become embedded and robust in the day-to-day operations?
- What types of firm capabilities are important for building effective internal control process management?
- What are the critical success factors associated with effective internal control process management?

6.2.2 A Co-extensive with Risk Management

A stream of high-profile fraud cases and corporate scandals around the world has been a key driver for improved corporate governance (Hermanson & Rittenberg, 2003, p. 39). Supported by regulators and other stakeholders, organizations are struggling to organize an uncertain world into manageable risks (Power, 2007). As a result, a new fully-fledged management function has entered onto the corporate governance scene under the leadership of the chief risk officer (see Power, 2004; Hutter & Power, 2005; Power, 2007; Mikes, 2009) and recent studies suggest that enterprise risk management (ERM) practices are growing and evolving (see studies such as Beasely, Clune, & Hermanson, 2005; Sarens & DeBeelde, 2006; Fraser & Henry, 2007; Woods, 2009; Mikes, 2009; Woods, 2009).

An associated development with these emerging risk-based practices has been that internal control has become more closely tied to risk management practices, and therefore also the strategy formulation and execution process of firms. The introduction of new risk-related regulations, the explosion of operational risk (Power, 2005) and practical frameworks for risk (COSO, 2004) have all contributed to the *transformation of internal control into an extension of risk management* (Power, 2007, p. 35). This focus on risk management practices during recent years may leave strategy experts relatively unimpressed, since risk lies at the heart of value creation and has for a long time been an explicit part of strategy development and execution (Power, 2007, p. 8).

Nevertheless, a "new form" of internal control-based risk management practices has developed. Recent case studies (Woods, 2009; Mikes, 2009) suggest that these practices may develop as a result of institutional pressures (see Chap. 2, Sect. 2.4) and that their design is contingent upon variables such as firm size, technology, management attitudes towards risk and risk practices, environment and strategy (see Chap. 5, Sect. 5.3.3). The case study by Mikes (2009) reveals that companies may adopt different approaches to risk management. Mikes defines these approaches as either ERM by the numbers or holistic ERM, and argues that the former is driven by a shareholder value approach to corporate governance, and the latter by a risk based internal control approach.

Since risk management is inherently a co-extensive with strategy, this also binds internal controls closer to the formulation and execution of strategies. Internal control is now regarded as a risk treatment whereby inherent risk may by be increased, accepted or decreased through the design and application of controls (Picket, 2001, p. 45). The beneficial nature of internal controls is thus becoming increasingly recognized and emphasised, by which it is meant that controls have a promotional and enabling effect and no longer only restraining or containing firm activity and related risk exposures (pp. 217–259).

6.2.2.1 Future Research Opportunities

The key research questions in this area are associated with the *application of internal controls as a risk-treatment* in firms risk assessment processes. How do firms go about applying internal controls as a part of their risk assessments? We have earlier mentioned a few studies which have been made on risk management and recently interesting case studies have shed additional light on the risk management practices of firms (see for example Woods, 2009; Mikes, 2009). However much remains to be learned, which is why more research is needed in this area (Mikes, 2009, p. 19). One way forward could perhaps be to build on studies such as those mentioned above and examine in-depth how internal controls are applied based on risk assessment processes. Specific research questions include:

- How do firms apply internal control in their emerging risk assessment processes?
- What are the critical success factors associated with internal control risk treatments in firms?
- How do risk officers, internal control officers, managers an directors co-operate with reference to assessment of risk and control treatments?
- How do control treatments adapt based on changes in contingent factors such as strategy and risk?

6.2.3 A Regulatory Object

The influence of the regulatory environment on internal control practices cannot be overestimated. Power (2007) uses the telling phrase "turning organizations inside out" (p. 34) to describe how regulatory requirements have forced organizations to disclose their internal control systems – systems which previously remained private to firms. For the last 15 years governance has been a dominating theme in corporate regulation and internal control now forms part of public policy and formal law (p. 62). Power (p. 55) concludes very interestingly on this development that:

> It remains to be seen whether this emphasis on reporting on the process of producing financial statements will become more significant for regulators than the financial statements themselves; internal control systems now have the potential to become the **primary** regulatory and managerial reporting object.

Even though in the United States, the SOX with its strict internal control reporting requirements has received much attention worldwide, mandatory and semi-mandatory regulations on internal control have also been introduced in other countries, including Sweden (see Jonnergård & Larsson, 2007). There is a trend towards a global standardization of corporate governance principles (Davies, 2008) and corporate governance codes of today often include provisions for external reporting and disclosure of the design and effectiveness of internal controls. The public disclosure of risk-related information is closely associated with the term decision-usefulness (see Scott, 2003) and agency theory (see Chap. 1, Table 2.1), which suggests that users such as analysts, investors and other financial market stakeholders need this information to improve their decision-making process.

Regulatory requirements on internal controls, and perhaps specifically any internal control disclosure requirements, have proven to be somewhat controversial however. Power (1997) described for example, how one of the pioneers in this field, The Cadbury Code (1992) in the United Kingdom, generated fundamental problems at the time it was introduced and that directors were reluctant to make any public statements. It was specifically the provisions prescribing public reporting on internal controls that generated substantial debate about what internal control was and what is really meant when they are described as effective (p. 55). A somewhat similar trend may be observed in the Swedish case following the introduction of the Swedish code of Corporate Governance in 2004. Statements made by the Swedish Corporate Governance Board, based on stakeholder feedback, suggest that the strict internal control provisions from the original Code caused concerns at the time.

The original internal control provisions were subsequently downsized (Kollegiet för Svensk Bolagsstyrning, 2005, 2006a). The design and usefulness of corporate governance code requirements, including disclosure requirements on internal control, remain a source of debate in Sweden (see Brandinger, 2008a, 2008b; Lekvall, 2008).

We mentioned above that any internal control requirements imposed on firms by regulators will necessarily be associated with how firms design, manage and oversee their internal controls. Spira and Page (2003) claim that if the regulatory internal control requirements are not aligned with firms' internal audit and control environments, substantial adjustment costs may incur. This indicates the importance of minimizing any gap between internal control regulations and business practices with regard to this matter, and to ensure that any disclosure requirements are useful to the user-groups concerned.

Naturally, law makers and supervisory authorities perform vital regulatory and supervisory functions. They impose requirements and restrictions on companies with reference to risk management and internal controls and are also charged with the responsibility of enforcing such restrictions. The distinctive attributes of financial services firms make law makers and the financial supervisory authorities' imperative. Their influence on financial services firms, with regard to internal control practices, seems to increase. We have previously claimed that supervisory authorities increasingly recommend and enforce practices of internal control which companies within the financial services sector should adhere to. This development is not only restricted to the financial sector however, but is becoming visible in other sectors and areas as well.

6.2.3.1 Future Research Opportunities

The research questions in this area seem closely associated with the design and value of internal control disclosure requirements. Research questions may be also associated with how *internal control as a regulatory object* may influence internal control practices of firms. From a local Swedish perspective, this might be a particularly interesting and beneficial research area since the corporate governance code, including the internal control-related provisions, is still rather new. Studies which examine the association between internal control reporting requirements and how firms and report-users respond to those requirements would be beneficial. Both quantitative and qualitative research approaches may be applied to gain understanding about the perceptions held by preparers and users of the usefulness of internal control disclosure requirements.

Moreover, the special features of the financial services sector (Handley-Schachler, Juleff, & Paton, 2007) would perhaps motivate research into the internal control practices by financial services firms. In the financial sector, internal control and risk management practices are primary regulatory objects today and an examination of the practices that firms are expected to adopt here would be interesting. In particular perhaps the application and outcomes of Financial Supervisory Authority-regulations and other banking regulation could be beneficial for our understanding in this area. Are the risk management and internal control practices that firms are expected to adopt perceived as compliance hurdles or are they effectively integrated into strategic management (p. 632; see also Doyle, 2007)? Financial institutions have pioneered the development of enterprise risk management, so, building on recent case studies such as Mikes (2009) and Woods (2009), it would be interesting to explore what approaches they have adopted in their practices (Fraser & Henry, 2007, p. 407). Specific research questions include.

- What kind of risk-related information do users value? How do users perceive different forms of internal control disclosure requirements?
- Do users value the risk-related information currently disclosed by companies?

- How do preparers go about responding to internal control disclosure requirements? How do preparers perceive different forms of internal control disclosure requirements?
- How do preparers regard and respond to the fact that internal control increasingly is becoming a primary regulatory object for supervisory authorities?
- What are the outcomes from internal control disclosure requirements on business practices?

6.2.4 A Corporate Governance Mechanism

With the rise of internal control (Maijoor, 2000; Spira & Page, 2003: Power, 2007), the concept of internal control now lies at the heart of contemporary governance thinking (Power, 2007, p. 35) and is often considered to be a key corporate governance mechanism (Rae & Subramaniam, 2008, p. 146). Maijoor (2000) however, claims that our understanding of internal control from a wider corporate governance perspective is incomplete (p. 102). We have earlier claimed that little research has been done on how different internal control elements may affect overall internal control quality (Rae & Subramaniam, 2008, p. 106). This may also be true with regards to the "next level", in other words, how internal control is associated with corporate governance quality (Maijoor, 2000, p. 102).

Corporate governance rating systems (including governance rating research) usually take their point of departure in established governance best practices and focus on the formal governance structures and arrangements of firms, covering areas such as board of directors and committee characteristics, ownership and shareholder protection and disclosure and transparency (see Khanchel, 2007, pp. 741–743).[1] In a recent paper on corporate governance, Khanchel (2007) provides an overview of firm-specific determinants of strong corporate governance: independent directors, independent committees, board characteristics (including variables such as size, roles, competence and meetings), and auditor and audit committee meetings (for a more detailed review, see pp. 743–745). The implied assumption is that better audit committee competence, better audit quality and better board arrangements will drive internal control quality thus improving corporate governance quality. Researchers have however examined internal control more explicitly as a governance mechanism. See for example the study by Turley and Zaman

[1] Governance rating systems builds on agency-ideas (see Chap. 1, Table 2.1) where disclosure about the level of corporate governance quality will reduce information-asymmetries between investors and firms thus enabling investors to make better investment-decisions. Corporate governance ratings and disclosures thus provides opportunity to compare companies within themselves and also to show companies which may be involved with non-best practices. It should also be pointed out that researchers have also examined informal processes and arrangements related to certain governance structures and how they impact governance outcomes, see for example Turley and Zaman (2007).

(2007) where through a case-study approach they examine the workings of directors and the audit committee members and how they deal with, and consider, internal control issues from a governance perspective. Since internal control is considered to be a vital governance mechanism, additional studies such as this one would be of interest in order to improve our understanding of how internal control serves the overall corporate governance system. Since the audit committee is chiefly responsible for overseeing the adequacy and effectiveness of the internal controls (Hermanson & Rittenberg, 2003, p. 50), it is natural that the committee's work in discharging their duties is crucial to examine.

6.2.4.1 Future Research Opportunities

The key research questions in this area are related to *how internal control is associated with corporate governance quality*. Quantitative research approaches may build on frameworks and findings established by prior research (see Khanchel, 2007). Qualitative research approaches may use case-study methods, as done by for example Turley and Zaman (2007), in order to examine how executive management, auditors, audit committee members and directors consider internal control to improve governance of firms.

Examining internal control as a governance mechanism may be further motivated by the increasing attention that is being paid to the audit committees. We have earlier claimed that the responsibilities of audit committees for risk and control appear to be expanding, a fact which recognizes their growing importance for oversight of risk and control. At the same time, concerns have been raised as to whether audit committees possess the adequate skills and capabilities necessary for reviewing the risk management process and non-financial internal controls (Fraser & Henry, 2007, p. 407). Specific research questions include:

- How is internal control associated with corporate governance quality?
- What are the determinants of effective oversight over internal control?
- What necessary skills must directors and committee members possess to discharge their duties with reference to risk and control?
- How is effective internal control disclosure associated with corporate governance quality?
- How may effective working relationships between internal audit, risk management and audit committees improve corporate governance quality?
- What are the key determinants for an effective working relationship, with reference to internal control, between the key *internal* corporate governance actors as outlined in Fig. 5.8? How do effective working relationships between these actors contribute to corporate governance quality and what are the key success factors and issues?

6.2.5 A Contingent-Based Concept

Kinney (2000) claimed great research opportunities for PhD-students and senior researchers within the field of internal controls. Based on his knowledge and experience, Kinney concluded that a "well developed internal control process was essential for the management decision making process and the protection of assets in general" (p. 84). However, Kinney pointed to a number of stumbling blocks, the biggest one being the complexity of the concept and the fact that it draws upon different theoretical concepts found in different academic fields. Kinney claimed that:

> The main barrier for doing important research into internal control is our own limited knowledge (as auditing researchers) of business strategy and organization design, management processes, risk and risk measurement..(. . .). . .In addition. . .(. . .). . .many of us lack knowledge of internal control alternatives and conceptual knowledge about process verification. These limitations in our background might be overcome through study of risk and strategy, through reading about internal control alternatives, and perhaps by borrowing process verification techniques from other disciplines (p. 88).

Undoubtedly this is a rather telling statement and sums up much of the complexity and challenges surrounding the practice of internal controls. What Kinney refers to is the fact that although internal control is primarily associated with the fields of accounting and auditing, is not limited to these fields but also incorporates concepts from other disciplines. This may however apply to most concepts and fields within business administration. According to Power (2007) the concept of internal control has never received any significant intellectual attention from researchers.

> The topic of internal control in organizations has never been part of mainstream management research, reflecting no doubt its position in the hierarchy of management knowledge and its primary association with auditing. Compared with the body of scholarship on management accounting and management control more generally, this is surprising since there is considerable overlap. . .(. . .). . .For many years, the subject of internal controls has been a private matter for a sub-group of technical control assurance specialists. . .(....) The practice by which corporations, corner shops, clubs and churches maintain a basic level of financial and non-financial control over resources, has hardly been worthy of serious intellectual attention (p. 62).

This close connection between internal control and other academic fields outside accounting and auditing is also clear from recent comments made by researchers from both the fields of auditing and management control regarding the similarities between internal control and general management control. Rae and Subramaniam (2008) state that the internal control system is *a feature of management control systems* (p. 104) while Fadzil, Haron and Jantan (2005) argue that "the definition of internal control systems reveals that it is not fundamentally different from management control, which has an essential component of control such as planning, organizing, staffing and directing" (p. 846). However, a potential implication of the inherent complexity of the concept is that examination and measurement of internal control quality becomes difficult.

> A second major research barrier is the inherent complexity of the internal control process. Internal control is extremely broad by definition and is operationalized in complex, dynamic organizations that differ substantially across time, across organizations, and across cultures. Due to this inherent complexity, it is difficult to capture measures of internal control process quality in an experiment, and archival study, or even a survey (Kinney, 2000, p. 88).

This may certainly have contributed to any shortcomings in research in this area. As we mentioned earlier, Rae and Subramaniam (2008) also concluded in a recent paper on the subject that there is little empirical evidence about the factors that may be associated with internal control quality. Since research in this area is insufficient, it seems important that we obtain a better understanding of how internal control designs are established *in action* and how they may be associated with different levels of internal control quality. Kinney (2000) seems to recommend more qualitative approaches to internal control research, which perhaps would enable more relevant and complete measurements of internal control process quality. Rae and Subramaniam (2008) suggest that more holistic approaches to internal control quality might be necessary instead of relying on single sources for measurement, such as the perceptions of controllers for example.

In Sect. 5.3.3 we claimed that internal control will vary from firm to firm, unless two of more firms are identical. Thus firms will have different types of intern control arrangements. Figure 5.1 in that section suggested that internal control process designs are *contingent* upon a number of firm-specific and external variables such as corporate objectives and strategies, risk appetite, management attitudes and the regulatory environment. We argued that those variables necessarily influence and drive internal control designs.

Figure 5.4 also suggested that firms may be capable of producing different forms, or levels, of internal control process quality, depending on how successful they are in applying their internal control capabilities within the firm. Action-oriented studies in this area could develop these models and the associated assumptions and relationships about internal control design and quality. In addition, we might like to find out more about the building of internal control capabilities. Section 5.3.3 suggested that such capabilities may be of importance for firms if cost-effective, balanced, integrated and dynamic controls can be installed (see Oliviero, 2002). The term *capability* emphasizes the key role of management in integrating, balancing, adapting and re-configuring organizational skills and resources for internal control (based on Teece, Pisano, & Shuen, 1997, p. 515).

6.2.5.1 Future Research Opportunities

How do firms design and apply internal controls and what are their effects? These questions may very well be the most interesting and important questions for internal control researchers. The complexity of the concept may require certain research strategies however. While all research methods are valid, case studies could potentially be a way forward in developing theories and relationships between relevant variables (see Eisenhardt, 1989b, 2007). Building on recent case studies in the related area of risk management (see for example Woods, 2009; Mikes, 2009) would be useful.

Based on their study of the quality of internal control procedures, Rae and Subramaniam (2008) recommend researchers to find better and more holistic measurements of internal control, rather than to rely on one single source, such as the perceptions of internal control quality according for example to the financial controller.

Since prior research, as well as most regulatory and practical texts, suggest that internal controls are contingent upon variables, additional studies that examine relationships between controls and the contingent variables seem important. A *contingency-based perspective* to internal control could therefore be fruitful. We seem also to be in the need of additional studies that examine how internal control capabilities are developed and applied within firms and how those capabilities may be associated with internal control quality. Future research enterprises could thus take their point of departure in a *resource-based approach* to internal control and examine how organisations build and develop their internal control capabilities in order to create strong, cost-effective and sustainable assurance (see studies such as Teece, Pisano, & Shuen, 1997; Eisenhardt & Jeffrey, 2000; Winter, 2003; Ethiraj, Kale, Krishnan, & Singh, 2005). To gain an understanding of how such capabilities are developed would truly be beneficial for expanding knowledge in the field. Specific research questions may include:

- What are the factors associated with internal control designs?
- How do firms apply internal controls?
- What are the factors associated with internal control quality?
- How do firms develop and apply internal control capabilities?
- How do we measure internal control quality?
- What are the outcomes of internal control?

6.3 A Research Agenda

The present chapter consists of a number of key observations that have been derived from the previous chapters that make up this thesis. In connection to the concluding observations, we have provided in total 25 suggestions for future research into the area of internal control. In this final section of the thesis, we end by proposing a high-level research agenda for the future.

Internal control is considered to be a key corporate governance mechanism where adequate and effective internal controls may provide reasonable assurance that objectives will be met. From a management control perspective, it seems important to learn more about the following:

- Which variables influence the design and use of internal controls?
- How are internal controls applied by an organization?
- What are the outcomes of the application of internal controls?

While we do not exclude other research methods, we recommend researchers to perform additional case studies into internal controls so that we may gain deeper understanding of how managers, directors and other specialists are working with internal controls in their day-to-day activities. Another research agenda relates more to the regulatory aspects of the concept. It seems crucial that we find out more about the design and value of risk-related disclosure requirements. We recommend a focus on the following questions:

- What are the factors associated with high-quality internal control reporting requirements?
- What are the factors associated with high-quality internal control reports?

In this area, both qualitative and quantitative approaches are valid for finding out more about the perceptions held by both preparers and users on this matter. Results from such studies could also have potential benefits for regulators.

References

af Ekenstam, A.-C. (2009, August 17). Modernisera riskarbetet. *Dagens Industri.*

Agarwal, S. (1993). Influence of formalization on role stress, organizational commitment, and work alienation of sales persons: A cross-national comparative study. *Journal of International Business Studies, 24*(4), 715–739.

Ahmed, A. S., McAnally, M. L., Rasmussen, S., & Weaer, C. D. (2010). How costly is the Sarbanes Oxley act? Evidence on the effects of the act on corporate profitability. *Journal of Corporate Finance, 16*, 352–369.

Ahrne, G., & Brunsson, N. (eds.). (2004). *Regelexplosionen.* Ekonomiska Forskningsinstitutet, Handelshögskolan i Stockholm. Elanders Gotab

Aktiebolagslagen (2005) Swedish Law 2005:551 [Limited Liability Companies Act].

Allegrini, M., DÓnza, G., Paape, L., Melville, R., & Sarens, G. (2006). The European literature on internal auditing. *Managerial Auditing Journal, 21*(8), 845–853.

Anderson, S. W., Christ, M. H., & Sedatole, K. L. (2006). Risky business. *Internal Auditor, 63*, 47–52.

Anthony, R. N. (1965). *Planning and control systems: A framework for analysis.* Boston: Graduate School of Business Administration, Harvard University.

Apostolou, B., Hassell, J. M., & Webber, S. A. (2001). Fraud risk factors: Ratings by forensic experts. *The CPA Journal, 71*, 48–52.

Arwinge, O., & Munkby, T. (2011). Intern kontroll i finansiell sector – en studie av brister [Internal control in the financial sector – a study of deficiencies]. *Balans, No.6/7*, 25–29.

Ashbaugh-Skaife, H., Collins, D. W., & Kinney, W. R., Jr. (2007). The discovery and reporting of internal control deficiencies prior to SOX-mandated audits. *Journal of Accounting and Economics, 44*, 167–192.

Ashbaugh-Skaife, H., Collins, D. W., Kinney, W. R., Jr., & LaFond, R. (2008). The effect of SOX internal control deficiencies and their remediation of accrual quality. *The Accounting Review, 83*(1), 217–250.

Ashbaugh-Skaife, H., Collins, D. W., Kinney, W. R., Jr., & Lanfond, R. (2009). The effect of SOX internal control deficiencies on firm risk and cost of capital. *Journal of Accounting Research, 47*(1), 1–43.

Ashton, R. H. (1974). An experimental study of internal control judgments. *Journal of Accounting Research, 12*(1), 143–157.

Baiman, S. (1990). Agency research in managerial accounting: a second look. *Accounting, Organizations and Society, 15*(4), 341–371.

Baker, R. L., Bealing, W. E., Jr., Nelson, D. A., & Staley, A. B. (2006). An institutional perspective of the Sarbanes-Oxley act. *Managerial Auditing Journal, 21*(1), 23–33.

Bannister, S. J., Engvall, D. H., & Martin, D. B. H. (2007). Retooling the internal control process – A welcome relief. *Insights, 21*(8), 2–15.

O. Arwinge, *Internal Control*, Contributions to Management Science,
DOI 10.1007/978-3-7908-2882-5, © Springer-Verlag Berlin Heidelberg 2013

Barnard, C. I. (1938). *The functions of the executive*. Cambridge: Harvard University Press.

Basel Committee on Banking Supervision. (1998). *Framework for internal control systems in banking organizations*. Available at www.bis.org

Beasley, M. S., Clune, R., & Hermanson, D. R. (2005). Enterprise risk management: an empirical analysis of the factors associated with the extent of the of implementation. *Journal of Accounting and Public Policy, 24*, 521–531.

Bebbington, J., Larrinaga, C., & Moneva, J. M. (2008). Corporate social reporting and reputation risk management. *Accounting, Auditing and Accountability Journal, 21*(3), 337–361.

Berger, P. L., Luckmann, T., (1966): *The social construction of reality*, Garden City, New York: Anchor books

Berle, A. A., & Means, G. C. (1932). *The modern corporation and private property*. New York: Harcourt, Brace & World.

Bhasa, M. P. (2004). Global corporate governance: Debates and challenges. *Corporate Governance, 4*(2), 5–17.

Bierstaker, J. L. (2003). Auditor recall and evaluation of internal control information: Does task-specific knowledge mitigate part-list interference? *Managerial Auditing Journal, 18*(2), 90–99.

Bierstaker, J. L., Brody, R. G., & Pacini, C. (2006). Accountants' perceptions of fraud detection and prevention methods. *Managerial Auditing Journal, 21*(5), 520–535.

Bierstaker, J. L., Hunton, J. E., & Thibodeau, J. C. (2009). Do client-prepared internal control documentation and business process flowcharts help or hinder an auditor's ability to identify missing controls? *Auditing: A Journal of Practice and Theory, 28*(1), 79–94.

Bierstaker, J. L., & Thibodeau, J. C. (2006). The effect of format and experience on internal control evaluation. *Managerial Auditing Journal, 21*(9), 877–891.

Bihmani, A. (2009) Risk management, corporate governance and management accounting: Emerging interdependencies. *Management Accounting Research*, 20, Editorial, p. 2–5.

Birkenshaw, J., & Jenkins, H. (2009). *Risk management gets personal. Lessons from the credit crisis*. Executive Briefing. Advanced Institute of Management Research (AIM Research). Available at www.aimresearch.org

Boessa, G., & Kumar, K. (2007). Drivers of corporate disclosures: A framework and empirical evidence from Italy and the United States. *Accounting, Auditing and Accountability Journal, 20*(2), 269–296.

Borthick, A. F., Curtis, M. B., & Sriram, R. S. (2006). Accelerating the acquisition of knowledge structure to improve performance in internal control reviews. *Accounting, Organizations and Society, 31*, 323–342.

Bower, J. B., & Schlosser, R. E. (1965). Internal control – Its true nature. *The Accounting Review, 40*(2), 338–344.

Bowling, D. M., & Rieger, L. A. (2005, February–March). Making sense out of COSO's new framework for enterprise risk management. *Bank Accounting and Finance*, 29–34.

Braiotta, L., Gazzaway, R. T., Colson, R. H., & Ramamoorti, S. (2010). *The audit committee handbook* (5th ed.). New Jersey: Wiley.

Brandinger, R. (2008a). Kodens ansvar finns i betraktarens öga. *Dagens Industri*.

Brandinger, R. (2008b, September 1). Riskhantering – inget för koden. *Dagens Industri*.

Bronson, S. N., Carcello, J. V., & Raghunandan, K. (2006). Firm characteristics and voluntary management reports on internal control. *Auditing: A Journal of Practice and Theory, 25*(2), 25–39.

Brown, R. (1962): Changing audit objectives and techniques. *The Accounting Review, 37*(4), 696–703. In Lee, T. A. (ed.). (1988). *The evolution of audit thought and practice*. New York: Garland.

Bryman, A. (2004). *Social research methods* (2nd ed.). Oxford: Oxford University Press.

Bryman, A. (2006). Paradigm peace and the implications for quality. *International Journal of Social Research Methodology, 9*(2), 111–126.

Bryman, A. (2007). The research question in social research: What is its role? *International Journal of Social Research Methodology, 10*(1), 5–20.

Bryman, A., Becker, S., & Sempik, J. (2008). Quality criteria for quantitative, qualitative and mixed methods research: A view from social policy. *International Journal of Social Research Methodology, 11*(4), 261–276.

Burns, J., & Nixon, W. A. J. (2005). Introduction: Management control in the 21st century. *Management Accounting Research, 16*, 260–268.

Cain, A. (2009, December). Financial industry leads in fraud increases. *Internal Auditor*, 15.

Callaghan, J. H., Savage A., & Mintz, S. (2007, March). Assessing the control environment using a balanced scorecard approach. *The CPA Journal*, 58–63.

Carcello, J. V., Hermanson, D. R., & Raghunandan, K. (2005). Factors associated with US public companies' investment in internal auditing. *Accounting Horizons, 19*(2), 69–84.

Cardinal, L. B., Sitkin, S. B., & Long, C. P. (2004). Balancing and rebalancing in the creation and evolution of organizational control. *Organization Science, 15*(4), 411–431.

Carmichael, D. R. (1970). Behavioral hypotheses of internal control. *The Accounting Review, 45*(2), 235–245.

Chambers, A. (2006). Assurance of performance. *Measuring Business Excellence, 10*(3), 41–45.

Changchit, C., Holsapple, C. W., & Madden, D. L. (2001). Supporting managers internal control evaluations: An expert system and experimental results. *Decision Support Systems, 30*, 437–449.

Chapman, C. (1997). Reflections on a contingent view of accounting. *Accounting, Organizations and Society, 22*(2), 189–205.

Chapman, C. (2003a, February). Let there be light – an interview with Sir Adrian Cadbury. *Internal Auditor*, 38–44.

Chapman, C. (2003b). Bringing ERM into focus. *Internal Auditor, 60*, 30–35.

Chapman, C., Hopwood, A., & Shields, M. D. (Eds.). (2007). *Handbook of management accounting research.* Oxford: Elsevier.

Cheney, G. (2007, October 31). Assurance: COSO queries concepts in monitoring internal control. *Accounting Today*, 14.

Cheney, G. (2008, May 26). Controlling internal controls. *Investment dealers' Digest*, 20–21.

Chenhall, R. (2003). Management control systems design within its organizational context: Findings from contingency-based research and directions for the future. *Accounting, Organizations and Society, 28*, 127–168.

Clikeman, P. M. (2009, February). Audit evidence. *Internal Auditor*, 19–20.

COCO (Canadian Institute of Chartered Accountants). (1995). *Guidance on control.* Canada

Cohen, J., Krishnamoorthy, G., & Wright, A. (2004). The corporate governance mosaic and financial reporting quality. *Journal of Accounting Literature, 23*, 87–152.

Coleman, J. W. (2001). *The Criminal Elite. Understanding White-Collar Crime.* New York: St Martin's Press.

Coletti, A. L., Sedatole, K. L., & Towry, K. L. (2005). The effect of control systems on trust and cooperation in collaborative environments. *The Accounting Review, 80*(2), 477–500.

COSO (Committee of Sponsoring Organizations of the Treadway Commission). (1992). *Internal control – Integrated framework.* New York: AICPA.

COSO (Committee of Sponsoring Organizations of the Treadway Commission). (2004). *Enterprise risk management – Integrated framework, executive summary.* New York: AICPA.

COSO (Committee of Sponsoring Organizations of the Treadway Commission). (2006). *Internal control over financial reporting – Guidance for smaller public companies, volume 1: executive summary.* New York: AICPA.

COSO (Committee of Sponsoring Organizations of the Treadway Commission). (2007). *Internal control – integrated framework, guidance on monitoring internal control systems, Discussion document*, 2007–09

COSO (Committee of Sponsoring Organizations of the Treadway Commission). (2009a). *Internal control – integrated framework. Guidance on monitoring internal control systems – introduction.* New York: AICPA. Available at www.coso.org

COSO (Committee of Sponsoring Organizations of the Treadway Commission). (2009b). *Effective enterprise risk oversight – the role of the board of director.* New York: AICPA. Available at www.coso.org

COSO (Committee of Sponsoring Organizations of the Treadway Commission). (2009c). *Strengthening Enterprise Risk Management for Strategic Advantage*. New York: AICPA. Available at www.coso.org

COSO (Committee of Sponsoring Organizations of the Treadway Commission). (2010a, December). *Board risk oversight – a progress report. Where boards and directors currently stand in executing their risk oversight responsibilities*. Research commissioned by COSO. Available at www.coso.org

COSO (Committee of Sponsoring Organizations of the Treadway Commission). (2010b). *Developing key indicators to strengthen enterprise risk management. How key risk indicators can sharpen focus on emerging risks*. Research commissioned by COSO. Available at www.coso.org

COSO (Committee of Sponsoring Organizations of the Treadway Commission). (2011). *Embracing enterprise risk management. Practical approaches to getting started*. Research commissioned by COSO. Available at www.coso.org

D'Aquila, J. M. (1998). Is the control environment related to financial reporting decisions? *Managerial Auditing Journal, 13*(8), 472–478.

Davies, M. (2008). The impracticality of international "once size fit all" corporate governance of best practice. *Managerial Auditing Journal, 23*(6), 532–544.

Davies, M. (2009). Effective working relationships between audit committees and internal audit – The cornerstone of corporate governance in local authorities, a Welsh perspective. *Journal of Management and Governance, 13*, 41–73.

De Haas, M., & Algera, J. A. (2002). Demonstrating the effect on strategic dialogue: Participation in designing the management control system. *Management Accounting Research, 13*, 41–69.

De La Rosa, S. (2007, June). Moving forward with ERM. *Internal Auditor*, 50–54.

DeFond, M. L., & Francis, J. R. (2005). Audit research after Sarbanes-Oxley. *Auditing: A Journal of Practice and Theory, 24*(Supplement: 5–30), 5–40.

DesJardins, J. R., & McCall, J. J. (2005). *Contemporary issues in business ethics* (5th ed.). Belmont: Wadsworth/Thomson.

DeSantis, G., & Monge, P. (1999). Introduction to the special issue: Communication processes for virtual organizations. *Organization Science, 10*, 693–703.

Dewar, R. D., Whetten, D. A., & Boje, D. (1980). An examination of the reliability and validity of the Aiken and Hage scales of centralization, formalization and task routineness. *Administrative Science Quarterly, 25*(1), 120–128.

Dicksee, L. R. (1892). *Auditing: A practical manual for auditors* (1st ed.). London: Gee.

Dicksee, L. R. (1905). *Auditing: authorized American edition* (R. H. Montgomery, ed). New York: Arno Press

Dillard, J. F., Rigsby, J. T., & Goodman, C. (2004). The making and remaking of organization context. Duality and the institutionalization process. *Accounting, Auditing and Accountability Journal, 17*(4), 506–542.

DiMaggio, P. J., & Powell, W. W. (1983). The iron cage revisited; Institutional isomorphism and collective rationality in organizational fields. *American Sociological Review, 48*(2), 147–160.

Dolphin, R. R. (2004). Corporate reputation – A value creating strategy. *Corporate Governance, 4*(3), 77–92.

Donaldson, T. (2007). Closing reflection. "Ethical blowback": The missing piece in the corporate governance puzzle – the risks to a company which fails to understand and respect its social contract. *Corporate Governance, 7*(4), 534–541.

Doyle, E. (2007). Compliance obstacles to competitiveness. *Corporate Governance, 7*(5), 612–622.

Drazin, R., & Van de Ven, A. H. (1985). Alternative forms of fit in contingency theory. *Administrative Science Quarterly, 30*, 514–539.

Eisenhardt, K. M. (1985). Control: organizational and economic approaches. *Management Science, 31*(2), 134–149.

Eisenhardt, K. M. (1988). Agency-and institutional-theory explanations: The case of retail sales compensation. *Academy of Management Journal, 31*(3), 488–511.

Eisenhardt, K. M. (1989a). Agency theory – An assessment and review. *The Academy of Management Review, 14*(1), 57–74.

Eisenhardt, K. M. (1989b). Building theories from case study research. *The Academy of Management Review, 14*(4), 532–550.

Eisenhardt, K. M. (2007). Theory building from case studies: Opportunities and challenges. *Academy of Management Journal, 50*(1), 25–32.

Eisenhardt, K. M., & Martin, J. A. (2000). Dynamic capabilities: What are they? *Strategic Management Journal, 21*(10), 1105–1121.

Ernst & Young (2009). The future of risk. Protecting and enabling performance. EYGM limited. Available at http://www.ey.com

Ekonomistyrningsverket [Swedish Financial Supervisory Authority]. (2008). *Handledning intern styrning och kontroll. Ett stöd vid myndigheters tillämpning av förordningen om intern styrning och kontroll, 2008:*13 *[Guidance on internal control. A support for governmental agencies in the application of the regulation on internal control, 2008:13]*, Stockholm. Available at www.esv.se

Ethiraj, S. K., Kale, P., Krishnan, M. S., & Singh, J. V. (2005). Where do capabilities come from and how do they matter? A study in the software services industry. *Strategic Management Journal, 26*, 25–45.

European Commission. (2010). Green Paper. Corporate governance in financial institutions and remuneration polices, COM (2010)284.

European Commission. (2011). Green Paper. The EU corporate governance framework, COM (2011)164.

Fama, E.F, & Jensen, M.C. (1983). Separation of ownership and control. *Journal of Law and Economics*, Vol. *26*

Fadzil, F. H., Haron, H., & Jantan, M. (2005). Internal auditing practices and internal control system. *Managerial Auditing Journal, 20*(8), 844–866.

Fagerberg, J. (2008). *Occupational Fraud – Auditors´ perceptions of red flags and internal control.* (diss.) [Licenciat avhandling]. Linköping University, Linköping Studies in Science and Technology, Thesis No. 1369.

Far, S. R. S. (2009). *Samlingsvolymen 2009 Revision [Swedish Audit Standards 2009]*. Stockholm/Sverige: FAR SRS Förlag.

FFE (The Federation of European Accountants). (2007). *Selected issues in relation to financial statement audits. Inherent limitations, reasonable assurance, professional judgement and its documentation, and enforceability of auditing standards.* Available at www.ffe.be

Finansinspektionen [The Swedish Financial Supervisory Authority]. (2005). *Allmänna råd om styrning och kontroll i finansiella bolag. FFFS 2005:1 [General guidelines regarding governance and control of financial undertakings]*, Stockholm. Available at www.fi.se

Finansinspektionen [The Swedish Financial Supervisory Authority]. (2011, Maj 24). *Tillsynsrapport 2011. Erfarenheter från tillsyn och regelutveckling [Oversight report 2011. Learnings from oversight and policy development]*, Finansinspektionen, Stockholm. Available at www.fi.se

Flint, D. (1988). *Philosophy and principles of auditing – An introduction.* London: Macmillan Education.

Fogarty, T. J., & Kalbers, L. P. (1998). Organizational and economic explanations of audit committee oversight. *Journal of Managerial Issues, 10*(2), 129–150.

Foster, B. P., Ornstein, W., & Shastri, T. (2007). Audit costs, material weaknesses under SOX section 404. *Managerial Auditing Journal, 22*(7), 661–673.

Franck, P., & Sundgren, S. (2010). Den upplevda nyttan med intern kontroll: En studie av svenska noterade bolag. *Ekonomiska Samfundets Tidskrift, 2*, 81–93.

Fraser, I., & Henry, W. (2007). Embedding risk management: Structures and approaches. *Managerial Auditing Journal, 22*(4), 392–409.

FRC (Financial Reporting Council). (2005). *Internal control. Revised guidance for directors on the combined code*. London. Available at www.frc.org.uk

FRC (Financial Reporting Council). (2008, June). *The combined code on corporate governance*, London. Available at www.frc.org.uk

Fredrick, W. R. (2011). Enhancing the role of the boards of directors of state-owned enterprises. OECD Corporate Governance Working Papers, No.2.

Gadh, V. M., Krishnan, R., & Peters, J. M. (1993). Modeling internal controls and their evaluation. *Auditing: A Journal of Practice and Theory, 12*(Supplement), 113–129.

Garbade, W. H. (1944). Internal control and the internal auditor. *The Accounting Review, 19*(4), 416–421.

Gee, W., & McVay, S. (2005). The disclosure of material weaknesses in internal control after the Sarbanes-Oxley Act. *Accounting Horizons, 19*(3), 137–158.

Gerkes, J., Van der Werf, W. J., & Van der Wijk, H. (2007, October). Entity-level controls. *Internal Auditor*, 50–54.

Goldberg, D. M. (2007, December). Focus on high-risk controls. *Internal Auditor*, 69–71.

Grant Thornton (2009b). *ISEQ corporate governance review 2009*. Available at www. grantthornton.ie

Grant Thornton. (2009a, Summer). *Corporate governance series: enterprise risk management: creating value in a volatile economy*. Available at www.grantthornton.com

Grant Thornton (2012). Intern kontroll i finansiell sektor 1999-2011 [Internal control in the financial sector 1999–2011]. Available at www.grantthornton.se

Gupta, P. P., & Thomson, J. C. (2006). Use of COSO 1992 in management reporting on internal control. *Strategic Finance*, 27–33.

Hall, R. H., Johnson, N. J., & Haas, E. (1967). Organizational size, complexity and formalization. *American Sociological Review, 32*(6), 903–912.

Hambrick, D. C., Werder, A., & Zajac, E. J. (2008). New directions in corporate governance research. *Organization Science, 19*(3), 381–385.

Hammer, M. (2007, April). The process audit. *Harvard Business Review*, 111–123.

Hammer, M., & Champy, J. (1993). *Reengineering the corporation. A manifesto for business revolution*. London: Nicholas Brealey.

Handley-Schachler, M., Juleff, L., & Paton, C. (2007). Corporate governance in the financial services sector. *Corporate Governance, 7*(5), 623–634.

Haron, H., Chambers, A., Ramsi, R., & Ismail, I. (2004). The reliance of external auditors on internal auditors. *Managerial Auditing Journal, 19*(9), 1148–1159.

Hass, S., Abdolmohammadi, M. J., & Burnaby, P. (2006). The Americas literature review on internal auditing. *Managerial Auditing Journal, 21*(8), 835–844.

Haun, R. D. (1955). Broad vs. narrow concepts of internal auditing and internal control. *The Accounting Review, 30*(1), 114–118.

Hay, D. (1993). Internal control: How it evolved in four English-speaking countries. *The Accounting Historians Journal, 20*(1), 79–102.

Heier, J. R., Dugan, M. T., & Sayers, D. L. (2005). A century of debate for internal controls and their assessment: A study of reactive evolution. *Accounting History, 10*(3), 39–70.

Hermanson, H. M. (2000). An analysis of the demand of reporting on internal control. *Accounting Horizons, 14*(3), 325–341.

Hermanson, D. R., & Rittenberg, L. E. (2003). *Research opportunities in internal auditing chapter 2: Internal audit and organizational governance*. Florida: IIA (Institute of Internal Auditors) Research Foundation.

Hofstede, G. (1984). *Culture's consequences: International differences in work-related values*. Beverly Hills: Sage.

Hoitash, R., Hoitash, U., & Bedard, J. C. (2009). Corporate governance and internal control over financial reporting: A comparison of regulatory regimes. *The Accounting Review, 84*(3), 839–867.

Holland, T. R. (2009, December). Reputation risk is tricky. *Internal Auditor*, 11.

Holme, I. M., & Solvang, B. K. (1991). *Forskningsmetodik. Om kvalitativa och kvantitativa metoder*. Studentlitteratur. Lund.
Holmes, S. A., Langford, M., Welch, O. J., & Welch, S. T. (2002). Associations between internal controls and organizational citizenship behavior. *Journal of Managerial Issues, 14*(1), 85–99.
Holmström, B., & Kaplan, S. N. (2003). The state of U.S. corporate governance: What's right and what's wrong? *Journal of Applied Corporate Finance, 15*(3), 8–20.
House, J. D. (1975). Organization without formalization: The case of a real estate agency. *The Canadian Journal of Sociology, 2*(2), 19–31.
Humphrey, C. (2007). Auditing research: A review across the disciplinary divide. *Accounting, Auditing and Accountability Journal, 21*(2), 170–203.
Hutter, B., & Power, M. (Eds.). (2005). *Organizational encounters with risk*. Cambridge: Cambridge University Press.
IAASB (International Auditing and Assurance Standards Board). (2006, December). *Redrafted International Standards on Auditing 240, 300, 315, 330*. New York
IIA (Institute of Internal Auditors). (2004). *The professional practices framework*. Florida: The IIA Research Foundation. Global Practices Center.
IIA (Institute of Internal Auditors). (2009). *International professional practices framework (IPPF)*. Florida: The IIA Research Foundation.
Jagan Krishnan, Dasaratha Rama, and Yinghong Zhang (2008, May) osts to Comply with SOX Section 404. *A Journal of practice & theory, 27(1)*, pp. 169–186
Jackson, R. A. (2004, October). Principles vs. rules. *Internal Auditor*, 56–61.
James, K. L. (2003). The effect of internal audit structure on perceived financial statement fraud prevention. *Accounting Horizons, 17*(4), 315–327.
Jensen, M. C., & Meckling, W. H. (1976). Theory of the firm: managerial behaviour, agency costs and ownership structure. *Journal of Financial Economics, 3(4)*, 305–360.
Johnson, T. H., & Kaplan, R. S. (1987). *Relevance lost. The rise and fall of management accounting*. Boston: Harvard Business School Press.
Jokipii, A. (2006). *The structure and effectiveness of internal control – A contingency approach*. (diss.) Åbo Akademi University, Turku.
Jokipii, A. (2010). Determinants and consequences of internal control in firms: a contingency theory based analysis. *Journal of Management and Governance, 14*(2), 115–144.
Jonnergård, K., & Larsson, U. (2007). Developing codes of conduct: Regulatory conversations as means for detecting institutional change. *Law & Policy, 29*(4), 460–492.
Khanchel, I. (2007). Corporate governance: Measurement and determinant analysis. *Managerial Auditing Journal, 22*(8), 740–760.
Kinney, W. R., Jr. (2000). Research opportunities in internal control quality and quality assurance. *Auditing: A Journal of Practice and Theory, 19*(Supplement), 83–90.
Kinney, W. R., Jr. (2005). Twenty-five years of audit deregulation and re-regulation: What does it mean for 2005 and beyond? *Auditing: A Journal of Practice and Theory, 24*, 89–109.
Kirkpatrick, W. W. (1962). The adequacy of internal corporate controls. *The ANNALS of the American Academy of Political and Social Science, 343*(1), 75–83.
Kjellberg, A.-C. (2009, September). Ledningen måste ta helhetsgrepp på riskerna. *Dagens Industri*.
Knechel, W.R. (2007) The business risk audit: Origins, obstacles and oppurtunities, Accounting, Organizations and Society, 32, p.383–408.
Kodgruppen [The Code group]. (2004). *Svensk kod för bolagsstyrning [Swedish code of Corporate Governance]*, Stockholm.
Kollegiet för Svensk Bolagsstyrning [The Swedish Corporate Governance Board]. (2005). *Anvisning Nr.1-2005 [Guidance No.1-2005 regarding board reporting on internal control]*, Stockholm, December 15, 2005.
Kollegiet för Svensk Bolagsstyrning [The Swedish Corporate Governance Board]. (2006a). *Anvisning Nr.1-2006 [Guidance No. 1-2006 on the application of code provisions regarding*

reporting and disclosure of internal controls], Stockholm, September 6, 2006. Available at www.corporategovernanceboard.se

Kollegiet för Svensk Bolagsstyrning [The Swedish Corporate Governance Board]. (2006b). *Årsrapport 2006 [Annual Report 2006]*. Stockholm, June 2006. Available at www.corporate-governanceboard.se

Kollegiet för Svensk Bolagsstyrning [The Swedish Corporate Governance Board]. (2006c). *Kodbarometern 2006 [Survey on the attitudes towards the Swedish code, 2006]*, Stockholm, June 2006. Available at www.corporategovernanceboard.se

Kollegiet för Svensk Bolagsstyrning [The Swedish Corporate Governance Board]. (2008a). *Jämförelse mellan den tidigare koden och den reviderade koden 2008-05-05 [Comparison between the revised Swedish code of Corporate Governance Code and the previous Code]*. Available at www.corporategovernanceboard.se

Kollegiet för Svensk Bolagsstyrning [The Swedish Corporate Governance Board]. (2008b). *Svensk kod för bolagsstyrning. Gällande från 1 juli 2008 [The Swedish code of Corporate Governance: Applicable from July 1 2008]*, Stockholm. Available at www.corporategovernanceboard.se

Kollgiet för Svensk Bolagsstyrning [The Swedish Corporate Governance Board]. (2009, June). *Årsrapport 2009 [Annual Report 2009]*, Stockholm. Available at www.bolagsstyrning.se

Kollgiet för Svensk Bolagsstyrning [The Swedish Corporate Governance Board]. (2010). *Årsrapport 2010 [Annual Report 2010]*, Stockholm. Available at www.bolagsstyrning.se

Koutoupis, A. G. (2007, October). Documenting internal controls. *Internal Auditor*, 23–27.

Krishnan, J., Rama, D., & Zhang, Y. (2008). Costs to comply with SOX section 404. *Auditing: A Journal of Practice and Theory, 27*(1), 169–186.

Langfield-Smith, K. (1997). Management control systems and strategy: A critical review. *Accounting, Organizations and Society, 22*(2), 207–232.

Langfield-Smith, K., & Smith, D. (2003). Management control systems and trust in outsourcing relationships. *Management Accounting Research, 14*, 281–307.

Lazarides, T., & Drimpetas, E. (2008). The missing link to an effective corporate governance system. *Corporate Governance, 8*(1), 73–82.

Lee, T. A. (1971). The historical development of internal control form the earliest times to the end of the seventeenth century. *Journal of Accounting Research, 9*(1), 150–157.

Lee, T. A. (Ed.). (1988). *The evolution of audit thought and practice*. New York: Garland.

Lekvall, P. (2008, September 6). Intern kontroll kvar i fokus. *Dagens Industri*.

Leone, A. J. (2007). Factors related to internal control disclosure: A discussion of Ashbaugh, Collins and Kinney (2007) and Doyle, Ge, and McVay (2007). *Journal of Accounting and Economics, 44*, 224–237.

Lightle, S. S., Castellano, J. F., & Cutting, B. T. (2007, December). Assessing the control environment. *Internal Auditor*, 51–56

Linseley, P. M., & Lawrence, M. J. (2007). Risk reporting by the largest UK companies: Readability and lack of obfuscation. *Accounting, Auditing and Accountability Journal, 20* (4), 620–627.

Little, A., & Best, P. J. (2003). A framework for separating duties in an SAP R/3 environment. *Managerial Auditing Journal, 18*(5), 419–430.

MacCahery, J., Picciotto, S., & Collin, S. (Eds.). (1993). *Corporate control and accountability – Changing structures and the dynamics of regulation*. New York: Oxford University Press.

Maijoor, S. (2000). The internal control explosion. *International Journal of Auditing, 4*, 101–109.

March, J. G., & Simon, H. A. (1958). *Organizations*. New York: Wiley.

Malmi, T., & Brown, D.A. (2008) Management control systems as packages: Opportunities, challenges and research directions. *Management Accounting Research 19*, 287–300.

Matyjewicz, G., & DÀrcangelo, J. R. (2004, October). Beyond Sarbanes-Oxley. *Internal Auditor*, 67–72.

Mautz, R. K., & Sharaf, H. A. (1961). *The Philsophy of Auditing, American Accounting Association*. Monograph No.6, Sarasota FL.

McEvily, B., Perrone, V., & Zaheer, A. (2003). Trust as an organizing principle. *Organization Science, 14*(1), 91–103.
McMullen, D. A., Raghunandan, K., & Rama, D. V. (1996). Internal control reports and financial reporting problems. *Accounting Horizons, 10*(4), 67–75.
Merchant, K. A., & Otley, D. T. (2007). A review of the literature on control and accountability. In C. Chapman, A. G. Hopwood, & M. D. Shields (Eds.), *Handbook of management accounting research* (1st ed., Vol. 2). Oxford: Elsevier.
Meyer, J. W., & Rowan, B. (1977). Institutionalized organizations: Formal structure as myth and ceremony. *The American Journal of Sociology, 83*(2), 340–363.
Michaels, R. E., Cron, W. L., Dubinsky, A. J., & Joachimsthaler, E. A. (1988). Influence of formalization on the organizational commitment and work alienation of salespeople and industrial buyers. *Journal of Marketing Research, 25*(4), 376–383.
Mikes, A. (2009). Risk management and calculative cultures. *Management Accounting Research, 20*, 18–40.
Mintzberg, H. (1983). *Power in and around organizations*. Englewood Cliffs: Prentice-Hall.
Mintzberg, H. (1990). The design school: Reconsidering the basic premises of strategic management. *Strategic Management Journal, 11*(3), 171–195.
Mock, T. J., Sun, L., Srivastava, R. P., & Vasarhelyi, M. (2009). An evidential reasoning approach to Sarbanes-Oxley mandated internal control risk assessment. *International Journal of Accounting Information Systems, 10*(2), 65–78.
Monks, R.A.G., & Minow, N. (2004). *Corporate Governance*, Third edition, Blackwell Publishing, USA.
Netter, J., Poulsen, A., & Stegemoller, M. (2009). The rise of corporate governance in corporate control research. *Journal of Corporate Finance, 15*, 1–9.
O'Leary, C., Iselin, E., & Sharma, D. (2006). The relative effects of elements of internal control on auditors' evaluations of internal control. *Pacific Accounting Review, 18*(2), 69–96.
O'Reilly, M., & McMullen, D. (2002, January). Internal control reporting and users' perceptions of financial statement reliability. *American Business Review*. 100–107.
OECD (Organization for Economic Co-operation and Development). (2004). *OECD principles of corporate governance*. Paris: OECD Publications Service. Available at www.oecd.org
OECD (Organization for Economic Co-operation and Development). (2009a). *The corporate governance lessons from the financial crisis*. OECD Publications. ISSN 1995–2864. Financial Market Trends. Available at www.oecd.org
OECD (Organization for Economic Co-operation and Development). (2009b, June). *Corporate governance and the financial crisis: Key findings and main messages*. OECD Publications. Available at www.oecd.org
Oliviero, M. E. (2001). Internal control – Integrated framework: How is responsible? *Critical Perspectives on Accounting, 12*, 187–192.
Oliviero, M. E. (2002, February). The architect is missing. *Internal Auditor*, 76.
Olve, N.-G., Petri, C. J., Roy, J., & Roy, S. (2003). *Making scorecards actionable: Balancing strategy and control*. England: Wiley.
Organ, D. W., & Greene, C. N. (1981). The effects of formalization on professional involvement: A compensatory process approach. *Administrative Science Quarterly, 26*(2), 237–252.
Otley, D. T. (1980). The contingency theory of management accounting: Achievement and prognosis. *Accounting, Organizations and Society, 5*(4), 413–428.
Otley, D. T. (1994). Management control in contemporary organizations: Towards a wider framework. *Management Accounting Research, 5*, 289–299.
Otley, D. T. (1999). Performance management: A framework for management control systems research. *Management Accounting Research, 10*, 363–382.
Otley, D. T. (2003). Management control and performance management: Whence or whither? *The British Accounting Review, 35*, 309–326.
Otley, D. T. (2008). Did Kaplan get it right? *Accounting, Auditing and Accountability Journal, 21* (2), 229–229.

Ouchi, W. G. (1977). The relationship between organizational structure and organizational control. *Administrative Science Quarterly, 22*, 95–113.

Ouchi, W. G. (1979). A conceptual framework for the design of organizational control mechanisms. *Management Science, 25*(9), 833–848.

Ouchi, W. G. (1980). Markets, bureaucracies and clans. *Administrative Science Quarterly, 25*, 129–141.

Parker, L. D., & Roffey, B. H. (1997). Methodological themes. Back to the drawing board: Revisiting grounded theory and the everyday accountant's and manager's reality. *Accounting, Auditing and Accountability Journal, 10*(2), 212–247.

Pathak, J. (2005). Guest Editorial: Risk management, internal controls and organizational vulnerabilities. *Managerial Auditing Journal, 20*(6), 569–577.

Patterson, E. R., & Smith, J. R. (2007). The effects of Sarbanes-Oxley on auditing and internal control strength. *The Accounting Review, 82*(2), 427–455.

PCAOB (Public Company Accounting Oversight Board). (2004). *Auditing Standard No.2 – An audit of internal control over financial reporting performed in conjunction with an audit of financial statements*

PCAOB (Public Company Accounting Oversight Board). (2007). *Auditing Standard No.5 – An audit of internal control over financial reporting that is integrated with an audit of financial statements*. Available at www.pcaob.org

PCAOB (Public Company Accounting Oversight Board). (2009, September). *Report on the first-year implementation of the audit standard No.5: An audit of internal control over financial reporting that is integrated with an audit of financial statements*. Available at www.pcaob.org

Pfister, J. A. (2009). *Managing organizational culture for effective internal control, from practice to theory*. Heidelberg: Physica-Verlag.

Pharoah, A. (2003). Corporate reputation: The board room challenge. *Corporate Governance, 3*(4), 46–51.

Picket, K. H. S. (2001). *Internal control: A manager's journey*. New York: Wiley.

Podsakoff, P. M., Williams, L. J., & Todor, W. D. (1986). Effects of organizational formalization on alienation among professionals and nonprofessionals. *The Academy of Management Journal, 29*(4), 820–831.

Porter, M. E. (1985). *Competitive advantage*. New York: Free Press.

Power, M. (1996). Making things auditable. *Accounting, Organizations and Society, 21*(2), 289–315.

Power, M. (1997). *The audit society: Rituals of verification*. New York: Oxford University Press.

Power, M. (2000). The audit society – Second thoughts. *International Journal of Auditing, 4*, 111–119.

Power, M. (2003a). Auditing and the production of legitimacy. *Accounting, Organizations and Society, 28*, 379–394.

Power, M. (2003b). Evaluating the audit explosion. *Law & Policy, 25*(3), 185–202.

Power, M. (2004). The nature of risk: The risk management of everything. *Balance Sheet, 12*(5), 19–28.

Power, M. (2005). The invention of operational risk. *Review of International Political Economy, 12*(4), 577–599.

Power, M. (2006). Special research symposium: Organizations and the management or risk. *Journal of Management Studies, 43*(6), 1331–1337.

Power, M. (2007). *Organized uncertainty: Designing a world of risk management*. New York: Oxford University Press.

Power, M., Scheytt, T., Soin, K., & Sahlin, K. (2009). Reputational risk as a logic or organizing in late modernity. *Organization Studies, 30*, 301–324.

Quinn, L. R. (2006, July). COSO at a crossroad. *Strategic Finance*, 42–49.

Radin, A. J. (2008). A practical approach to finding management override. *The CPA Journal, 10*, 6–9.

Rae, K., & Subramaniam, N. (2008). Quality of internal control procedures: Antecedents and moderating effect on organizational justice and employee fraud. *Managerial Auditing Journal, 23*(2), 104–124.

Raghunandan, K., & Rama, D. V. (1994). Management reports after COSO. *Internal Auditor*, 54–58.

Raghunandan, K., & Rama, D. (2006, May). SOX Section 404 Material Weakness Disclosures and Audit Fees. *Auditing: A Journal of Practice and Theory, 25*(1), 99–114.

Ramamoorti, S. (2003). *Research opportunities in internal auditing, chapter 1: Internal auditing: History, evolution and prospects*. Florida: IIA (Institute of Internal Auditors) Research Foundation.

Ramos, M. (2004, May). Evaluate the control environment. *Journal of Accountancy*, 75–78.

Regeringskansliet [Government Offices of Sweden]. (2008). *Styrelseansvaret i företag med statligt ägande [Board responsibility in state-owned companies]*. Produktion: Edita Communication. Tryck: Edita Västra Aros. Available at www.regeringen.se

Rittenberg, L. E., & Miller, P. K. (2005). *Sarbanes-Oxley 404 work: looking at the benefits*. Florida: IIA (The Institute of Internal Auditors) Research Foundation.

Roberts, J., & Scapens, R. (1985). Accounting systems and systems of accountability – understanding accounting practices in their organisational context. *Accounting, Organizations and Society, 10*(4), 443–456.

Sarens, G., & De Beelde, I. (2006). Internal auditors' perception about their role in risk management: A comparison between US and Belgium companies. *Managerial Auditing Journal, 21*(1), 63–80.

Schipper, K. (1989, December). Earnings management. *Accounting Horizons*, 91–102.

Schnatterly, K. (2003). Increasing firm value through detection and prevention of white-collar crime. *Strategic Management Journal, 24*, 587–614.

Scott, W. R. (2003). *Financial accounting theory* (3rd ed.). Toronto: Prentice Hall.

Scott, S. V., & Walsham, G. (2005). Reconceptualizing and managing reputation risk in the knowledge economy: Toward reputable action. *Organization Science, 16*(3), 308–322.

SEC (United States Securities and Exchange Commission). (2009a, September). *Study of the Sarbanes-Oxley Act of 2002 section 404 internal control over financial reporting requirements*. Available at www.sec.gov

SEC (United States Securities and Exchange Commission). (2009b). *Proxy disclosure enhancements*, Release No: 33–9089, Proposed Rule Release No. 33–9052. Release date December 19, 2009, Effective date: February 28, 2010. Available at www.sec.gov

Sen, A. (1993). Does business ethics make economic sense? *Business Ethics Quarterly, 3*, 45–54.

Senior Supervisors Group. (2009, October 21). *Risk management lessons from the global banking crisis of 2008*. Available at www.sec.gov

Shapiro, B., & Matson, D. (2008). Strategies of resistance to internal control regulation. *Accounting, Organizations and Society, 33*, 199–228.

Shaw, H. (2006, March). The trouble with COSO. *CFO*, 75–77.

Sherer, M., & Turley, S. (1997). *Current issues in auditing* (3rd ed.). London: Sage.

Simon, H. A. (1948). *Administrative behavior: A study of decision-making processes in administrative organizations*. New York: The Free Press.

Simons, R. (1987). Accounting control systems and business strategy: An empirical analysis. *Accounting, Organizations and Society, 12*(4), 357–374.

Simons, R. (1990). The role of management control systems in creating competitive advantage: New perspectives. *Accounting, Organizations and Society, 15*(1/2), 127–143.

Simons, R. (1991). Strategic orientation and top management attention to control systems. *Strategic Management Journal, 12*(1), 49–62.

Simons, R. (1995). *Levers of control: How managers use innovative controls systems to drive strategic renewal*. Boston: Harvard Business School Press.

Skinner, D., & Spira, L. (2003). Trust and control – A symbiotic relationship? *Corporate Governance, 3*(4), 28–35.

Smith, A. (1776). *An inquiry into the nature and cause of the wealth of nations*. Cannan edition. New York: Random House Inc.

Smith, K. A. (1972). The relationship of internal control evaluation and audit sample size. *The Accounting Review, 47*(2), 260–269.

Solomon, J., Solomon, A., Norton, S., & Joseph, N. (2000). A conceptual framework for corporate risk disclosure emerging from the agenda for corporate governance reform. *British Accounting Review, 32*, 447–478.

SOU (Statens Offentliga Utredningar). (2004a, April). *Svensk kod för bolagsstyrning. Förslag från Kodgruppen [Swedish code of corporate governance: A proposal from the Code Group]*, Stockholm, Fritzes, p. 46.

SOU (Statens Offentliga Utredningar). (2004b, December). *Svensk kod för bolagsstyrning. Betänkande av Kodgruppen [Swedish code of corporate governance: Consideration by the Code Group]*, Stockholm, Fritzes, p. 130

Spira, L. F., & Page, M. (2003). Risk management: The reinvention of internal control and the changing role of internal audit. *Accounting, Auditing and Accountability Journal, 16*(4), 640–661.

Steffee, S. (2009, December). Reforms reduced compliance costs. *Internal Auditor*, 17.

Strauss, A., & Corbin, J. (1990). *Basics of qualitative research. Grounded theory procedures and techniques*. London: Sage.

Swayze, W. S. (1946). Internal control in industrial organizations. *The Accounting Review, 21*(3), 272–277.

Tacket, J., Wolf, F., & Claypool, G. (2006). Internal control under Sarbanes Oxley: A critical examination. *Managerial Auditing Journal, 21*(3), 317–323.

Tackett, J., Wolf, F., & Claypool, G. (2004). Sarbanes-Oxley and audit failure: A critical examination. *Managerial Auditing Journal, 19*(3), 340–350.

Taiariol, R. (2000, February). Segregated duties in fashion. *Internal Auditor*, 23–25.

Tannenbaum, A. (1968). *Control in organizations*. New York: McGraw-Hill.

Taylor, F. W. (1911). *The principles of scientific management*. New York: Harper and Brothers.

Taylor, B. (2003). Board leadership: Balancing entrepreneurship and strategy with accountability and control. *Corporate Governance, 3*(2), 3–5.

Teece, D. J., Pisano, G., & Shuen, A. (1997). Dynamic capabilities and strategic management. *Strategic Management Journal, 18*(7), 509–533.

The Cadbury Code (1992) The Committee on the Financial Aspects of Corporate Governance and Gee and Co Ltd. (1992): Report of the committee on the financial aspects of corporate Governance, 1 December, 1992. The corporate governance committee, Financial Reporting Council.

The Sarbanes-Oxley Act of 2002, Public Law 107-204, 107th Congress, July 30, 2002, 116 STAT, 745

The Turnbull Report (1999). *Internal control: Guidance for directors on the Combined Code*. published by ICAEW in September 1999, Great Britain.

The Walker Review. (2009). *A review of corporate governance in UK banks and other financial industry entities, Final recommendations*, 26 November 2009.

Trenerry, A. (1999). *Principles of internal control*. Sydney: University of New South Wales Press.

Turley, S., & Zaman, M. (2007). Audit committee effectiveness: Informal processes and behavioural effects. *Accounting, Auditing and Accountability Journal, 20*(5), 765–788.

Vinten, G. (2001). Corporate governance and the sons of Cadbury. *Corporate Governance, 1*(4), 4–8.

Vinten, G. (2002). The corporate governance lessons of Enron. *Corporate Governance, 2*(4), 4–9.

Vinten, G. (2003). Enronitis – Dispelling the disease. *Managerial Auditing Journal, 8*(6/7), 448–455.

Walker, P. L., Shenkir, W. G., & Barton, T. L. (2003, August). ERM in practice. *Internal Auditor*, 51–55.

Wallace, W. A. (1981). Internal control reporting practices in the municipal sector. *The Accounting Review, 56*(3), 666–689.
Waller Shelton, S., & Whittington, O. R. (2008). The influence of the auditor's report on investors' evaluations after the Sarbanes-Oxley act. *Managerial Auditing Journal, 23*(2), 142–160.
Watts, R. L., & Zimmerman, J. L. (1983). Agency problems, auditing and the theory of the firm: Some evidence. *Journal of Law and Economics, 26*(3), 613–633.
Wells, J. T. (2002). Let them know someone's watching. *Journal of Accountancy, 5*, 106–110.
Whitley, J. (2006, December). COSO to develop further internal control guidance. *Internal Auditor*, 18.
Wiesen, J. (2003). Congress enacts Sarbanes-Oxley Act of 2002: A two-ton gorilla awakes and speaks. *Journal of Accounting, Auditing and Finance, 18*(3), 429–448.
Williamson, O. E. (1985). *The economic institutions of capitalism: Firms, markets, relational contracting*. New York: The Free Press.
Winter, S. G. (2003). Understanding dynamic capabilities. *Strategic Management Journal, 24*, 991–995.
Woods, M. (2009). A contingency theory perspective on the risk management control systems within Birmingham city council. *Management Accounting Research, 20*, 69–81.
Yakhou, M., & Dorweiler, V. P. (2004). Dual reforms: Accounting and corporate governance. *Managerial Auditing Journal, 19*(3), 361–377.
Zandstra, G. (2002). Enron, board governance and moral failings. *Corporate Governance, 2*(2), 16–19.
Zannetos, Z. S. (1964). Some thoughts on internal control systems of the firm. *The Accounting Review, 39*(4), 860–868.

FSC
www.fsc.org
MIX
Papier | Fördert gute Waldnutzung
FSC® C083411

Kolibri 360 GmbH
Ferdinand-Jühlke-Straße 7
99095 Erfurt, Deutschland
produktsicherheit@kolibri360.de